Introduction
to

FRENCH PHONOLOGY
AND MORPHOLOGY

To the memory of my father —
Jacques Jacob Valdman

Introduction
to
FRENCH PHONOLOGY AND MORPHOLOGY

Albert Valdman

Professor of French/Italian and Linguistics
Indiana University

NEWBURY HOUSE PUBLISHERS, INC. / *ROWLEY* / *MASSACHUSETTS*

Library of Congress Cataloging in Publication Data

Valdman, Albert.
    Introduction to French phonology and morphology.

    1. French language--Phonology. 2. French lan-
guage--Inflection. 3. French language--Word formation. I. Title.
PC2131.V3   441'.5   76-1888
ISBN 0-88377-054-7

Cover design by Wendy Doherty
Artwork by Stanley Russo

NEWBURY HOUSE PUBLISHERS, Inc.

 Language Science
Language Teaching
Language Learning

Rowley, Massachusetts 01969

Printed in the U.S.A.   First Printing: September 1976   5   4   3

PREFACE

In the course of the last three decades many linguists have turned to French to exemplify new models of linguistic analysis. These studies have brought to light new facts and generated illuminating insights in the area of phonology and morphology. Yet these contributions are not readily accessible to the beginning student in French linguistics, the teacher of French curious about the structure of the language he is imparting to others, and the general linguist who seeks documentation. They are obliged to turn, on the one hand, to traditional handbooks of phonetics in which the scope is too narrow and some of the facts are obsolete or have been proven erroneous by more recent research, and on the other, to traditional grammars with the primary objective to prescribe adherence to restricted varieties and styles of French rather than to describe and analyze forms in use.

    This book aims to review for the non-specialist generally accepted facts about the pronunciation and the system of spoken forms of Standard French, the variety of the language accepted as an idealized norm in France and by many segments of French-speaking communities outside of France. The approach adopted is frankly eclectic. Facts about French do not serve to illustrate a particular theoretical position or to demonstrate its superiority over others. Rather various theoretical approaches—American structuralism, European functionalism, generative phonology—serve to highlight aspects of the structure of the pronunciation and form systems of French and to reveal interesting relationships between sounds and forms. An attempt has been made to shy away from polemic discussions and to avoid the presentation of views which are too personal or facts discovered by the author which have not been subjected to careful scrutiny by fellow specialists. However, *Introduction to French Phonology and Morphology* may also serve as an introduction to phonological theory since it provides, with examples from French, discussions of current issues such as the incorporation of variation in linguistic descriptions or the motivation of abstract underlying forms. Particular emphasis has been placed on language variation. In Chapter 2 it is emphasized that there exist considerable variation and fluctuation in Standard French, that other languages are spoken within metropolitan France, and that communities outside of the Hexagon employ diverse varieties of French.

This is not a book in applied linguistics. No claim is made that the description and analysis presented of the French sound system or adjective and verb inflection can contribute directly to more effective teaching of these aspects of the structure of French. Nonetheless, since one must describe and talk about what one teaches, persons involved in the planning and preparation of materials and syllabi for the teaching of French and even classroom instructors would derive much practical benefit from familiarity with the material presented in this introductory treatment.

Each chapter ends with a set of study questions. These have proven useful in permitting the reader to check on his understanding of the material presented and, in the context of university classes, channeling discussions.

Introduction to French Phonology and Morphology developed from class notes expanded to constitute the basic text reference in a graduate course in applied French linguistics and advanced undergraduate and beginning graduate courses in French phonology and morphology at Indiana University and several other institutions. I am deeply grateful to colleagues, particularly Marvin Moody of Indiana University and John Rea of the University of Kentucky, who tried out preliminary drafts of the material and provided many valuable suggestions and constructive criticism. I am also indebted to Fred Jenkins of the University of Illinois who subjected the final draft to careful scrutiny and brought to my attention inaccuracies, inconsistencies and infelicities of style. I must bear full responsibility for the failure of the published version to incorporate the advice so generously given. Finally, I should like to acknowledge with gratitude a Grant-in-Aid of Research from the Office of Research and Advanced Studies at Indiana University which supported in part research leading to the preparation of the book and clerical services.

Albert Valdman

Bloomington, Indiana
August 1975

CONTENTS

PART I

PHONOLOGY

1

INTRODUCTION

1.1   THE AIMS OF LINGUISTIC DESCRIPTION

The fundamental aim of linguistics is to present in a precise, rigorous, and explicit form facts about a language which those who speak it as a native language know intuitively. The striking feature of native control of a language is the ability to produce an infinite number of sentences from a finite stock of elements and rules of combination of these elements and the converse ability to understand an equally infinite number of sentences which other speakers of the same language may produce. Too often passed over is the equally admirable ability of speakers of one language to acquire, in a relatively short time, the ability to understand and to produce sentences in several other languages.

There are several assumptions that every linguist brings to the description of a language:

1.   Language is amenable to objective and systematic study; in other terms, language is a system.

2.   Directly observable phenomena are only partial data on the basis of which the internal system is to be inferred. What all members of a linguistic community share is a linguistic *competence* which partially determines the outward form of utterances. The linguistic performance on the basis of which the linguist describes the internal system is conditioned by many external and linguistically irrelevant facts. In his analysis the linguist will need to disregard what are clearly errors, lapses, or fragments. On the other hand, similarities of outward form often camouflage differences at the underlying level.

3.   Linguistic analysis yields an orderly and accurate description of a language. The grammatical categories and the totality of forms of a language must be clearly revealed. Thus, any satisfactory analysis of French must state at least that the adjective *grand* has a total of six different phonetically observable forms (*un grand* [grã] *restaurant, un grand* [grãt] *hôtel, une grande*

3

[grɑ̃də] *hache, une grande* [grɑ̃d] *maison, les grands* [grɑ̃] *restaurants, les grands* [grɑ̃z] *hôtels, les grandes* [grɑ̃d] *maisons, les grandes* [grɑ̃dz] *usines).*

4. A linguistic description must lead to insights and understanding of the structure of a language, and it must bring together under a single comprehensive explanation a variety of seemingly unrelated observations. Thus, a description of French adjective inflection with explanatory power would account for the totality of form in terms of the affixation of an underlying feminine marker which "protects" the final consonant of the adjective base from loss or change.

In describing a language a linguist proceeds very much like any other scientist. He first looks at his data and makes detailed observations. After collecting a sufficient sample of language (termed the *corpus*) and on the basis of his experience with other languages and his own intuition, he attempts to generalize beyond the collected data and make statements about the underlying system, the linguistic competence of the native speakers of the language he is attempting to describe. He next attempts to generate forms and sentences he has not directly observed in the data; that is, he verifies his predictions by testing them against additional data and modifies his generalizations if necessary.

1.2   PHONOLOGY

This book attempts to present an up-to-date description of some aspects of the structure of a particular language—French. The aspects of the structure of French that will be treated are the spoken form of French morphemes and the pronunciation system of the language: morphology and phonology. Since this is an introductory treatment, no attempt will be made at exhaustive treatment, and only facts and interpretations about which there is general agreement will be presented. In addition to an accurate description of the most important aspects of French morphology and phonology, an attempt will be made to reveal the general processes that determine the form of French morphemes (basic meaningful units).

When one first listens to a foreign language, one is left with the impression that it is composed of an array of strange noises, and in the case of unfamiliar tongues, one is hard put to isolate units that coincide with the words of familiar languages and to identify individual sounds that resemble those of one's native language. Thus, in characterizing the differences between pronunciation systems of two languages, one is tempted to ascribe them to the presence of different sounds—often, the more unfamiliar of the two languages will be said to contain strange and difficult sounds.

Indeed, languages do differ in terms of constituent sound types. For example, as compared to English, French contains a set of vowels produced in the front part of the mouth cavity and with lip rounding: *du* [dy], *deux* [dø], *leur* [lœr]. On the other hand, the initial consonant sounds of such English words as *them* [ðɛm] and *three* [θri] are alien to French ears. Languages also differ in the way phonetically identical sounds function. English and French both have nasal vowels, vowels produced with the lowering of the velum which separates the oral and nasal cavities. In French, nasal vowels contrast with oral (non-nasal) vowels and serve to distinguish words from each other; compare *beau* [bo] and *bon* [bõ]. The latter word contains the nasal vowel [õ] which differs from the vowel [o] of *beau* only by its nasal articulation. While English has a large variety of nasal vowels (compare the vowels of each of the following paired words: *pat/pant; sit/sin; sad/sang; at/aunt*), they occur only before a nasal consonant (*m, n,* or *ng*) and never contrast with oral vowels. In other words, the nasality of English vowels is automatic: before non-nasal consonants, nasal vowels do not appear; before a nasal consonant, only nasal vowels may appear.

The pronunciation systems of two languages may also differ in the type of sound sequences that are permissible. English is characterized by quite complex groups of consonants occurring at the end of words: *prints* [nts], *laughed* [ft], *lasts* [sts], *asked* [skt]. While French has fewer final consonant clusters of this type, it allows very complex initial clusters: *je prends* [ʒpr], *ce cuisinier* [skч], *le troisième* [ltrw].

Finally, an important aspect of the pronunciation system of a language is the function of the prosodic features: stress—the relative prominence of the various syllables of a word or group of words; intonation—the rise and fall of the voice; as well as the relative degree of juncture and separation between the constituent vowels and consonants of phonological units. Languages also differ with regard to the length of phonological units and the degree to which grammatical units that correspond more or less to the word are clearly demarcated in the speech chain. Except for short function words such as *the, to, an,* etc., English words are delineated by stress and junctural phenomena; in French, on the other hand, words lose their individuality, and the smallest phonological unit above the level of individual vowels and consonants is a group of three to six syllables containing a variable number of words.

To accurately and adequately characterize the pronunciation system of a language, a phonological description must have a four-fold aim:

1. It must specify the stock of contrastive sound units (phonemes). In this book, the contrastive vowels and consonants of French are presented in Chapters 2 to 5 and in Chapter 8.

2. It must describe how phonemes are produced in terms of positions and movements of the vocal organs (Chapters 2-5 and 8). It is also possible to describe phonemes in terms of the acoustic properties of the sounds they subsume, although this type of specification is not as useful as an articulatory one for the purposes of an introductory treatment.

3. It must specify variations in the number of phonemes or the phonetic realization of phonemes determined by regional or social class differences as well as, for the same speakers, variations correlating with the setting in which speech takes place (situation, interlocutors, etc.). Variations in the French phonological system are taken up in Chapter 6.

4. It must state the restrictions on the distribution of vowels and consonants relative to each other and to prosodic features. Constraints on permissible sequences of vowels and consonants and the description of the role of stress and junctural phenomena are presented in Chapter 9. No satisfactory theory has yet been proposed to account for intonational distinctions in French and, short of listing intonational curves for various types of French sentences, no coherent and simple description is yet possible for that area of the phonology of French. Therefore, that area has not been treated in this book.

1.3 MORPHOLOGY

Morphology deals with the composition of words in terms of constituent morphemes and with the phonological representation of morphemes. Many morphemes can be specified in terms of a given set of phonemes: for example, *sac* is made up of three phonemes /sak/ and *cassé* of four /kase/. (You have no doubt observed that the pronunciation of morphemes is sometimes indicated by [ ] or by / /. The different point of view implied by the choice between these two types of transcriptions will be taken up in Chapter 4.) In other words, these morphemes show a one-to-one relationship with a single set of phonemes. But this straightforward relationship does not always obtain. The same set of phonemes may represent several morphemes, as is the case with French /vɛr/ which is the phonological output of the following morphemes: *vert* "green," *vair* "many-colored," *verre* "glass," *vers* "toward," *(le) vers* "verse," *ver* "worm." On the other hand, a morpheme may be represented by two or more sets of phonemes. In English, the definite and indefinite determiners *the* and *a/an* have two spoken forms each, the difference in form being determined by whether the word that follows begins with a vowel or a consonant. This type of alternation, however, affects only these two morphemes. In French there is an alternation between two phonological representations also determined by whether the following word begins with a vowel (or semivowel) or a consonant: compare *deux* /dø/ *mois* vs. *deux* /døz/ *ans.* This type of alternation which characterizes all types of French morphemes is termed liaison and will be discussed in Chapter 10. Another type of alternation also determined by whether the following word begins with a consonant or vowel (semivowel) and found in all types of morphemes affects only the phonological unit called mute *e* (*e muet*): compare *le train* vs. *l'avion.* The realization of mute *e* as either no sound (zero) or a vowel that varies between those of *deux* and *peur* is called elision and must be differentiated from the loss or retention of mute *e* before a consonant, as in *c'est l¢ train* vs. *ils prennent le train*; both of these types of alternations are treated in Chapter 11.

English and French have the reputation of being difficult languages to learn because the official spellings used to represent them are inconsistent and fail to provide a one-to-one relationship between the phonemes of these languages and the letters of the alphabet used by the spellings. Of course the type of spelling employed to represent a language plays no role in determining the relative ease or difficulty of acquisition of that language on the part of speakers of particular languages. The fit between the representation of French morphemes in terms of phonemes and the conventional spelling is notoriously bad. For instance, the sequence of two phonemes /sã/ corresponds to the following graphic representations: *sang, sans, cent, (je) sens, (il) sent.* But, as will be shown in Chapter 12, in view of the existence of liaison in French, the morphemes *sans* and *cent* have different pronunciation potentials. The latter may be pronounced as /sã/ *(cent francs)* or /sãt/ *(cent ans)* whereas the former is realized as /sã/ *(sans travail)* or /sãz/ *(sans argent).* This is to say that in some cases the so-called "silent" letters of French spelling stand in fact for liaison consonants which appear in certain contexts.

Certain classes of French morphemes show a variation in phonological form conditioned by grammatical factors. Like English nouns, French nouns may be pluralized, but seldom does the addition of the plural morpheme to French noun result as it does in English in an overt change in pronunciation; compare *the dog* vs. *the dogs* and *le chien* vs. *les chiens.* In English the determiner remains invariable whereas /z/ is added to the noun; in French, the singular and plural forms of the determiner differ by their vowel, but the noun remains invariable. As will be shown in Chapters 13 and 14, in French the plural marker appears generally with determiners and adjectives.

French nouns belong to one of two gender classes: masculine and feminine. Because the feminine ending consists of a mute *e* added to the masculine form (or, more precisely to the base of a morpheme) the difference between masculine and feminine spoken forms of determiners and adjectives usually appears as the absence opposed to the presence of a final consonant. Chapter 14 will point out that an understanding of feminine and plural inflection in adjectives depends on a certain view of liaison and elision.

French verbs appear in a large number of forms and show several classes of variation in form determined by the addition of various sets of morphological formatives. In Chapters 15 and 16 it will be shown that, although the traditional description of French verbs in terms of four or five classes (conjugations) is fundamentally sound, the relationship among spoken forms can be fully understood only if reference is made to the concepts of liaison and elision.

Finally, in Chapter 17 deeper level alternations between variant forms of morphemes will be studied in the context of derivation. The question will be raised as to whether in a morphological description of French one would want to relate formally such forms as *fleur* and *floral* or *frère* and *fraternel*.

1.4 TOWARD THE EMPIRICAL STUDY OF FRENCH PHONOLOGY AND MORPHOLOGY

French is one of the world's best described languages, and phonology and morphology are the aspects of that language that have received the most extensive and detailed treatment. Yet at the present time the linguist who attempts to present a description of French phonology and morphology readily accessible to the non-specialist is hard put to find statements about the phonological and morphological structure of French as used by specific groups of speakers in carefully delimited situations. As set forth in Chapter 2, French is used by a large and complex linguistic community encompassing not only the various regions of France but many other countries on several continents. In many areas of the francophone domain French co-exists with other languages and many closely related speech varieties. The term "French language" refers in fact to the speech of a very limited geographical and sociocultural group, the educated, upper middle-class speakers of Paris.

Not only does the speech of this minority not reflect the linguistic competence of the majority of people who use French as a means of communication and expression, but, because of the nature of the observations on which descriptions of "Standard" French are based, these descriptions in fact portray an idealized version of the speech of the "happy few" that does not correspond to reality. Available descriptions of French are based on the intuitions of speakers representing the dominant sociocultural group or on the observation of the careful, monitored style of these speakers. In their more normal spontaneous style these speakers use features which they are likely to attribute to members of less prestigious sociocultural groups. Although the data presented in this book necessarily share the limitations of the standard reference works and existing detailed studies currently available, an attempt has been made, particularly in Chapter 6, to describe features present in more representative varieties of French.

2

LANGUAGE VARIATION IN FRANCE AND THE GEOGRAPHICAL DISTRIBUTION OF FRENCH

2.1   WHO SPEAKS FRENCH?

Most students of French view it as the national tongue of the French people, but French is also, with English, the world's major vehicular language. As such, it permits communication between people who, on other occasions, use other languages. On the other hand, there are more than ten million Frenchmen who make extensive use of languages other than French for many of their daily communicative needs. In addition, Frenchmen have available for use in appropriate situations a wide variety of pronunciation features, grammatical constructions, and vocabulary items that are not usually reflected in the variety of French taught to foreigners in the classroom. In this chapter, we will define briefly the types of variations languages show; inventory the languages spoken in France in addition to French; and discuss the distribution of French outside of France and the main types of variations French itself shows in and outside of France.

2.2   LANGUAGE VARIATION

Within any human community language varies according to the geographical location of its speakers and their social status on the one hand, and the circumstances that attend the use of language, on the other. That the members of a linguistic community understand one another in spite of extensive differences is an important aspect of the use of language. Speakers of the same language pay attention to the meaning of the message that is being communicated and, in the decoding process, ignore many aspects of the form it takes. No two members of the same linguistic community use their language in exactly the same way: one speaker may be a more skillful user of the language than another; a second may have a speech impediment; a third may know a foreign language and adopt some words from it. That effective communication is maintained despite extensive variation is due to the redundancy inherent in language. Language is supported by auxiliary communicative systems such as gestures—"body language"—and greatly aided by the situational context. Thus, to interpret sentences correctly it is not necessary to pick out from the sound wave all significant sound features or to identify all grammatical formatives present in the speech chain.

Yet members of a linguistic community are not wholly unaware of speech differences, for these signal information about the speaker's geographical provenience, his social class, his state of mind, etc. Speech variants are alternative ways of expressing the same meaning, but the fact that they play no cognitive function does not mean that they are devoid of interest for the student of language. Awareness of the function of language variants is quite subtle, yet the fact that speakers of a language are sensitive to the geographical, social, or stylistic correlates of speech variation is amenable to empirical demonstration. Several examples from American English will serve as illustration.

In New York City many speakers do not pronounce the *r* of such words as *car* or *guard,* so that for them such pairs of words as *God* vs. *guard* sound alike. The facts attending the pronunciation or non-pronunciation of word-final *r* are quite complex. All New York City speakers pronounce such words as *car* and *guard* with or without *r.* The relative frequency of the *r*-less pronunciation varies according to at least two factors: (1) social class, and (2) situational context or style. Different styles may be defined, for instance, by varying the circumstances attending the recording of speech: spontaneous and informal conversation, formal discussion, the reading of connected discourse, the reading of paired words. Figure 2.1 shows the social stratification of the pronunciation of word-final *r* in New York City. On the vertical axis are represented average index scores ranging from *r*-less pronunciations (0 index score) to frequent pronunciation; on the horizontal axis are represented five different contextual styles ranging from the most spontaneous to the most formal. It will be noted that speakers from all social classes are likely to pronounce more *r*'s as the formality of the context increases, but that in any one contextual style middle-class speakers have fewer *r*-less pronunciations than working-class and lower-class speakers. From these data it may safely be concluded that *r*-less pronunciations are **stigmatized** in New York City, that is *all* New Yorkers ascribe lower-class status to speakers who show a high proportion of *r*-less pronunciations. On the other hand, the pronunciation of word-final *r* is **prestigious:** speakers who show a high proportion of pronunciations with *r* are ascribed higher social status. In one of his studies on the sociolinguistic implications of variations in pronunciation in New York City, William Labov asked a group of speakers to assign a group of fellow speakers to a set of hierarchically ranked occupations (for example, office manager, administrative assistant, clerk-typist, machine operator) on the basis of recorded samples only. The higher the proportion of final *r*'s pronounced by a given speaker, the higher the status of the occupation to which he was assigned.

2.3   TYPES OF LANGUAGE VARIATION

Western societies such as that of France have undergone a long process of linguistic unification. As a corollary to this process there has developed a strong monolingual and normative bias. It is assumed that a national state must as a matter of natural course have a single language, used by all citizens, for all communicative needs, and in a fairly homogeneous form. But as one surveys the nations of the world, one discovers that linguistic diversity, *not* linguistic uniformity is the natural state of affairs.

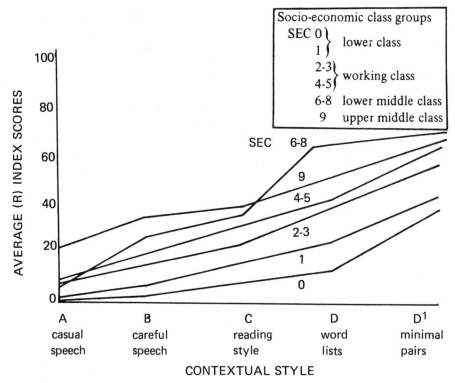

Figure 2.1 Class stratification of (r) in *guard, car, beer, beard,* etc. for native New York City adults.

(from William Labov, *The Social Stratification of English in New York City.* Washington, D.C.: Center for Applied Linguistics, 1966)

Linguistic diversity manifests itself in many forms. A nation may be **bilingual**: speakers use two languages (or more than two languages, in which case one speaks of **multilingualism**) in the same contextual situations. Or two or more languages may be used by all speakers but not in all situations: one language is used for one set of situations and the other for others. This type of situation is termed **diglossia,** and nations characterized by this type of situation are said to be **diglossic**. It is important to distinguish between official and actual bilingualism and diglossia. In Belgium, for example, French and Flemish (a variety of Dutch) are recognized as official languages and are used in government administration, in schools and universities, etc. But only a small minority of Belgians possess the ability to use the two languages interchangeably for all of their communicative needs. More accurately, there is in Belgium official bilingualism, but only a small minority of the population is bilingual.

Linguistic diversity usually takes the form of the use by the total population of several varieties of the same language. A distinction needs to be made, however, between several types of language variation. The term **dialect** is used to refer to varieties of the same language that show differences in pronunciation, grammar, and vocabulary small enough as to usually not interfere with mutual intelligibility. That is, speakers of dialects of the same language usually can understand one another. Dialects may be geographical or social, depending on whether variable features are characteristic of a region or a social class. Often, one of the geographical and/or social dialects is the only one recognized as suitable for official functions—administration, education—or situations generative of social prestige—formal speeches, literature. In such cases the dialect for which these various functions are reserved is referred to as the **standard** variety or dialect of the language. Only standard dialects are codified (normative grammars that specify their grammatical structure, and dictionaries that list their words are prepared) and endowed with a writing system. Non-standard varieties of a language show less uniformity, they become fragmented into a large number of sub-varieties spoken by small groups of speakers, and even people who have recourse to them for their daily communicative needs will assume a depreciative attitude toward them. Devalorized dialects are called **patois.** As the standard dialect of a nation becomes the prime means of communication of a larger proportion of the population, and as it spreads to new social strata and into new geographical areas, it becomes subject to minor variations—variations that affect pronunciation and vocabulary rather than the grammatical system. These variations within the standard dialect are so small as never to interfere with mutual intelligibility, and speakers are always conscious of the fact that they refer to the same overall speech norm. This situation characterizes most varieties of English. It is therefore preferable not to use the term **dialect** to refer to these varieties of a language (usually, varieties of a dialect of a language); the term **accent** will be used.

There are other variations in language that correspond to differences in the situational context and in the relationship between the speaker and his interlocutors. When one speaks about matters of daily life with one's peers, one uses a spontaneous level of speech or **style;** when one discusses less mundane matters, when one speaks in formal circumstances, when one feels that judgments are made about him on the basis of his speech, or when one engages in conversation with interlocutors that are not one's intimates or peers, one employs a monitored style. Finally, it is important to bear in mind that the most coherent language or variety of language (dialect, accent, style) and the one that is less subject to variation is that used spontaneously for everyday communication, one's **vernacular.**

2.4   BILINGUAL AND DIGLOSSIC AREAS OF FRANCE

There are many parts of France where some speakers are bilingual or diglossic. That is, in some areas speakers are able to use a speech variety that is not a dialect of Standard French in domains of use where both French and the other variety of language are admitted. This constitutes **bilingualism.** In other areas a speech variety that is not a dialect of Standard French is employed for daily communicative needs but Standard French in domains generative of prestige and for administrative or educational purposes; this constitutes **diglossia.**

2.4.1   Non-Romance Languages

In the extreme corner of southwestern France (see Figure 2.2) all but young persons speak **Basque,** a language of mysterious origins that has no apparent link to any other language of Europe. Though the number of its speakers is small, Basque is buttressed by the strong ties between French speakers of Basque and the much larger communities in the Spanish Basque provinces on the other side of the

Figure 2.2

Pyrenees. In the western half of Brittany there are still many speakers of **Breton,** a Celtic language closely related to Welsh and, more distantly to Gaelic. The inhabitants of ancient Gaul at the time of the Roman invasion also spoke a Celtic language, but Breton is not a direct descendant of the language of the Gauls. It was introduced at a later date by speakers of Celtic who migrated from Cornwall. In northern and eastern France there are two groups of speakers of Germanic languages, **Flemish** and **Alsatian.** Flemish, spoken in the Dunkirk and Lille area, close to the Belgian frontier, is related to Dutch, which serves as its standard dialect. In Alsace and the northern and eastern part of Lorraine, Alsatian—a dialect of German—is widely spoken. Standard German serves as the standard dialect for Alsatian, and, because of its wide use as a written form stemming from periods of German control during which it was the official language (1870-1918 and 1940-1945), it is widely understood and spoken. In Alsace there is effective French-German bilingualism: all administrative acts are drafted in both languages; Church sermons are often delivered in German; and one of the major newspapers has a German edition published in 200,000 copies as opposed to 20,000 copies for its French edition. But Alsatian is in a diglossia relationship with French and German, for it is not admitted to domains of use generative of prestige. Like Breton, Flemish and Alsatian are related to French, but the relationship is quite distant, as is shown by the genetic tree of Figure 2.3.

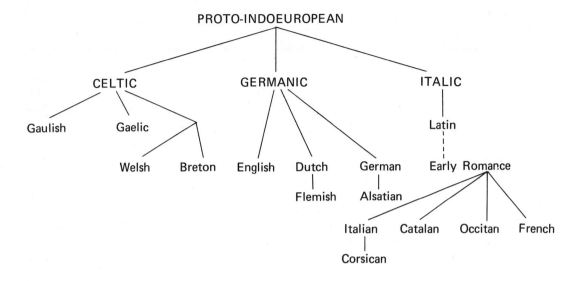

Figure 2.3

2.4.2   Romance Languages

The other varieties of language spoken in France that differ markedly from Standard French are, like that language, derived ultimately from Latin. The most divergent of these are the dialects spoken in the island of Corsica which are closely related to the varieties of Italian in the Florence area (Tuscan), although southern **Corsican** dialects also show the influence of Sardinian dialects. In the department of Pyrénées Orientales (from Perpignan and its vicinity to the Spanish border) most of the native population speak Rousillonnais, a variety of **Catalan.** Catalan is a standardized language with an extensive body of literature spoken in the Spanish province of Cataluña where the feeling of cultural and linguistic autonomy is very strong.

In the rest of Southern France (see Figure 2.2) are spoken a wide variety of **Occitan** dialects. Occitan (also termed Provençal) shares affinities with both French and Catalan. In the medieval period it enjoyed greater prestige than French. It was well codified and served as the expression of a flourishing literature whose apogee was the poetry of the troubadours. But the defeat of the Occitan-speaking areas by the northern French feudal lords during the Albigensian Crusade marked the beginning of the demise of Occitan. Increased political domination by the North was accompanied by the spread of Standard French southward. The elite of Southern France gradually became bilingual and discarded the use of Occitan for official functions and for literary creation. No longer buttressed by a literary standard, it diverged and fragmented into a multitude of local dialects. In the late nineteenth century Frédéric Mistral tried to reconstitute a new literary standard based on the dialects of the Rhône valley (medieval literary Occitan was based on the speech of Limousin and Languedoc). Mistral's attempts were unsuccessful, and Occitan has continued to recede before Standard French.

Local varieties of language spoken in northern France (see Figure 2.2) are referred to as *Oïl* dialects (as opposed to the Oc or Occitan dialects of the South). They are closely related to Standard French, and, because of the large number of linguistic features they share with that dialect, they have ceased to constitute clearly demarcated speech norms, except in such peripheral areas as Picardy, western Lorraine, Burgundy, Poitou and Charentes, and western Normandy. In the rural areas of southeastern France there exist local varieties of speech that contain features characteristic of both Oïl and Occitan dialects. These dialects, grouped under the term Franco-Provençal, constitute a buffer area between the two main groups of Gallo-Romance dialects.

2.5   THE PRESENT STATUS OF NON-FRENCH VARIETIES OF SPEECH

Standard French is for all intents and purposes the only official language of France, and the authorities of that highly centralized state have always strongly discouraged the use of local varieties of speech. Before the French Revolution, French had not permeated down to the lower social strata outside of the area around Paris. Commenting on the absence of mutual intelligibility between the speech of Paris (Standard French) and that of the Rhône valley he had visited and the problems in oral communication that resulted as a consequence, the playwright Racine wrote his friend La Fontaine, noted for his adaptation of Aesop's fables in French, in 1661:

> "Je vous jure que j'ai autant besoin d'interprète qu'un Moscovite en aurait besoin dans Paris. . . . Cela irait à l'infini si je voulais vous dire tous les inconvénients qui arrivent aux nouveaux venus en ce pays comme moi."

In the early stages of the Revolution no political significance attached to linguistic diversity. In fact, a certain Garat, representative to the Constituent Assembly, advocated the creation of a Basque department on the basis of the linguistic particularism of that area, and the equal status of the local dialects and Standard French was so much taken for granted by the Constituent Assembly that it decided to have all laws translated in local dialects. But the Convention, controlled by the Jacobins and intent on total centralization, quickly launched a war of annihilation on local varieties of speech. The Jacobins' advocacy of complete linguistic uniformity was no doubt motivated by the following demagogic argument: Under the old Regime fluency in Standard French was one of the attributes of the privileged classes; full equality of all citizens could be achieved only if the masses abandoned their vernaculars for Standard French. Under the direction of the Abbé Grégoire, local authorities were requested to complete a questionnaire providing information about local varieties of speech, including their relationship to Standard French, their geographical distribution, their literary expression, and even their influence on morality (sic). Armed with the results of the questionnaire, Grégoire proclaimed:

> "La féodalité a conservé pieusement cette disparité d'idiomes pour mieux river les chaînes de ses serfs. Leur suppression importe au maintien de la liberté. . . . Il faut consacrer au plus tôt, dans une république une et indivisible, l'usage invariable de la langue de la liberté."

And he urged that a crusade be undertaken against the instruments of the forces of reaction:

"Citoyens, qu'une sainte émulation vous anime pour bannir de toutes les contrées de France ces jargons qui sont encore des lambeaux de la Féodalité et de l'Esclavage."

The revolutionary zeal had little immediate effect, but the credo of linguistic equality through linguistic uniformity was accepted by all subsequent governments. It was the spread of compulsory primary education that spelled the eventual demise of non-French varieties of speech. Local schoolteachers imbued with anticlerical and antireactionary fervor banned the use of local dialects from the classroom since they held, rightly or wrongly, that their use interfered with their students' acquisition of fluency in Standard French. The diffusion of French was also fostered by massive population movements occasioned by the two world wars; the extension of paid summer vacations to all levels of the population; and the development of radio and television.

Today there is scarcely any Frenchman who does not speak Standard French, and very few young people have a fluent control of the local language. While the French census forms do not contain questions on the use of languages other than French, the following figures reflect accurately the number of persons in France who have a passive knowledge and some active mastery of a local language not directly related to French:

Language	Number of estimated speakers
Basque	75,000-100,000
Breton	800,000-1,000,000
Alsatian	1,250,000
Flemish	200,000
Catalan	200,000
Corsican	200,000
Occitan	7,500,000

France's force of unskilled laborers is made up mostly of an estimated two million migrant workers mainly from Portugal and North Africa. These speakers of Portuguese and Arabic dialects do not comprise integrated and localized communities, and a discussion of their linguistic problem is outside the scope of a description of language variation indigenous to France.

The sentiment of linguistic particularism has not been completely rooted out from the Basque-, Breton-, Catalan-, and Occitan-speaking areas. In Occitania there have existed, since Mistral's attempted revival of a literary form of Occitan, local societies of Felibriges who have devoted themselves to the maintenance of the local vernacular, its codification, and its illustration by means of literary productions. Because of Alsace's special political status, its local vernacular was never subjected to massive attempts at eradication from Paris, although it was relegated to inferior, patois status by the implantation of Standard German. In Alsace, movements for local linguistic particularism strive to maintain the official status of German rather than to revalorize Alsatian dialects. In the Basque-, Breton-, Catalan-, and Occitan-speaking areas local pressure movements initiated in the late 1930's resulted in the passage in 1951 of a decree allowing the introduction, under local option, of vernacular languages in primary and secondary schools. This decree was carefully drafted so as to subordinate the teaching of the vernaculars to ultimate improvement of the pupils' competence in French:

"Des instructions pédagogiques seront adressées aux recteurs en vue d'autoriser les maîtres à recourir aux parlers locaux dans les écoles primaires et maternelles chaque fois qu'ils pourront en tirer profit pour leur enseignement, notamment pour l'étude de la langue française. Tout instituteur qui en fera la demande pourra être autorisé à consacrer, chaque semaine, une heure d'activités dirigées à l'enseignement de notions élémentaires de lecture et d'écriture du parler local et à l'étude de morceaux choisis de la littérature correspondante. . . . Dans les lycées et collèges, l'enseignement facultatif de toutes les langues et dialectes locaux, ainsi que du folklore, de la littérature et des arts populaires locaux, pourra prendre place dans le cadre des activités dirigées."

Recent demands for regional autonomy have been accompanied by a revalorization of local patois. This movement has been fervently embraced by young intellectuals and it distinguished itself from former attempts, such as that of the Occitan Felibriges, by a more militant tone and an interest centered on the current language rather than older stages. Efforts are being made to work at the grassroots' level by establishing contacts with rural and worker groups and by organizing classes designed to impart fluency in everyday speech. New spelling systems are advocated and lexical modifications are proposed that tend to more clearly demarcate the vernacular from French, and attempts are made to define new norms embracing several local varieties so that they may transcend their patois status. Finally, the vernacular is no longer viewed as a quaint survival from past eras of glory but as a means to achieve local autonomy and self-respect.

2.6   FRENCH OUTSIDE OF FRANCE

French is the official language of more than a dozen countries outside of France. A distinction must be made, however, between Belgium, Switzerland, and Canada, where French is not only an official language but is spoken in several varieties by compact communities, and the other so-called francophone nations, where it is also an official language but is spoken by only a small minority. The latter situation obtains particularly in French-influenced countries of Africa. Indeed, the use of the term francophone for these countries is grossly misleading, since French is used only for administrative and educational purposes and where the vernacular languages spoken by the preponderant part of the population usually do not bear any relationship to it. In these multilingual countries French also serves as a neutral national language accepted by all linguistic and ethnic groups and provides a means of wider communication for the educated elite.

In Belgium, French and Flemish (Dutch) share the status of official language. French, both in its standard form and in many regional dialects, is spoken by the Walloon ethnic group in the southern part of the country. Belgian non-standard varieties of French belong to the Oïl group of dialects and are closely related to those spoken in eastern France, and their divergences from Standard French do not stem from contact with Flemish. In Switzerland, French is one of four officially recognized languages. It is spoken in its standard form and in regional varieties in several cantons, notably those in which are located the cities of Geneva, Lausanne, and Neuchâtel. A variety of French, related to Franco-Provençal dialects is also spoken in the valley of Aosta in northeastern Italy, close to the French and Swiss borders.

Varieties of French are spoken in widely separated areas of North America. In addition to the French overseas departments of Guadeloupe and Martinique in the Antilles and Guiana on the northeastern coast of South America, there are varieties in Canada, the United States, and Haiti. In Canada, French shares with English the status of official language, and it is spoken by more than five million persons residing principally in the province of Quebec. While Canada is officially a bilingual state, only twelve per cent of the population according to the 1961 census figures speak both English and French. That French is a minority language in Canada is reflected by the fact that, whereas about thirty per cent of Franco-Canadians are bilingual, only about four per cent of Anglo-Canadians speak French in addition to their own language. The linguistic situation in Quebec province is complicated by the existence side by side with Standard French of several varieties closely related to it. Regional varieties of French in Canada fall into two main groups of dialects: **Acadian** in the Maritime Provinces and eastern Quebec, and **Laurentian** in the rest of Quebec province, including Quebec City and Montreal. In Montreal particularly there is a social dialect belonging to the Laurentian group, called **Joual**—from the pronunciation of *cheval* in that dialect—characterized by many pronunciation and grammatical features that deviate from Standard French and by heavy lexical borrowing and syntactic adaptations (calques) from English. Standard French is spoken with a regional accent by the tradition-ally-oriented middle class, whereas a more cosmopolitan segment of that class follows the Parisian norm.

In Haiti, French is the official language, but it is spoken fluently by less than five per cent of the population. The preponderant mass of the estimated five million inhabitants of the world's first black republic are monolingual in **Creole** (Creole French). Creole is a language whose genesis and development are still not satisfactorily explained. It has generally been characterized as constituted of French words organized according to the syntax of West African languages and whose pronunciation has also been influenced by these languages. Creole most likely represents the evolved form of a contact language used by speakers of lower-class varieties of seventeenth- and eighteenth-century (Northern) French and speakers of West African languages; in the Indian Ocean this vernacular variety of French came in contact with speakers of Malagasy (Madagascar) languages and Indo-Portuguese. In its pronunciation, grammar, and vocabulary Creole shows its double origin as well as certain features characteristic of the learning of a foreign language under natural (as opposed to classroom) conditions. Creole also functions as the vernacular in the French overseas departments of Martinique, Guadeloupe, and Guiana; in the British-influenced Leeward islands of Dominica, Saint-Lucia and, marginally, in Trinidad and a group of smaller islands to the north; in the Indian Ocean islands of Mauritius (a newly independent multilingual nation), Réunion (an overseas French department), the Seychelles and Rodriguez. All of these territories are former plantation colonies controlled by France during some period of the seventeenth or eighteenth centuries when the majority of the work force consisted of imported slaves from West Africa. To return to Haiti, the middle class of that country is more properly characterized as diglossic: they use French in official and formal situations but Creole in other situations. The variety of Standard French which they use, and which differs from that of the Parisian norm only by the presence of a few local pronunciation features and vocabulary items, strikes metropolitan Frenchmen as somewhat stilted and pompous. This is no doubt because francophone Haitians use Creole in situations where metropolitan Frenchmen would switch to a more spontaneous style and have available only a monitored style of Standard French.

There are two main French-speaking communities in the United States: New England and Southwestern Louisiana. The former is composed mostly of emigrants from Laurentian-speaking areas of Quebec province, and its speech shows many of the features characteristic of Joual. In the nineteenth century and in the beginning of the present century the speech of the Franco-American communities of New England was buttressed by Standard French employed by the Catholic church for religious services, in parochial schools, and in the local press. But as Franco-Americans became assimilated to their surrounding environment, this support gradually disintegrated, and today the varieties of French spoken in New England have been more profoundly affected by English than related Franco-Canadian dialects. Only the older generation speak the local dialect fluently and use it for their basic communicative needs; other members of the Franco-American ethnic group have mostly a passive knowledge.

The linguistic situation is more complex in Southwestern Louisiana. In addition to Creole (referred to as Negro French), two varieties of French are found: **Cajun** dialects and a local variety of Standard French termed "français grammatical." Louisiana Creole is mutually intelligible with most other varieties of Creole, and shows particular affinities with the dialects of Haiti, French Guiana, and Mauritius. Spoken only by older blacks, it is on the verge of extinction.

"Français grammatical" is spoken in Southwestern Louisiana and in New Orleans primarily by some members of the upper middle class descended from white French settlers from France and the former French West Indian colonies, mostly Saint-Domingue (present-day Haiti). A source of confusion is that these persons are called Creoles. The most widely distributed variety of French in Southwestern Louisiana is Cajun. The term is derived from the local pronunciation of *Acadien* and stems from the fact that a large proportion of speakers of Cajun dialects are descendants of settlers who fled from Acadia (present-day Nova Scotia) when that then French colony was ceded to Great Britain in the eighteenth century. Cajun evolved for nearly a century in relative isolation from Standard French, so that today it differs greatly from Standard French as well as from Acadian varieties of Franco-Canadian. Its sociolinguistic status is similar to that of New England dialects of French: it is inferiorized vis-à-vis both English and Standard French and has been abandoned by younger generations of speakers. The number of Louisianans who have some degree of competence in Cajun is estimated to be between 400,000 and 1,000,000. Through the efforts of a local group called Council for the Development of French in Louisiana (CODOFIL), the Louisiana Legislature has recently promulgated an act declaring the teaching of French obligatory starting in primary schools in all parishes where the majority of the population is of French ethnic background. Cajuns now take pride in their ethnicity, and this has been translated into a revalorization of French. The result of the introduction of French in the schools and the beginning of its diffusion by the mass media may result in the preservation of a local variety of Standard French rather than the direct continuation of Cajun.

2.7   ACCENTS AND STYLES OF STANDARD FRENCH

It is important to distinguish between the French dialects spoken in Belgium, Switzerland, and North America, all of which, like Standard French, belong to the Oïl group and accents of Standard French. In the medieval period several competing Oïl dialects existed in a fairly well codified form, and all were used for administrative and literary purposes. But concurrent with the growing economic and political hegemony of Ile-de-France (Paris) the Oïl dialect of that region, Francian, assumed an overwhelming prestige, and by the middle of the fourteenth century had displaced its rivals in the administrative and literary domains. The other dialects ceased to be standards, they became devalorized by their speakers, and were relegated to handling communication dealing with home, hearth, and field. Today, in all francophone countries, Parisian Standard French is the variety that all persons strive to imitate. As it is adopted as a second language or dialect Standard French is modified in the direction of the variety of speech it displaces. These modifications appear principally at the level of pronunciation and vocabulary. For instance, in Canada and Haiti *t* and *d* are pronounced with affrication before the vowels *i* and *y: tu dis* [t^{s}yd^{z}i]; in most Occitan areas nasal vowels are produced with an intercalated nasal consonant when they occur before a consonant: *un peu* [oe^{m}pø] *chante* [ʃa^{n}t], *oncle* [ɔ̃ŋkl]. Regional accents of Standard French contain numerous terms referring to local artifacts, culture, flora and fauna, words borrowed from other languages spoken in the community as well as survivals from displaced varieties of French. For example in Quebec province *industriel* is replaced by *manufacturier* and the expression *faire des courses* or *faire du shopping* by *magasiner.*

Intersecting with regional varieties of Standard French are variations in speech correlating with social status. From a sociolinguistic point of view one may identify two varieties of Standard French: one characteristic of middle-class speakers and the other of the working and lower classes. The former will be referred to as *bon usage* and the latter as *français populaire.* The adjective *populaire* means here "referring to the *peuple,* the plebian masses" rather than "popular." Formerly the line of demarcation between these two social varieties was very sharp, but the gradual breakdown of a strict separation between social classes in France has resulted in the establishment of a fluid continuum between them. It is more realistic to consider *bon usage* and *français populaire* as two idealized polar varieties of Standard French. The distance between individual speech samples and one or the other of these two poles depends on several factors to be discussed below.

The prestige variety of Standard French is *bon usage* spoken with a Paris accent, and its typical speakers are upper middle-class Parisians. *Français populaire* also varies according to geographical location, but as was the case for *bon usage,* the variety that is imitated throughout the francophone domain has radiated from Paris. The two social varieties of Standard French have spread by means of two different sets of channels: *bon usage* by means of the schools, government administration, and the mass media; *français populaire* by means of population movements occasioned by military service, migration from rural areas to urban centers, vacation travel, etc.

Regional and social accents of Standard French also intersect with style and medium of expression. Many of the features of spontaneous style are located close to the *français populaire* pole whereas those of monitored style are nearer the *bon usage* pole. *Français populaire* is a less elaborated form of Standard French whose normal means of expression is the spoken language. On the other hand, *bon usage* is marked by numerous redundant features whose presence in written texts may be considered equivalent to the features of sentence organization and semantic distinctions signalled in speech by changes in intonation and other prosodic phenomena. A middle-class Frenchman is likely to shift toward the *français populaire* pole when engaged in a casual conversation, while a worker will adopt many features of *bon usage* when he is committing his language to writing. Thus, it would be incongruous for a middle-class speaker who notices that his wife requires help to utter *Puis-je t'être utile, ma chère?*, most likely, he would say *Je peux t'aider, mon chou?* A lower-class speaker who normally pronounced [ʒʃepɑ] for *Je ne sais pas* would be conscious of committing a gross error in grammar if he attempted to represent exactly what he had said by means of *j'sais pas* or even *je sais pas.*

Of the two varieties of Standard French, *français populaire* is the most dynamic. Its vocabulary, and to a lesser extent, its pronunciation and grammatical structure, are subject to change through the influence of external and internal linguistic forces. The external forces take the form of pressure from other languages or dialects spoken in the particular geographical area, but one of the important sources of lexical renewal of *français populaire* is **slang** *(argot)*. Slang is a coded variety of *français populaire* achieved by maintaining the same grammatical structure and pronunciation but changing the meaning of words or substituting new words. The result is a loss of mutual intelligibility, as the following examples attest:

Les huiles sont au parfum. Les gens en haut lieu sont au courant.

S'il est pas clamcé, poirotte un peu et reviens dans une plombe. S'il est pas mort, attends un peu et reviens dans une heure.

Bon usage is codified by normative grammars and dictionaries and thus undergoes very few changes. Speakers may depart from a well-established norm only by a modest number of borrowings from foreign languages or by the use of vocabulary items and grammatical constructions from older stages of the language. The latter type of borrowing is characteristic of the literary uses of *bon usage* which contain, depending on the taste of individual authors, a variable number of lexical and grammatical features of **Classical French.**

The sources of influence and modification of *français populaire* and *bon usage,* and the factors that determine the relative number of features from one or the other of these two polar varieties of Standard French used in a particular speech sample are summarized in Figure 2.4.

Figure 2.4

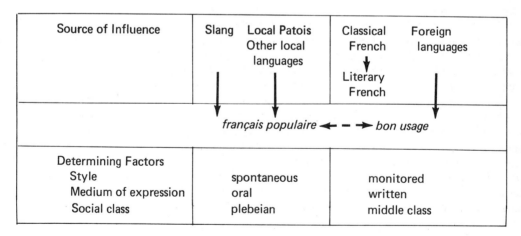

Source of Influence	Slang Local Patois Other local languages	Classical Foreign French languages ↓ Literary French
français populaire ◄ — ► *bon usage*		
Determining Factors Style Medium of expression Social class	spontaneous oral plebeian	monitored written middle class

Sociolinguistic differentiation also exists within patois. For example, in Nice there are upper middle-class and lower-class varieties of the local Occitan, Niçart. Usually, outside of Paris, members of the upper and middle classes use a variety of *bon usage* which differs little from that of Paris, and the working and lower classes speak a variety of *français populaire* more markedly influenced by the local patois or non-French variety of speech. What might be considered the purest forms of *bon usage* and *français populaire* are found in Paris—the myth that the most prestigious variety of *bon usage* is spoken in the Loire valley, particularly in Touraine, is without empirical foundation. However, the pronunciation, grammar and lexicon of educated *Tourangeaux* very closely matches that of Parisian *bon usage.*

We complete this chapter with two sample cases that illustrate that members of French-speaking communities have available a variable range of speech types and that, often out of awareness, they select from this range a variety congruent with the situational context.

Consider first the case of a middle-class speaker residing in Nice who has local family ties going back several generations. With his peers, he uses a regional accent of *bon usage,* except that in spontaneous style he might shift down toward the *français populaire* pole or insert features from a form of Niçart, the local Occitan patois, that enjoys a certain degree of local prestige. Often, his shift to Niçart takes the form of complete sentences. In his dealing with working- or lower-class speakers he will accommodate to their speech by a greater shift to *français populaire,* and depending on his interlocutor's proficiency in the local patois, he might shift completely to a more plebeian variety of Niçart. The totality of his speech repertoire—his linguistic range—shows features that enable the knowledgeable observer (that is to say, a member of the same linguistic community) to identify him as a resident of Occitania, as a member of the middle class, etc.

Consider next the case of a working-class resident of Montreal, Canada. His basic, everyday communicative needs are met by Joual, a local variety of *français populaire* which differs from the varieties of France by the presence of massive lexical borrowings from English, numerous syntactic calques, and divergences at the level of pronunciation. In fact, the degree of mutual intelligibility between Joual and Parisian *français populaire* is quite limited. If he has lived outside of Montreal for some period of time, this typical working-class Montreal speaker might be able to shift to a rural Laurentian dialect of French. In addition, he would be able to understand the local variety of *bon usage* as well as the Paris variety which is used on certain radio and television programs.

In conclusion, although in this textbook we will be describing the *bon usage* variety of Standard French, the variety of French most suitable for acquisition on the part of foreigners, the reader should always bear in mind that actual speech samples will deviate considerably from this norm. Some of the implications of the relatively heterogeneous nature of the object of our study will be taken up in later chapters.

STUDY QUESTIONS

1. Provide examples from English of:
   a) differences in the pronunciation of words that distinguish speakers from different geographical areas;
   b) differences in the pronunciation of words that distinguish speakers living in the same area but belonging to two clearly demarcated social levels;

     c)   grammatical features that are characteristic of working- or lower-class speakers but which may also be used on certain occasions by all speakers;

     d)   differences in vocabulary that are characteristic of the part of the U. S. in which you live.

2. How can it be shown that *r*-less pronunciations within the New York City speech community are stigmatized in New York City? Is *r*-lessness also stigmatized in your area?

3. What is the difference between a bilingual and a diglossic linguistic community?

4. In what way is Canada not a bilingual country?

5. How does an accent differ from a dialect?

6. Define the term *patois.*

7. In such English-influenced Caribbean islands as Dominica, Trinidad, and Saint-Lucia, French Creole is referred to as patois. What attitudes toward the language are implied by the choice of this term?

8. List the languages spoken in France which do not belong to the Romance group of languages.

9. Where is Catalan spoken in France? How is it related to the language of Cataluña, on the one hand, and to Occitan dialects, on the other?

10. In your opinion, what motivated the campaign for the eradication of local speech varieties launched by later Revolution governments? Why would subsequent governments such as the Empire of the Third Republic have adopted the same attitude?

11. What is the current status of Occitan dialects?

12. How are the local French dialects spoken in Belgium, Switzerland, and the valley of Aosta related to Standard French?

13. Define the term *Joual.*

14. Describe the linguistic situation in Haiti and Martinique.

15. Why is the use of the term Creole in the Louisiana context misleading?

16. Distinguish between *bon usage* and *français populaire* from a sociolinguistic point of view.

17. List some features that set off *français populaire* from *bon usage.*

18. Describe the varieties of speech available to a farmer living in Brittany and the circumstances of their use.

3

THE ARTICULATORY DESCRIPTION
OF CONSONANTS

3.1   SPEECH PRODUCTION

Speech sounds are produced by the modification of a vibrating column of air as it moves outward from the lungs. Most significant modifications of the column of expelled air take place between the larynx and the lips. The vocal tract is shown in Figure 3.1.

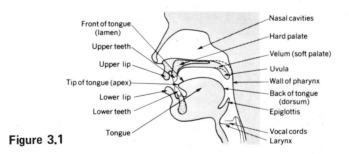

Figure 3.1

Speech souhds are divided into two main classes: **consonants** and **vowels.** Consonants are produced by stopping or impeding the airstream; vowels are produced with unobstructed airstream. From the point of view of acoustics, consonants are noisy (non-harmonic) sounds, whereas vowels are musical (harmonic) sounds.

Consonants are classified by reference to three sets of articulatory variables:

1.   the role of the vocal cords (**voicing**);

2.   the manner in which the airstream flows out of the vocal tract (**manner of articulation**);

3.   the place in the vocal tract where the airstream is stopped or impeded (**point of articulation**).

3.2   VOICING

The **larynx**, which juts out as the Adam's apple, is a cartilaginous structure located at the top of the windpipe, or **trachea**. The larynx contains the **vocal cords**, two elastic bands of tissue attached to its side walls. The vocal cords come together at the front of the larynx, but in the back they are attached

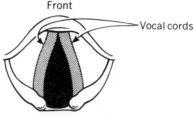

Front

Vocal cords

Figure 3.2   Back

to two different movable cartilages; they can thus move from side to side as the two cartilages to which they are attached are spread apart or drawn together. This is illustrated in Figure 3.2.

The vocal cords may be drawn apart so that the airstream can pass through freely, as is the case in normal breathing; they can be drawn together closing the passageway (glottis) completely; or they may be partially drawn together leaving a small opening for the airstream. In the last case the pressure of the outgoing air will cause the vocal cords to vibrate; this is called **voicing**. Since the vocal cords are elastic they may be set to different tensions, just like the strings of a violin, and will vibrate at different frequencies. These variations in the vibration frequency of the vocal cords produce changes in pitch: with greater tension, the frequency of vibration increases, and **pitch** rises; with reduced tension, the frequency of vibration decreases and pitch falls.

Sounds produced with vibration of the vocal cords are **voiced** sounds; sounds produced without any vibration of the vocal cords are **voiceless** sounds. For instance, English *p* as in *pin,* contrasts with *b* as in *bin* only with regard to voice: voiceless versus voiced respectively. The three main positions of the vocal cords are illustrated in Figure 3.3.

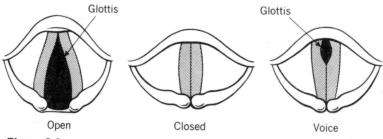

Glottis   Glottis

Open   Closed   Voice

Figure 3.3

3.3 MANNER OF ARTICULATION

French consonants fall into three main classes on the basis of their manner of articulation: **stops, fricatives,** and **resonants.** Stop consonants are produced by the complete closure of the airstream channel. Typically, a stop consonant is characterized by three phases: in the **onset** phase the organs that form the closure—say, the upper and the lower lip if the consonant is *b* or *p*—move toward each other; there is then a very brief **hold** phase, during which the airstream channel is closed; finally during the **release** phase the organs separate, and the air held back by the obstruction rushes out, producing the noise perceived as the consonant. French and English have six stops each: [p b t d k g].

For fricative consonants the organs forming the obstruction to the airstream do not form a complete closure. The channel through which the airstream passes is narrowed, and as the air escapes through it, a friction noise is produced. Unlike stops, fricatives can be prolonged, but like stops they may be voiced or voiceless. The fricative consonants of English and French are compared below; each fricative is illustrated by a key word where it occurs as the first sound:

French	[f] fin	[s] sel	[ʃ] chou				
	[v] vin	[z] zèle	[ʒ] joue				
English	[f] fin	[θ] thin	[s] so	[ʃ] shoe			
	[v] vin	[ð] then	[z] zoo	[ʒ] measure			

Stops and fricatives together constitute the class of **obstruent** consonants. In both French and English, obstruents pair off in a series where the only distinctive feature between the elements of each pair is the presence or absence of voice. Resonants are consonants produced without complete closure of the vocal tract nor any friction noise. They include the nasal consonants, sounds like [l] and [r], and the semivowels. When the airstream has progressed through the glottis, it may go through either the mouth or both the mouth and the nose. The back portion of the roof of the mouth, the **velum,** is flexible and may be raised or lowered. If the velum is raised, it presses against the back wall of the pharynx and closes the passageway between the pharynx and the nasal cavities. The air can then travel only through the mouth, and the sound thus produced is said to be **oral,** or non-nasal. If the velum is lowered, the passageway from the pharynx to the nasal cavities is open, and the airstream can pass through both the mouth and the nose; the sound thus produced is termed **nasal.** Try to lower and raise your velum as you utter the sound *ah;* note the difference in quality produced. Now contrast *dough* and *no.* The phonemes *n* and *d* differ only in that *n* is produced with the velum lowered and *d* with the velum raised (see Figure 3.4). Nasalization can be detected easily by the "pinch" test. Pinch your nose above the nostrils and say first *dough,* then *no,* then *dough* again. You will observe that the pronunciation of *no* is accompanied by vibration in the nose. English nasal consonants include the first segment of *me* and *no* and the last of *sing.* French nasal consonants include the first segment of *mou* [mu] and *nous* [nu] and the last segment of *peigne* [pɛɲ]. In the pronunciation of French [l] the front of the tongue forms a closure against the **alveoles** or gum ridge, and air passes on both sides of the tongue. For that reason [l] is termed a **lateral.** The pronunciation of [R] varies greatly in French, depending on a speaker's geographical provenience, his social level, or his style of speech.

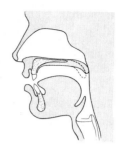

Figure 3.4 Velum raised and lowered.

The normal variant found in the speech of educated Paris speakers is a resonant produced with slight friction. Semivowels will be discussed in Chapter 6. In addition to [R], French has another resonant produced with slight friction, [j], which occurs at the end and in the middle of words and which must be distinguished from the semivowel [j] for reasons which will be discussed in Chapter 5.

3.4   POINT OF ARTICULATION

The third criterion in the definition of consonants is the **point of articulation,** a convenient way to refer to the organs involved in the formation of the obstruction or modification of the airstream channel. Two organs are involved in the articulation of a consonant: a movable articulator moving toward a fixed articulator. Movable articulators include the lower lip and the three main parts of the

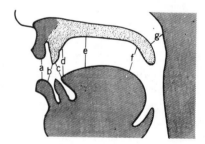

Figure 3.5
(a) Bilabial; (b) labiodental; (c) dental; (d) alveolar;
(e) palatal; (f) velar; (g) nasal

tongue: the tip or **apex,** the front, or **blade**, and the back, the **dorsum.** Fixed articulators include the upper lip, the upper front teeth, the alveoles, the hard palate, the soft palate or velum, and the uvula, the extreme back of the velum. (In the production of the uvular trill [r] found in some French dialects, the uvula is set into a series of rapid vibrations and thus functions as a movable articulator.) Articulators taken in movable (lower) and fixed (upper) pairs define the various points of articulation; for the sake of convenience the name of the fixed articulator is generally used. A convenient classification and description of points of articulation is provided in Figure 3.5.

Consult the classification of French consonants provided in Table 3.1. The stops [p] and [b] and the nasal [m] are produced with a closure formed by the upper and lower lip; these consonants are termed **bilabials.** Remember that in the pronunciation of nasals there is no complete closure of the vocal tract, since air may pass through the nasal cavities. The fricatives [f] and [v] are produced with contact between the upper lip and the lower front teeth and are therefore called **labiodentals.** French has six consonants produced with contact between the tip of the tongue (**apex**) and the upper

Table 3.1 The Consonant System of French

Manner of Articulation			Point of Articulation					
			Bilabial	Labio-dental	Dental	Palatal	Velar	Pharyngal (uvular)
Obstruents	Stops	Voiced	b		d		g	
		Voiceless	p		t		k	
	Frica-tives	Voiced		v	z	ʒ		
		Voiceless		f	s	ʃ		
Resonants		Fricatives				j		R
		Nasals	m		n	ɲ		
		Lateral			l			
		Semivowels	ɥ			j	w	

Key Words

[b]	bain	[d]	daim	[g]	gain
[p]	pain	[t]	teint	[k]	quint
[v]	vain	[z]	zône	[ʒ]	geint
[f]	faim	[s]	sain	[ʃ]	chien
		[j]	yacht; paille	[R]	rein; par
[m]	main	[n]	nain	[ɲ]	pagne
		[l]	lin; pâle		
[ɥ]	puis	[j]	pied	[w]	pois

front teeth, the **dentals** [t], [d], [s], [z], [n], [l]. Sometimes [t] and [d] may be produced with contact of the tip of the tongue against the gum ridge (alveoles) rather than the upper front teeth and are referred to as **alveolars**. Another large group of French consonants are **palatals;** they involve a relatively large area of contact between the blade of the tongue and the hard palate. French palatals are [ʃ], [ʒ], the nasal [ɲ], and the fricative resonant [j]. The stops [k] and [g] are **velars**, produced with a closure formed by the back of the tongue and the soft palate (velum).   Finally [R] is produced with movement of the back of the tongue toward the back wall of the mouth or pharynx and is termed a **pharyngal**. The semivowels are best described in terms of features of articulation of the vowel system. Figures 3.6, 3.7, and 3.8 illustrate typical (bi)labial, dental, and velar points of articulation exemplified by the voiceless stops [p], [t], and [k].

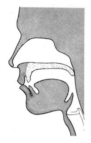

Figure 3.6
Position of articulation
for / p /.

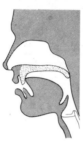

Figure 3.7
Position of articulation
tor / t /.

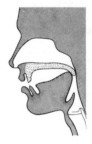

Figure 3.8.
Position of articulation
for / k /.

3.5   DISTINCTIVE ARTICULATORY FEATURES

An individual French consonant may be viewed as sets of articulatory features which distinguish it from any other consonant of the language. Sound serves to transmit meaning, and only those articulatory features that ultimately serve to distinguish French words from each other need to be considered in an introductory description. For example, we need to determine the feature of articulation that differentiates *pain* [pɛ̃] and *bain* [bɛ̃]. That feature is located in the first segment of each word and consists of the voicelessness of [p] as against the voicing of [b]. Voicing is then the distinctive feature that distinguishes all instances of [p] from all instances of [b]: *pont/bon, tapa/tabac.* But [p] is not only distinguished from [b] by voicing, it is distinguished from other voiceless stops by its labial place of articulation and from the voiceless labiodental [f] by its stop manner of articulation. Thus, the symbol [p] can be considered a shorthand notation for a set of three distinctive articulatory features.

$$\begin{bmatrix} \text{voiceless} \\ \text{labial} \\ \text{stop} \end{bmatrix} \quad [\,p\,]$$

There are other features of articulation that characterize all instances of [p] or certain instances of [p] occurring in particular positions in words, for example, initially. But these do not serve to distinguish words and need not be considered in an introductory description of the French sound system.

All obstruents are characterized by three distinctive articulatory features: one of voicing, one of point of articulation, and one of manner of articulation. As an illustration, we provide the distinctive articulatory characterization for [d], [v], and [ʃ]:

[d]	[v]	[ʃ]
voiced	voiced	voiceless
dental	labiodental	palatal
stop	fricative	fricative

Resonants need not be characterized by as many distinctive articulatory features as obstruents. All we need to state about [m], [n], and [ɲ], in addition to the fact that they are nasals, is their point of articulation. The resonant [l] is sufficiently characterized as a dental lateral, [R] as a pharyngal resonant, and [j] as a palatal resonant. Voicing need not be specified for resonants since they do not form voiced/voiceless pairs with otherwise identical articulatory features.

STUDY QUESTIONS

1. **Vocal Tract**
    Identify the parts of the vocal tract referred to in the diagram below.

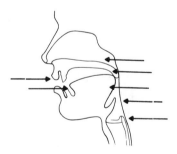

2. **Voicing**
    To test for the presence or absence of voicing, place a finger on your Adam's apple and say *z z z z z* then *s s s s s* several times in quick succession. You will feel a vibration when you say

z z z z z but none when you say *s s s s s*. Now try the "buzz" test and indicate whether the following French words begin with a voiced or a voiceless consonant.

pour   voiceless _____   quand   _____

vin   voiced _____   femme   _____

chaud _____   rond   _____

gare   _____   monde   _____

tire   _____   cinq   _____

3. **Manner of Articulation**

Transcribe in phonetic notation the final consonant of the following French words and state its manner of articulation

froide   [d] stop _____

belle   [l] lateral resonant _____

anglaise   _____

belge   _____

italienne   _____

turque   _____

russe   _____

yougoslave _____

4. **Place of Articulation**

Provide a consonant that has the same point of articulation as the consonants given.

[p]   [b]   _____

[t]   [d]   _____

[ʃ]   [ʒ]   _____

[f]   _____

[k]   _____

5. **Distinctive Articulatory Features**

a) Identify the consonants specified by the following distinctive articulatory features.

voiced dental stop   [d] _____

voiceless velar stop   _____

voiced labiodental fricative   _____

voiceless palatal fricative   _____

voiced dental fricative   _____

pharyngal fricative resonant   _____

palatal nasal   _____

palatal fricative resonant   _____

b) State the distinctive articulatory features for the following consonants.

[p]   voiceless _____   labial _____   stop _____

[f]   _____   _____   _____

[n]   _____   _____   _____

[l]   _____   _____   _____

[ʒ]   _____   _____   _____

[j]   _____   _____   _____

[R]   _____   _____   _____

4

DISTINCTIVE AND NON-DISTINCTIVE FEATURES OF FRENCH AND ENGLISH CONSONANTS

4.1   THE PHONEME

Behind the purely objective reality of articulatory motions and acoustic features is an "inner" system not available to direct observation but of which even linguistically naïve native speakers are aware, the phonological system of the language. The first step in the description of a language is the discovery of sound categories as they are perceived and interpreted by particular human speech communities. The fundamental unit of the sound system of a language is not the **phone,** a discrete class of sound within a narrowly defined articulatory and acoustic range, but the **phoneme,** a set of phones (which may sometimes consist of a single phone) which function as a single unit. We represent phones with square brackets [ ] and phonemes with parallel slant lines / /.

The discovery of the phonemic system of a language involves testing variation in phonetic substance against variation in meaning: two phones are shown to belong to two different phonemes if the substitution of one for the other results in a change of meaning. Consider the English word *pin.* This word consists of three phones we shall represent as [p], [i], and [n] respectively. At this stage of our discussion of sound systems, we need only state that [p] is a consonant produced without any vibration of the vocal cords and by complete closure of the mouth cavity at the lips; more technically, as we have seen in the preceding chapter, we say that it is a **voiceless bilabial stop.** If the vocal cords vibrate, a different phone, [b], a **voiced** bilabial stop, is produced. The substitution of [b] for [p], or, to put it more correctly, of voicing for voicelessness, produces a word, *bin* [bin], whose meaning is different from that of the original word, *pin.* Consequently the phones [p] and [b] must be assigned to two different phonemes / p / and / b / respectively.

Word pairs distinguished by a single segment are termed **minimal pairs,** and they constitute absolute proof for assigning two phones to separate phonemes. In English the contrast between the phonemes / p / and / b / determines many minimal pairs, and the two phonemes contrast with each other in a variety of positions: initially (*pat* versus *bat*), finally (*cap* versus *cab*), and medially (*rapid* versus *rabid*). Similarly French / p / and / b / determine the minimal pairs *pain* versus *bain, serpe* versus *Serbe,* or *tapa* versus *tabac.*

4.2   VARIATION IN THE ARTICULATORY RANGE OF PHONEMES

Phonemes of a language are not always pronounced alike in all positions in which they occur. They show minor variations in articulation which are not essential in differentiating one phoneme from another—and ultimately, one word from another—but which must be taken into account if one is to pronounce phonemes exactly the way native speakers do. Consider for example the pronunciation of / t / in the English words *team* and *steam.* As a speaker of English you are blissfully unaware of the fact that these two words contain two different *t* phones. Yet the difference in articulation between the / t / of *team* and that of *steam* can readily be demonstrated.

Place the palm of one of your hands in front of your mouth and say *team* loudly. You will notice that as you pronounce the / t /, a strong puff of air strikes the palm of your hand. This puff of air is called **aspiration,** and sounds characterized by it are termed **aspirated.** You will also note that the / t / of *steam* is not aspirated. English has at least two *t* phones: an aspirated [t'] and an unaspirated [t]. But these two phones can never contrast since unaspirated *t* occurs only after / s / and aspirated *t* in initial position and medially before a stressed vowel. They are positional variants (or **allophones**) of a single phoneme / t /.

Language is systematic, and a good phonological analysis should reveal the symmetrical relationships that exist between the phonetic features of a language. Let us consider the contrast between English / p / and / b / again. We observe that a single phone, a voiced bilabial stop [b], contrasts with a different type of voiceless bilabial stop in each of the following positions:

Initial		*Medial*		*Final*	
[p']	pin	[p]	rapid	[p=]	cap
[b]	bin	[b]	rabid	[b]	cab

In initial position—and within a word but before a strongly stressed vowel—/ p / is realized with aspiration; within a word but before a weakly stressed vowel, it is realized without any aspiration; in final position it is generally realized without any release of the closure. These three phonetic features that characterize / p / in various positions (aspiration, non-aspiration, and lack of release) are non-distinctive, for they cannot be used to differentiate words as can the features voiced and voiceless. They are in a sense mere accidents of pronunciation conditioned by the phonetic features that precede or follow. We also note that the features voiced and voiceless do not contrast after / s /, that is, matching *spin* (which contains unaspirated [p]) there is no **sbin.*

The other English stops (/ t /, / d /, / k /, / g /) pattern like / p / and / b /, with phonetically similar phones matching each other in the same positions. When we examine the velar stop pair / k / versus / g /, we note that in initial position and medially before a strongly stressed vowel / g / contrasts with aspirated [k'], that in medial position before a weakly stressed vowel it contrasts with unaspirated [k]; that in final position it contrasts with unreleased [k=], and that it does not occur after / s / to contrast with unaspirated [k]. These same facts characterize the dental pair / t / versus / d /. The following symmetrical scheme emerges for English stops:

	Initial (voiceless aspirated vs. voiced)	Medial (voiceless vs. voiced)	Final (voiceless unreleased vs. voiced)	After / s / (voiceless unaspirated)
Bilabial	pin bin	rapid rabid	cap cab	spin
Dental	tin din	attain addition	cat cad	stint
Velar	kill gill	lacking lagging	back bag	skin

Language may be conceived as a system of choices available to the speaker, but in that system each choice entails constraints on the speaker's linguistic behavior. If we choose to begin a sentence with the expression *I'm going,* our choice of the next sentence element is severely restricted: we need to select an adverb (away), a locative (*there to France*), some other adverbial (*tomorrow, with John*), or an infinitive (*to read, to see*). Unless we insert a pause (e.g., *I'm going, my friend*), we cannot select a nominal (*my friend, the house*) such as we could had we begun the sentence with another verb (*I see*). Similarly, at the phonological level we are in a sense free to select phonemes; but once a phoneme is selected the choice of the allophone that manifests the phoneme is conditioned by the structure of the language. For example, when we choose the vocabulary unit *kin* we also choose the phoneme / k / rather than the phonemes / p / or / t /, but the particular phonetic variety of / k / we produce is conditioned by the fact that in initial position English stops are realized by an aspirated phone rather than by an unreleased or unaspirated phone.

There are some instances, however, where a choice amongst several allophonic realizations is available to the speaker. In final position, voiceless English stops are realized by two allophones, an unreleased variant [p=], [t=], [k=] or an aspirated variant not unlike that found in initial positions and medially before a stressed vowel [p'], [t'], [k']. The choice between the unreleased or the aspirated variant is optional rather than conditioned, but it does not result in changes of meaning; it merely expresses a difference in style: in normal conversational style English voiceless stops are unreleased in final position, but in careful, formal pronunciation they are produced with a distinct aspirated release. Phones which co-occur in the same environment but which are not in contrast are said to be in **free variation.** This term is not altogether accurate since the choice among co-occurring phones is determined by choice of style, which, as we have seen in Chapter 2, is determined by the circumstances attending the speech act and the social relationships between speaker and hearer.

4.3   AIMS OF PHONOLOGICAL ANALYSIS

Learning to pronounce a foreign language with native accuracy and fluency involves: (1) acquiring the ability to perceive and reproduce the phonemic contrasts of the language; and

(2) producing the positional variants of phonemes in exactly the same way the native speakers of the language produce them. In addition, for languages where there are significant differences in pronunciation that correlate with education or socioeconomic prestige, to pronounce the language like educated speakers of the language requires the ability to shift styles in appropriate circumstances. A pedagogically useful phonological analysis should present the following information to the language teacher or the developer of teaching materials: (1) the **phonemic inventory,** that is the number of phonemic contrasts that must be posited for the language; (2) detailed phonetic specifications (primarily from an articulatory point of view) of the positional variants of the phonemes and a description of the environment in which they occur; (3) a statement of major dialect and stylistic variations involving differences in phonemic inventory or differences in articulation.

In Chapter 3 we have presented the inventory of French consonants, and we have given a description of their distinctive articulatory features. French consonants do not as a rule show marked positional variants, so that it will not be necessary to provide additional detail in specifying their articulation. In the remaining sections of this chapter we will compare the consonant systems of French and English for the purpose of identifying differences in phonemic inventory or in the articulation of corresponding consonants which might cause learning problems for the English learner of French.

4.4   THE ENGLISH CONSONANT SYSTEM

Table 4.1 gives the inventory and the distinctive articulatory features of English consonants. Note that in the obstruent system French and English differ in only four areas: (1) English differentiates between dental and alveolar fricatives. There is a pair of interdental fricatives / θ / and / ð / produced with the tip of the tongue between the lower and upper front teeth (although in fact the point of articulation varies and is often dental) which contrasts with an alveolar pair / t / and / d /; (2) / t / and / d / are pronounced with alveolar rather than dental point of articulation; (3) there is a glottal fricative / h / produced by constricted passage of the air through the vocal tract; (4) there are two palatals / tʃ / and / dʒ / produced with a stop articulation that shifts to a fricative articulation; unlike stops, / tʃ / and / dʒ / can be prolonged and they are termed **affricates.** (These two affricates function as single units and are often represented by a single symbol, / č / and / ǰ / respectively.) In the resonant system, English has a velar rather than a palatal nasal and only two semivowels. The latter are usually termed glides, and some linguists class / r / as a glide. As in French, the glides are best described within the frame of reference of vowels. In sections 4.5 and 4.6 we compare the French and English consonant systems in greater detail.

4.5   PHONEMIC INTERFERENCE

Every language selects a limited number of sounds from the almost unlimited number that human speech organs can produce and organizes them in a unique way. Two languages differ not only in the number of phonemes and the contrastive relations that obtain among the phonemes but also in the assignment of phonetic material to individual phonemes. Differences in the way two languages structure phonetic reality results in **phonological interference.**

Table 4.1 The Consonant System of English

Manner of Articulation		Bilabial	Labio-dental	Inter-dental	Alveolar	Palatal	Velar	Glottal
Obstruents	Stops — Voiced	b			d		g	
	Stops — Voiceless	p			t		k	
	Fricatives — Voiced		v	ð	z	ʒ		
	Fricatives — Voiceless		f	θ	s	ʃ		h
	Affricates — Voiced					dʒ		
	Affricates — Voiceless					tʃ		
Resonants	Nasals	m			n		ŋ	
	Lateral				l ⟶			
	Retroflex				r			
	Glides					j	w	

Key Words

[b] *b*in   [d] *d*in   [g] *g*ain
[p] *p*in   [t] *t*in   [k] *k*in

[v] *v*ain   [ð] *th*en   [z] *z*one   [ʒ] mea*s*ure
[f] *f*in   [θ] *th*in   [s] *s*in   [ʃ] *sh*in

                                                  [dʒ] *g*in
                                                  [tʃ] *ch*in
                                                  [h] *h*im

[m] *m*en   [n] *n*ame   [ŋ] si*ng*
                [l] *l*ane
                [r] *r*ain
                [j] *y*ou   [w] *w*oo

Difficulties in the perception and production of the phonemic contrasts of a foreign language are greatest in phonetic areas where the foreign language has more contrasts than the native language; in other words, when the foreign language is **overdifferentiated** with regard to the native language. For example, English is overdifferentiated with regard to French in the area of dental or alveolar stops and fricative consonants. In English there are six contrasts in that phonetic area: *tin, din, thin, then, sin, Zen*; but only four in French: *tant, dent, cent, zône*.

We can predict that French speakers will have difficulty in distinguishing between such pairs as *tin* versus *thin,* or *thin* versus *sin,* or *fin* versus *thin,* and in producing them so that they are clearly identifiable by English speakers. Characteristically, French speakers hear the / θ / of *thin* as their / s / or / f / and the / ð / of *then* as their / z / or / v /.

As Tables 3.2 and 4.1 show, the French consonant system is underdifferentiated in several areas with regard to the English consonant system, and speakers of English will experience few difficulties in perceiving French consonant contrasts, nor will it be difficult for them to produce most French consonants so that they are unambiguously interpreted by French speakers. In fact problems will be encountered with French phonemes that have English counterparts rather than with "new" phonemes. The problems are due in most instances to differences in the distribution or in the phonetic realization of matching phonemes.

4.5.1   Release of Final Consonants

In American English, voiceless stops (/ p t k /) are normally unreleased in final position, but their French counterparts always have a clearly audible release phase. American speakers have no difficulty distinguishing between words with different voiceless stops like *sap, sat,* or *sack* because the cue is contained in the transition between the vowel and the consonant and not in the release phase. In French the final release is essential for the identification of final consonants, and its absence is interpreted as absence of any consonant. For / p t k / final release consists of aspiration, i.e., / p t k / have aspirated allophones [p' t' k'] in final position; for all other consonants it consists of prolongation which sometimes is heard as a short [ə] vowel. The presence or absence of a final consonant plays an important differentiative role in French. For instance, it differentiates feminine and masculine forms of adjectives and the third person plural and the third person singular present indicative forms of verbs, e.g., *petite / petit; bonne / bon; ils viennent / il vient; ils finissent / il finit.*

4.5.2   / s / versus / z /

In American English, / s / and / z / contrast in all positions "sue" vs. "zoo," "racing" vs. "raising," "face" vs. "phase," but sometimes they are in free variation in medial position, and one hears words like "citizen" and "greasy" pronounced [sitəzən] or [sitəsən] and [grisiʲ] or [griziʲ] respectively. The extent of this variation depends on geographical location, but it is found among all American speakers. It is possible that confusion of such French minimal pairs as *le désert* vs. *le dessert* by English learners is due in part to the carrying over of this free variation.

4.5.3   Assimilation of / s / and / z /

In normal conversational style and in many areas of the United States, sequences / s / or / z / + / j / are assimilated to sequences / ʃ / or / ʒ / + / j /. "He'll pass you" is pronounced [hil pæ ʃjə] instead of [hil pæ sjə], "as you like" is pronounced [æ ʒjəlajk] instead of [æzyᵊlajk]. Only in carefully enunciated speech are / s / and / z / maintained without assimilation to the following / j /. Since in English the sequences / sj / and / zj / do not contrast with / ʃj / and / ʒj / respectively, this assimilation does not interfere with communication. In French / sj / contrasts with / ʃj /, e.g., *la sienne* vs. *la chienne, vous cassiez* vs. *vous cachiez,* and / zj / contrasts with / ʒj /, e.g., *la lésion* vs. *la légion,* and assimilation would eliminate the contrast. In French, to avoid assimilation, / s / and / z / should be articulated carefully with the tongue well fronted and its tip touching the back of the lower teeth. This will prevent the tongue from moving backward and upward to make contact with the palate under influence of the following / j /.

4.6   PHONETIC INTERFERENCE

The acquisition of near-native pronunciation accuracy—what the layman refers to as a "good accent"—entails the ability to produce the correct allophone of a phoneme in the appropriate environment. This ability is difficult to acquire for two reasons.

First, the articulatory habits of the foreign language partially overlap those of the native language, and the student must learn to make new responses to stimuli which are interpreted as identical to native language stimuli. For instance, French and English / s / differ with regard to place of articulation: the former is a dental, and the latter an alveolar. The partial similarities he perceives in the acoustic signal of French / s / will lead an English speaker to respond with the alveolar rather than the dental sound. Such problems are not encountered in the production of phonemes whose allophones involve the acquisition of complete sets of new articulatory habits.

Second, perfect control of articulatory habits is essential only insofar as they contribute to the differentiation of phonemes. Once the student has acquired the ability to produce phonemes with accuracy sufficient to permit the native speaker to identify them, he is not particularly motivated to exert the effort necessary to produce them with articulatory perfection.

4.6.1   Mode of Articulation

The articulatory habits of French converge to constitute two **modes of articulation** which contribute to give that language its characteristic overall phonetic quality: (1) **articulatory tension** and (2) **articulatory fronting.** French consonants are produced with a relatively high degree of tension of the muscles of the vocal tract, including not only the musculature of the mouth cavity and the tongue but of the chest wall as well. In the consonant system, articulatory tension manifests itself in clear transition in going from one segment to another and energetic onset of articulation in going from pause to a segment. The non-aspiration of voiceless stops is a special case of this tension. Three French consonants out of four have points of articulation located at the bilabial or dental positions.

4.6.2 Non-Aspiration of Voiceless Stops

English voiceless stops (/ p t k /) are aspirated in initial position and medially before a stressed vowel. In the same positions their French counterparts are unaspirated. Compare the allophone of the / p / phonemes of French and English; the same distribution obtains for / t / and / k /.

	Initial	Before Stressed Vowel	Medial	Before Unstressed Vowel	Final	After / s /
French	[p]		[p]		[p']	[p]
English	[p']	[p']		[p]	[p=]	[p]

Phonetic interference will occur in positions where French unaspirated allophones are matched by English aspirated allophones. In teaching English speakers to produce unaspirated voiceless stops, it is useful to start with English words containing a voiceless stop in medial position followed by an unstressed vowel or a voiceless stop preceded by / s / which have French cognates, e.g., *echo* [eko^W], *ski* [ski^Y], and then to have learners produce the stop without aspiration. The accuracy of the production is easily controlled by making the "puff" test: the palm of the hand is held in front of the mouth; if a puff of air is felt on the palm, aspirated stops are being produced. A more spectacular, albeit less practical, version of the "puff" test is to hold a lighted match in front of the mouth. The flame will waver but will never be extinguished by unaspirated voiceless stops, whereas aspirated voiceless stops will always extinguish it.

4.6.3 Dental Consonants

French / t d n s z l / are produced with contact between the tip of the tongue and the inner side of the upper or lower front teeth. For corresponding English phonemes the point of articulation is located further back, at the alveoles. There are other minor articulatory differences between matching pairs of some of these consonants. Intervocalic French / t / and / d / are always produced with full closure, whereas English (at least, American English) / t d / have flap allophones between a stressed and an unstressed vowel, e.g., *attitude/adder.*

English / l / has at least two allophones: (1) before front vowels, a front [l] ("clear") with distinct contact of the tip of the tongue against the alveoles, e.g., *light, million, lazy;* (2) before back vowel and in final position, a back ("dark") [l] produced by the movement of the tongue toward the rear of the mouth cavity with—sometimes in final position—no contact between the tongue and the roof of the mouth, e.g., *loom, low, bill, ball, belt.* French / l / has a single front allophone [l] always produced with energetic contact of the tip of the tongue against the inner side of the upper front teeth or the alveoles (see Figure 4.1).

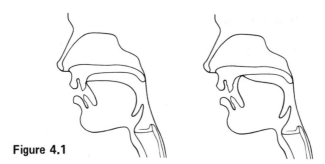

Figure 4.1

4.6.4   French / R /

The allophone realization of / R / varies greatly depending on the geographical location, social status of the speaker, and style. In standard French, / R / is realized by light contact between the back of the tongue and the wall of the pharynx—it is a **(dorso-)pharyngal**. Sometimes / R / is produced by vibration of the uvula and is then termed a **uvular trill**.

In English, / r / is realized as a retroflex: the tip of the tongue curls back, and the tongue assumes a concave shape. Figure 4.2 compares French and American English / r /. Note that in French during

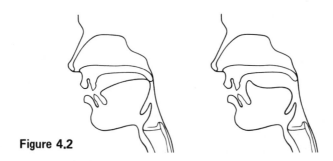

Figure 4.2

the articulation of / R / the tongue always assumes a convex position with the tip of the tongue resting against the inner side of the lower front teeth. It can thus rapidly assume the articulatory position of any vowel without affecting its acoustic quality. In English, / r / colors the acoustic quality of the vowels that precede or follow it, so that when it is substituted for French / R / it will influence the quality of French vowels and make it difficult for French speakers to identify them correctly. This is the case particularly for such vowels as / u / *(pour)*, / y / *(pur)*, / ø / *(peu)*, and / œ / *(peur)*.

STUDY QUESTIONS

1.   **Minimal Pairs**
   a)   Identify the consonants that differentiate the following minimal pairs.

1) faut/vaut / f / vs. / v /		5) came/cane _____
2) camp/gant _____		6) peigne/pèle _____
3) pris/cri _____		7) l'ail/lard _____
4) gâche/cache _____		8) sourd/soude _____

   b)   Provide minimal pairs that illustrate the following contrasts in initial position. You may use words or phrases.
   1)   / p / vs. / b /   pont/bon _____
   2)   / p / vs. / d /   _____
   3)   / k / vs. / g /   _____
   4)   / p / vs. / f /   _____
   5)   / b / vs. / v /   _____

   c)   Provide minimal pairs that illustrate the following contrasts in final position.
   1)   / m / vs. / n /   tome/tonne _____
   2)   / s / vs. / z /   _____
   3)   / f / vs. / v /   _____
   4)   / j / vs. / l /   _____
   5)   / ʃ / vs. / ʒ /   _____

   d)   Provide sentence length minimal pairs that illustrate the following contrasts.
   Medial Position
   / r / vs. / l /   Il est carré./Il est calé. _____
   / s / vs. / z /   _____
   / m / vs. / n /   _____

   Final Position
   / p / vs. / t /   Ça coupe./Ça coûte. _____
   / k / vs. / ʃ /   _____
   / j / vs. / r /   _____

   Initial Position
   / p / vs. / v /   Pends le jambon./Vends le jambon.
   / f / vs. / p /   _____
   / b / vs. / m /   _____

   e)   State the articulatory distinctive features that distinguish the following minimal pairs.
   1)   beau/veau   stops vs. fricative and labial vs. labiodental
   2)   bêche/beige   _____

3)	pont/fond	_____
4)	nord/mord	_____
5)	cale/caille	_____
6)	hameau/agneau	_____
7)	les eaux/les sauts	_____
8)	coule/court	_____

2. **Positional Variants of English Voiceless Consonants**
   Classify the positional variant of / p /, / t /, or / k / that occurs in the following English words.

	Aspirated	Unaspirated	Unreleased
spin		spin	
tack			
skin			
tin			
lip			
stain			
lit			
pass			
case			

3. **Comparison of French and English Consonants**
   a) Describe the difference in articulation between:
      1) French / p / of *pain* and English / p / of *pain*
      2) French / t / of *patte* and English / t / of *pat*
      3) French / l / of *belle* and English / l / of *bell*
      4) French / n / of *non* and English / n / of *noun*
      5) French / r / of *ruche* and English / r / of *rush*

   b) State the differences in inventory between French and English obstruents.

   c) Why might English speakers fail to differentiate:
      1) *légion* vs. *lésion*
      2) *les chiens* vs. *les siens*

5

THE FRENCH VOWEL SYSTEM

5.1   THE ARTICULATION OF VOWELS

Whereas most consonants are produced with the closure or the constriction of the vocal tract, vowels are articulated with a relatively open and unobstructed vocal tract. In the articulation of vowels, the vocal tract functions as a complex resonating chamber that modifies the column of air, already set in vibration by movements of the vocal cords, that passes through it. The various vowel sounds that the human vocal tract can produce are determined, ultimately, by the shape and volume of two main cavities—resonating chambers—that are formed in the front and back parts of the mouth, chiefly by the movement of the tongue from back to front or up and down (see Figure 5.1).

The following comparison will help you understand how the shape and volume of the front and back mouth cavities determine the acoustic quality of vowels. Compare the vowels of the words *lit* and *loup.* You will note that the vowel of *loup* is grave whereas that of *lit* is high pitched or acute. You have no doubt observed that when a bottle is being filled with a liquid, a sound with gradually rising pitch is produced. A bottle is also a resonating chamber. As it fills, the volume of the resonating chamber decreases and the pitch produced rises. That is, the larger the volume of a resonating chamber, the lower the pitch of the noise produced, and conversely. In the production of vowels, the front and back mouth cavities assume a wide variety of shapes and make possible the production of a large number of different vowel sounds. It is more useful to describe vowels indirectly, in terms of articulatory movements that determine the volume and shape of the two mouth cavities, rather than directly, in terms of their acoustic properties.

Before we proceed to describe the articulatory features of the vowels of French, it is important to distinguish between the **vowel letters** used to represent French vowels and the **vowel sounds** themselves. As is the case in English, only five letters (*i e a o u*) are available to represent a far larger

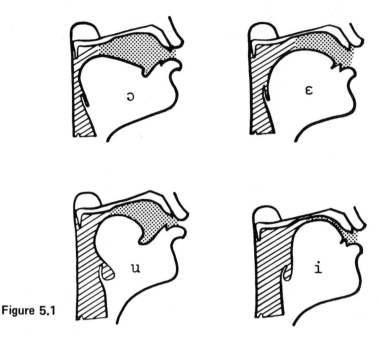

Figure 5.1

number of sound contrasts which speakers use to differentiate words. We will use the term vowel to refer to certain classes of sounds which serve to differentiate French words from each other, not to the letters used to represent them.

5.2   TONGUE POSITION

The vowel system of **Orthoepic** (Parisian) **Standard French**—the variety of Standard French that serves as a model in all francophone communities—contains fifteen units. These fifteen vowels are characterized by four articulatory parameters: (1) tongue fronting; (2) tongue height; (3) lip rounding; (4) nasalization.

Pronounce aloud the words *lit* and *loup*. In the pronunciation of the vowel of the latter word, the tongue is in its extreme backed position; in the pronunciation of the vowel of *lit*, it is in the most fronted position it can assume. These two vowels, represented by the symbols [i] and [u], are termed **front** and **back** respectively. Note that *lit* and *loup* are minimal pairs and they establish the two vowels / i / and / u / as phonemes.

Now observe the position your tongue takes in the pronunciation of *lit* and *loup,* as opposed to that of *là.* In the pronunciation of / i / and / u / the tongue is close to the roof of the mouth, and these two vowels are termed **high** vowels. In the pronunciation of / a / the tongue assumes a **low** position in the mouth. You will also note that / i / and / u / are produced with a small mouth opening or **aperture** whereas / a / is produced with a larger aperture. There is the following relationship between mouth aperture and tongue position: small mouth aperture corresponds to high tongue position; large mouth aperture corresponds to low tongue position.

Thus, tongue position determines two articulatory parameters: (1) tongue height or mouth aperture and (2) tongue fronting. The three vowel phonemes / i /, / u /, and / a / may now be characterized in terms of these two parameters as follows:

High

/ i /   / u /

Front   / a /   *Back*

Low

The tongue fronting parameter defines two features, front versus back. But the tongue height parameter must be expanded to four features in order to account for such minimally contrastive data as *gui* [gi] "mistletoe," *gué* [ge] "ford," *guet* [gɛ] "watch," *gars* [ga] "lad." These four words are differentiated by their vowel, and phonemic status must be given to / e / and / ɛ / as well as to / i / and / a /. In the pronunciation of / i /, / e /, / ɛ /, and / a / the tongue remains relatively fronted, so that the articulatory parameter that distinguishes them is tongue height. Four distinctive tongue height points must be posited, and these define both front and back vowels; for, contrasting with *saôule* [sul] "drunk, fem.," we find *saule* [sol] "willow tree" and *sol* [sɔl] "ground"; and contrasting with *paume* [pom] "palm" and *pomme* [pɔm] "apple" we find *pâme* [pɑm] *(elle se pâme)* "she is fainting." The latter vowel—[ɑ]—contrasts with / a / in such minimal pairs as *là* [la] "there" vs. *las* [lɑ] "tired" or *tache* [taʃ] "stain" vs. *tâche* [tɑʃ] "task." Tongue fronting and tongue height thus characterize eight vowel phonemes:

	Front	*Back*
High	i	u
High-mid	e	o
Low-mid	ɛ	ɔ
Low	a	ɑ

We have been using tongue position specifications (front, back, high-mid, etc.) as distinctive features rather than precise indications of points of articulation. Traditionally, French vowels are represented by a vowel "triangle" (more accurately a pentagon with unequal sides) indicating the exact location of the mass of the tongue during its articulation (see Figure 5.1). Figure 5.2 provides also an accurate representation of formant values that specify the acoustic properties of the front and back mouth cavities, which, as was stated in 5.1, ultimately determine vowel sounds.

But Figure 5.2 represents only about half the vowel contrasts in French. In order to describe the remaining vowels we need to add to the two articulatory parameters we have developed so far. Theoretically, we could add more points to the tongue fronting and tongue height parameters. In fact, for some languages such as English, three tongue fronting parameters—back, central, front—are posited, and additional tongue height distinctions can be perceived in French. For instance, the first vowel of *perron* "stoop" and those of *grève* "beach" and *terre* "earth" differ somewhat with regard to

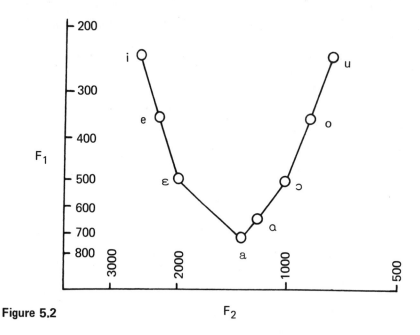

Figure 5.2

F_2

tongue height. But variations that may be observed within the tongue height points are not distinctive and do not serve to distinguish words from each other. Thus, were we to permute the vowels of *perron* and *grève,* the meaning would not be changed and French speakers would still be able to correctly identify the two words.

5.3   LIP ROUNDING

Compare the vowels of *vie* and *vue.* Both are front high vowels, but they differ with regard to the position of the lips. You will note that in the articulation of *vue* the lips are **rounded** and protrude forward; in the pronunciation of *vie* the lips are drawn back at the corners (spread or **unrounded**). Lip rounding, which is a two-point parameter—rounded vs. unrounded—serves to differentiate six front vowels:

	Unrounded	*Rounded*
High	i	y
High-mid	e	ø
Low-mid	ɛ	œ

These six vowel phonemes are required to account for contrasts such as: *vie* "life" vs. *vue* "view"; *fée* "fairy godmother" vs. *feu* "fire"; *sel* "salt" vs. *seul* "alone, masc."

All back vowels are rounded, but since there are no unrounded back vowels matching each rounded back vowel, lip rounding is not a distinctive feature for those vowels; nor is it distinctive for the low vowels / a / and / ɑ / which are differentiated by tongue fronting, although the latter is produced with the lips slightly more rounded than for the former. Also, lip rounding becomes less pronounced as tongue height is lowered: / ø / is produced with less protrusion and rounding of the lips than / y /, and / œ / with less than / ø /. We have now developed three articulatory parameters to characterize eleven vowels. Distinctive feature relationships among the eleven vowels described so far are best represented in three dimensions as in Figure 5.3. The high and mid vowels (high-mid and low-mid) are characterized by three distinctive features—one for each of the three articulatory parameters involved in their production—and the two low vowels are defined by only two since lip rounding is incompatible with wide mouth aperture.

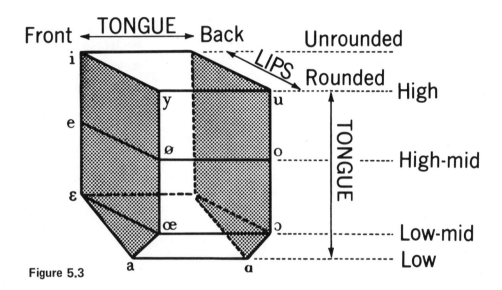

Figure 5.3

5.4   NASALIZATION

Nasal vowels are produced when the velum is lowered and the walls of the pharynx are relaxed. A passage is formed between the back mouth cavities and the nasal cavities. It is widely believed that it is the passage of air through the nasal cavities that results in the production of nasal vowels. In fact, in the production of the French nasal vowels little air egresses through the nasal cavities. The lowering of the velum results in the formation of a small cavity—the **velic** cavity—that modifies the resonance of the back mouth cavity. Figure 5.4 contrasts the articulation of the nasal vowels in *bain* and *bon* with that of their corresponding non-nasal (oral) vowels / ɛ / and / ɔ / and compares their formant specifications (formants describe the acoustic characteristics of the back and front mouth cavities).

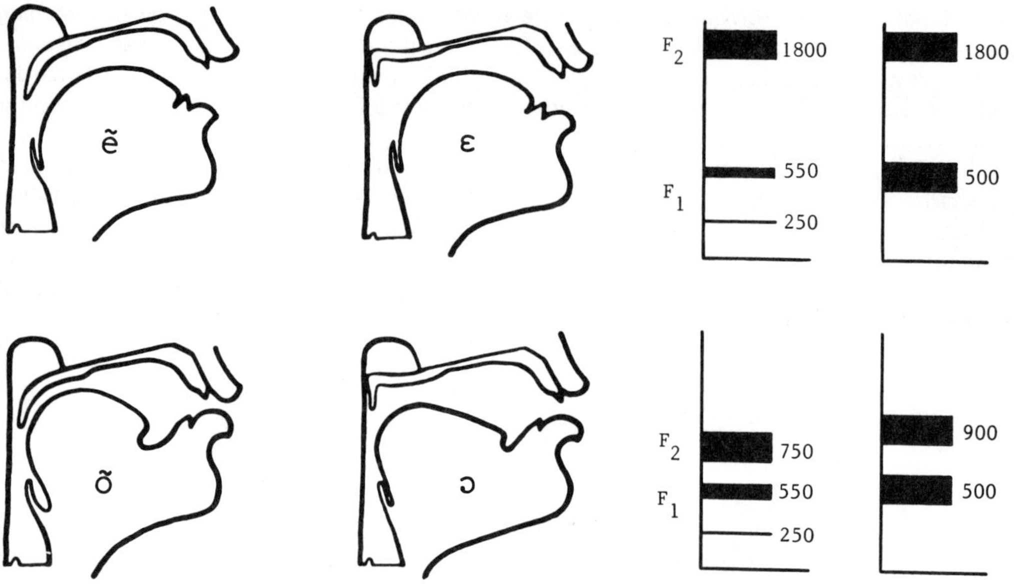

Figure 5.4

Note the velic cavity formed in the pronunciation of the nasal vowels and the reduction of formant one (F_1) which specifies the acoustic characteristics of the back mouth cavity that is modified by the velic cavity. The reduction of the intensity of F_1 accounts for the weak, diffuse, and indeterminate acoustic impression of French nasal vowels. That fact has been utilized by poets, particularly the Symbolists of the later nineteenth century, to derive special esthetic effects. Observe the frequency of nasal vowels, particularly in the last (rhyming) syllable, in Verlaine's famous poem "Chanson d'automne." Note, also, the occurrence of sequences of oral vowels plus nasal consonants, such as in *automne, monotone:*

Les s*an*glots l*on*gs
Des viol*on*s
 de l'au*tomne*
Blessent m*on* coeur
D'une l*an*gueur
 Mono*tone.*
Tout suffoqu*an*t
Et blê*me,* qu*an*d
 S*onne* l'heure,

Je me souvi*en*s
Des jours anci*en*s
 Et je pleure;
Et je m'*en* vais
Au v*en*t mauvais
 Qui m'*em*porte
 Deça, delà,
Pareil à la
 Feuille morte.

Four nasal vowels need to be posited for French in order to account for such contrastive data as *saint* [sɛ̃] "saint" vs. *sang* [sɑ̃] "blood" vs. *son* [sɔ̃] "sound" and *brin* [brɛ̃] "bit" vs. *brun*

[brœ̃] "brown." Traditional descriptions interpret the French nasal vowels as particular oral vowels to which has been added the feature of nasalization. This interpretation underlies the choice of phonetic symbols for the representation of the vowels: *saint* [ɛ̃] → [ɛ]; *brun* [œ̃] → [œ]; *sang* [ɑ̃] → [ɑ]; *son* [ɔ̃] → [ɔ]. In fact, the nasal vowels of French constitute a separate sub-system characterized by different distinctive feature relationships from those found among their so-called corresponding oral vowels. Tongue height is not significant for the nasal vowels since, for example, the pronunciation of the vowel of *sang* varies from [ɑ̃] to [ɔ̃] among various French speakers. (Most speakers of Standard French pronounce / ɑ̃ / as [ɑ̃]. But an apparently growing number of speakers realize that phoneme with a higher and more back vowel that overlaps with the phonetic realizations of / ɔ̃ /. It has been shown that speakers who pronounce / ɑ̃ / as [ɔ̃] instead of [ɑ̃] cannot consistently differentiate such minimal pairs as *blanc* vs. *blond* or *franc* vs. *front* out of context.) The relevant parameters in the distinctive feature characterization of French nasal vowels are tongue fronting and lip rounding:

	Front		Back	
Rounded	œ̃	l'un	ɔ̃	long
Unrounded	ɛ̃	lin	ɑ̃	l'an

The notation that we adopt for the representation of the nasal vowels does not reflect the assumption that, say, / ɔ̃ / is / o / plus nasalization. As the distinctive feature analysis of the nasal vowel indicates, / ɔ̃ /, in fact, corresponds to *both* / o / and / ɔ /. Like them, it is rounded and back, and precisely because it corresponds to both rather than one or the other, its tongue height is not distinctive. In Chapter 17 we will show that there are more meaningful oral-nasal vowel correspondences at a higher level of language structure, for example / ɛ̃ / and / in / in such forms as *fin* and *fine* or / ɛ̃ / and / ɛ / in such forms as *vient* and *viennent.*

5.5   SOME DIFFERENCES BETWEEN THE FRENCH AND ENGLISH VOWEL SYSTEMS

Differences in the articulatory nature of French and English corresponding vowels and differences in the distinctive feature relationships within the two vowel systems result in three main problems in the pronunciation of French vowels on the part of English learners: (1) the pronunciation of front rounded vowels; (2) the diphthongization of final high and mid vowels; (3) the confusion of nasal vowels and sequences—oral vowel plus nasal consonant.

5.5.1   Front Rounded Vowels

In English there are no front rounded vowels. Lip rounding is a non-distinctive feature which accompanies the production of back vowels such as those of *blue, so,* or *cot,* and English speakers will tend to replace French front rounded vowels by their back rounded corresponding vowels. This will lead to the confusion of such minimally contrasting words as *mule* and *moule, deux* and *dos, peur* and *port.* In addition, English speakers will tend to have difficulty in distinguishing among front rounded vowels such contrasts as *jus* vs. *jeu* or *pur* vs. *peur.*

5.5.2   Diphthongization of Final High and Mid Vowels

Compared to English vowels, French vowels are produced with greater articulatory tension and stability—the speech organs assume the position of articulation for a given vowel and remain in that position throughout its production. Below, we compare English and French words containing near-equivalent high and high-mid vowels pronounced normally and filmed using X-ray motion picture photography at twenty-four frames per second. Each symbol represents a position of articulation held during a single frame:

bee	[bbbɪɪiiij]	vs.	(ha)bit	[bbbiiii]
do	[dddʊ ʊ ʊ uuuw]	vs.	doux	[ddduuuuu]
Fay	[fffɛ ɛ ɛ eeeej]	vs.	vais	[vvveeee]
know	[nnnɔɔooow]	vs.	nos	[nnnooooo]

While these comparisons show that the English vowels are longer than corresponding French vowels—their articulation had to be filmed using a larger number of frames, for example, six for the vowel of *bee* versus only four for the vowel of *(ha)bit*—they also show that, whereas the French vowels remain unchanged during their entire articulation, the English vowels show three different configurations. Note, for example, that the vowel of *bee* starts as a lax [ɪ], moves to the position of a tense [i], and then to that of the glide (semivowel) [j]. As it were, the organs of articulation overshoot the characteristic position of the vowel—in this case, front high tense [i]—hold that position briefly, and then move toward the position of articulation of the glide.

   Related to the difference in mode of articulation between corresponding high and high-mid of English and French is a difference in distribution between English and French high and mid vowels: / i /, / e /, and / ɛ /. In the same area of articulation English has four vowels, those contained in the words *seat, sit, sate,* and *set.* But, whereas all three French vowels may occur in final position, only the longer, glided vowels of *seat* and *sate* may occur in that position in English:

English	*French*	
fee	fit	/ i /
	fée	/ e /
Fay	fait	/ ɛ /

English learners may at first fail to distinguish *fait* from *fée* or *fée* from *fit* since they will have a tendency to equate the vowel of *fit* to that of *fée* and the vowel *fait* with that of *Fay*. They might interpret the vowel of *fée* as identical with / ɛ / or / i / depending on whether it is presented paired with the latter or the former. No such problem will be encountered with the back vowels since in final position only English / u / *(do)* and / o / *(dough)* and French / u / *(doux)* and / o / *(dos)* occur.

5.5.3   Vowel Nasalization

Many English-speaking learners of French report that French strikes them as a "nasal" language. One might be tempted to explain this impressionistic judgment by the fact that French has nasal vowels while English does not. This explanation would be wrong, for, from a phonetic point of view, English (particularly American English) has more nasal vowels than French. If you compare the pronunciation of the following paired English words: *cap* vs. *camp, sit* vs. *sing, pod* vs. *pond, but* vs. *bunt,* or *woe* vs. *won't,* you will observe that the second member of each pair contains a vowel with nasal resonance. But, in each case, you will also note that the nasal vowel is followed by a nasal consonant (/ n /, / m /, or / ŋ /). In French, nasal vowels occur in many different positions, and, in fact, they usually do *not* occur before a nasal consonant. Both French and English have nasal vowel "sounds," but in English, nasalization of vowels is a feature predictable from the occurrence of a following nasal consonant. In the French vowel system, nasalization is a distinctive feature: that is, it serves to differentiate words, as is demonstrated by the following minimal pairs:

beau / bo / "handsome"	vs.	bon / bõ / "good"
las / la / "weary"	vs.	lent / lã / "slow"
la nuit / lanyi / "the night"	vs.	l'ennui / lãnyi / "the trouble"
patte / pat / "paw"	vs.	pente / pãt / "slope"
au nid / oni / "to the nest"	vs.	on nie / õni / "we deny"

The difficulties that American learners encounter with the French nasal vowels do not stem from the fact that they are not able to produce nasal vowels, but from the fact that they produce them automatically before a nasal consonant and that they interpret French nasal vowels as sequences of vowel plus nasal consonant. As a result they fail to perceive and reproduce contrasts between nasal vowels and sequences of oral vowels plus nasal consonant such as the following:

c'est le mien / ɛ̃ / "it's mine, masc."	c'est la mienne / ɛn / "it's mine, fem."
l'Américain / ɛ̃ / "the American, masc."	l'Américaine / ɛn / "the American, fem."
deux ans / ã / "two years"	deux ânes / ɑn / "two donkeys"
dix thons / õ / "ten tunas"	dix tonnes / ɔn / "ten tons"

Since in English, nasalization of vowels serves as a clue for the presence of a nasal consonant, and since moreover, nasal vowels do not occur in final position, American speakers may add a short [n] (epenthetic nasal closure) to French nasal vowels occurring at the end of a word. In this way, for example, both the masculine form *bon* and the feminine form *bonne* are realized as [bõn]. Exercises devised to train American learners to handle vowel nasalization correctly in French must deal with the following problems:

1. differentiation between nasal vowels and sequences consisting of corresponding oral vowels plus nasal consonant handled preferably as part of a grammatical problem: *fin* vs. *fine, sain* vs. *saine, commun* vs. *commune, paysan* vs. *paysanne, bon* vs. *bonne;*

2. production of nasal vowels without epenthetic nasal closure in: *pense* [pãs] vs. *[pãⁿse], tomber* [tõbe] vs. *[tõᵐbe], anglais* [ãglɛ] vs. *[ãⁿglɛ];*

3. differentiation of the four French nasal vowels in all positions; i.e., making contrasts such as *sang* vs. *son, penser* vs. *pincer, en train* vs. *entrons;*

4.   clearly audible release of nasal consonants in final position so that it serves to back up the contrast between nasal vowels and sequences oral vowel plus nasal consonant, e.g., *bon* [bõ] vs. *bonne* [bɔn].

STUDY QUESTIONS
Part I

1.   Identify the vowel contained in the following words.

a)	grand	__ã__	e)	clé	_____
b)	part	_____	f)	grue	_____
c)	grosse	_____	g)	yeux	_____
d)	songe	_____	h)	plein	_____

2.   Indicate whether the vowel contained in the following words is front or back.

a)	port	back	d)	train	_____
b)	fine	_____	e)	soute	_____
c)	oeuf	_____	f)	brun	_____

3.   Indicate whether the vowel contained in the following words is rounded or unrounded.

a)	gris	unrounded	d)	mont	_____
b)	flot	_____	e)	planche	_____
c)	beurre	_____	f)	singe	_____

4.   Indicate whether the vowel contained in the last syllable is nasal or oral.

a)	ils y vont	nasal	d)	les Allemands	_____
b)	c'est du lard	_____	e)	tu as tort	_____
c)	ça te plaît?	_____	f)	ils le prennent	_____

5.   State the tongue height feature of the vowel in the following words.

a)	pur	high	d)	part	_____
b)	tâche	_____	e)	deux	_____
c)	belle	_____	f)	boule	_____

6.   **Distinctive Features**
    a)   Identify the vowels specified by the following sets of distinctive features.

1)	front	high	rounded	/ y /
2)	back	low-mid	rounded	_____
3)	front	low		_____
4)	front	low-mid	unrounded	_____
5)	back	high	rounded	_____
6)	front	nasal	unrounded	_____
7)	back	nasal	rounded	_____

b)   Define the following vowels in terms of distinctive features.

1)   / i /   <u>front</u>   <u>high</u>   <u>unrounded</u>

2)   / e /   _____   _____   _____

3)   / a /   _____   _____   _____

4)   / o /   _____   _____   _____

5)   / y /   _____   _____   _____

6)   / œ /   _____   _____   _____

7)   / ẽ /   _____   _____   _____

8)   / ã /   _____   _____   _____

7.   **Minimal Pairs**

a)   Give one word length minimal pair for each of the following vowel contrasts.

1)   / i / vs. / u /   <u>à vie **vs.** à vous</u>

2)   / u / vs. / y /   _____

3)   / ɛ / vs. / ɔ /   _____

4)   / a / vs. / ɑ /   _____

5)   / a / vs. / õ /   _____

6)   / ∅ / vs. / y /   _____

b)   Give one sentence length minimal pair for each of the following vowel contrasts.

1)   / e / vs. / a /   <u>J'ai cinq francs. vs. J'ai cent francs.</u>

2)   / y / vs. / u /   _____

3)   / a / vs. / ɔ /   _____

4)   / o / vs. / õ /   _____

c)   Give one word length minimal pair for the following contrasts.

1)   / a / vs. / an /   <u>l'an vs. l'âne</u>

2)   / ɛ / vs. / e /   _____

3)   / o / vs. / ɔ /   _____

4)   / ẽ / vs. / œ̃ /   _____

Part II

1.   Explain briefly why American learners of French may have difficulty differentiating the following minimal pairs:

a)   le bourreau/le bureau

b)   quel jus/quel jeu

c)   le gué/le guet

2.   Would American learners have difficulty differentiating *loup* and *lot?*

3.   What basic difference between the French and the English mode of articulation accounts for possible inaccurate pronunciation of such words as *nid, né, nous,* and *nos* on the part of American learners?

4.   Which of the following minimal pairs are American learners not likely to differentiate?
   a)   cinq francs/cent francs
   b)   les bons/les bains
   c)   les ans/les ânes
   d)   ils vont/il vend
   e)   les bons/les bonnes
   f)   les vins/les veines
   g)   ses copines/ses copains

5.   Explain why American learners might have difficulty in reproducing the following minimal pairs accurately:
   a)   C'est Jeanne/C'est Jean
   b)   les marins/les maraines
   c)   qu'elle abandonne/quel abandon

6

VARIATION IN THE FRENCH MID VOWEL SYSTEM

As was indicated in Chapter 2, Standard French is marked by considerable geographical and social variation. Except for various articulations of / r /, the consonant system remains fairly uniform throughout the French-speaking world, and it is in its vowel system that French shows marked variation. Four areas of the French vowel system are subject to variation: (1) the mid vowels, (2) back / ɑ /, (3) the nasal vowel / œ̃ /, and (4) long vowels. In this chapter we shall discuss some of the structural factors that account in part for variation in the mid vowel system; we shall describe its geographical and social correlates; and we shall discuss some of its pedagogical implications. The other areas of variation in the French vowel system will be treated in Chapter 7.

6.1   THE DISTRIBUTION OF MID VOWELS

French vowels occur typically in a variety of positions within a word. Consider the vowels / i / and / u / . They occur in initial position (*image,* out*il*), within words (*vitesse,* arri*ver, s*ouve*nir, am*ou*reuse, laicité*), and in final position, both in **free** and in **checked** syllables. Free syllables end with a vowel (*vie, vous*), and checked syllables end with one or more consonants (*rite, route, siffle, souffle*). Thus, / i / and / u / contrast with each other in a variety of positions and can differentiate a great number of words and sentences. In charting the distribution of French vowels the key positions are: (1) medial position, e.g., *niveau* "level" vs. *nouveau* "new"; (2) final free syllable, e.g., *mie* "soft bread" vs. *moue* "pout"; (3) final checked syllable, e.g., *file* "file" vs. *foule* "crowd."

The distribution of mid vowels differs markedly from that of other vowels. In final position they have the distribution shown in Table 6.1. As the data presented in Table 6.1 show, there are many environments in which members of each of the three high-mid vs. low-mid vowel pairs cannot contrast

Table 6.1 Distribution of French Mid Vowels in Final Syllables

Vowel:	e	ɛ	ɔ	o	oe	ø
Environment:						
Free Syllable:	poignée	poignet	------	peau	--------	peu
Checked Syllable Ending With:						
ʒ	-------	aurai-je	loge	auge	--------	--------
t	-------	sept	hotte	hôte	--------	meute
z	-------	pèse	--------	pause	--------	creuse
d	-------	raide	rode	rôde	--------	--------
l	-------	sel	sol	saule	veulent	veule
n	-------	benne	bonne	Beaune	jeune	jeûne
f	-------	chef	étoffe	sauf	bœuf	--------
v	-------	lève	love	mauve	peuvent	--------
r	-------	serre	sort	--------	sœur	--------
j	-------	oreille	--------	--------	feuille	--------
p	-------	guêpe	tope	taupe	--------	--------
b	-------	plèbe	robe	aube	--------	--------
k	-------	sec	roc	rauque	--------	--------
ʃ	-------	pêche	poche	embauche	--------	--------
g	-------	bègue	vogue	--------	--------	--------
ʃ	-------	règne	grogne	--------	--------	--------

with each other. From the point of view of limitation of contrast the mid vowels fall into two sets: the front unrounded pair / e / vs. / ɛ / and the rounded pairs / ø / vs. / œ / and / o / vs. / ɔ /. In the case of the latter two pairs no contrast is possible in final free syllables since only the high-mid pair—/ ø / and / o /—occurs in that position. In other words, there is no */ pœ / matching *peu* / pø /, nor any */ pɔ / matching *peau* / po /. Another important limitation in the distribution of the rounded mid vowels (and, consequently, another reduction of their differentiative value) is the exclusive appearance of the high-mid member before / z /, e.g., *pose, rose, dose; creuse, peureuse, heureuse,* and of the low-mid member before / r /, e.g., *port, nord, fort; peur, sœur, meurt.* Thus high-mid and low-mid rounded vowels contrast only before a relatively small number of final consonants. With regard to the front unrounded mid vowels / e / and / ɛ /, they may contrast only in final free syllables since / e / does not occur in checked syllables, that is, there is no */ bel / matching *belle* / bɛl /, no */ per / matching *père* / pɛr /, etc.

The case of the pair / ø / vs. / œ / is particularly interesting. Were it not for the existence of two minimal pairs—*(il) jeûne* "he fasts" vs. *jeune* "young" and *(ils) veulent* "they want" vs. *veule* "lackadaisical"—/ ø / and / œ / could be analyzed as variants of a single phoneme: / ø / would occur in final free syllables and in final checked syllables ending with / z /, and / œ / in the other types of checked syllables. Thus, / ø / and / œ / would contrast as a pair with other vowels such as / i /, / u /, / y /, or / a / and function as a single vowel:

nœud	———	nid	nous	nu	n'a
———	peur	pire	pour	pur	part

In most Méridional accents of Standard French—not only in the Provence region but in all those areas in southern France where Occitan dialects were at one time spoken—the high-mid and low-mid members of mid vowel pairs do not contrast with each other. This does not mean that Méridional speakers can only produce three mid vowel sounds. They produce six phonetically distinct mid vowels, but each member of the three mid vowel pairs occurs in an environment from which the other member is excluded. The distribution of mid vowels in Méridional Standard French is quite symmetrical: high-mid vowels occur in free syllables and low-mid vowels in checked syllables (see Table 6.2).

Table 6.2 Distribution of Mid Vowels in Free and Checked Syllables in Méridional Standard French

	Free Syllable	Checked Syllable
e	fée, fait; j'irai, j'irais; l'aîné	
ɛ		belle, père; veston
ø	feu, deux; malheureux	
œ		jeune, jeûne; peur, heureuse; heurter
o	peau; dot; philoso-phie	
ɔ		sol, saule; port, rose; solfège

The distribution of the mid vowels characteristic of Méridional speakers is termed the *loi de position*; of course, it is not a "law" or principle of the phonological structure of French but a mere observational generalization. Note that the distribution described by the *loi de position* (the high-mid vowels [e], [ø], [o] in free syllables and the low-mid vowels [ɛ], [œ], [ɔ] in checked syllables) also applies to medial syllables.

Méridional speakers do not have contrasts of the type *jeune* vs. *jeûne* or *sol* vs. *saule* since in checked syllables only low-mid vowels are permitted; *jeûne* is pronounced [ʒœn] and *saule* [sɔl]. In free syllables only high-mid vowels occur, and contrasts of the type *gué* vs. *guet* or *j'irai* vs. *j'irais* cannot be made; in both members of each pair the final vowel used is [e]. The exclusive use of [e] in free syllables is very widespread in France and is found in many areas of Northern France as well as in Occitan-influenced areas. Even speakers who do pronounce [ε] in final free syllables are likely to vary in their use of [e] or [ε] in individual words. An interesting experiment you might perform is to ask a group of French speakers to individually read a list of, say, ten words which dictionaries list as pronounced with [ε], for example, *lait, sujet, il fait, près, prêt, trait, gai, geai, balai, ballet.* You will no doubt discover that seldom will two speakers pronounce the entire list identically.

It is important to note that the variation from the Parisian upper middle-class vowel system referred to as the **orthoepic norm** and used as a basis for dictionary listing and described in the above paragraph—is characteristic of Méridional speakers at all social levels (although it is probably the case that the higher the social class standing of a Méridional speaker, the more likely he is to conform to the orthoepic norm). Such pronunciation as [le] for *lait* or [ʒire] for *j'irais* are not stigmatized and would seldom be noticed by Paris speakers who adhere to the orthoepic norm. On the other hand, the use of low-mid vowels in such words as *heureuse, creuse, rose, saule, jaune,* etc. is a feature readily identified as Méridional, and it will often provoke amusement on the part of Northern speakers, particularly when used by a foreigner. It is also a feature that many Méridional speakers attempt to discard when they speak with persons from other parts of France or when they shift to a formal variety of speech.

It is sometimes claimed that the distribution of mid vowels that is characteristic of Méridional speakers—termed *la loi de position,* see Table 6.2—reflects a natural tendency in the development of the French language. It is also claimed that the distribution of mid vowels described by the *loi de position,* particularly the exclusive use of [e] in final free syllables, is found in the speech of lower-class speakers in many areas of the French-speaking world. Related to this claim is the belief that natural tendencies of a language manifest themselves in lower-class and rural speech, unfettered by academic purism and less subject to the influence of spelling than the speech of educated middle-class speakers. Finally, it is asserted that speakers who adhere to the orthoepic norm in formal situations will switch to the *loi de position* in spontaneous speech. That these claims are without foundation is easily shown by considering the speech of young teenagers from working-class families in the Paris area. Not only do those speakers pronounce such words as *lait, j'irais* according to the orthoepic norm, but they also pronounce future and past definite forms, e.g., *j'irai* and *j'allai,* with [ε] rather than the [e] indicated by the orthoepic norm. In other words, these speakers violate the *loi de position* by generalizing the use of the low-mid vowel in free syllables. Of course, like all other Northern French speakers, they contrast high-mid and low-mid rounded vowels in such minimal pairs as *saule* vs. *sol.* We shall return to these sociolinguistic considerations in our discussion of the pedagogical implications of variation in the mid vowel system in section 6.3 below.

6.2   NEUTRALIZATION OF MID VOWEL CONTRASTS

Neutralization describes a situation where a phonological contrast which obtains in one or more environments does not operate in some other environment or environments. In addition, in the environment where the two phonemes do not contrast a phonetic variant occurs which differs phonetically from the realizations of the two phonemes and which, therefore, cannot be assigned to one or the other on the basis of phonological considerations alone. For instance, in English, / t / and / d / contrast in initial and final position, e.g., *tin* vs. *din* and *bit* vs. *bid.* In most American dialects, these two phonemes do not contrast in medial position, so that *bitter* and *bidder* are not usually differentiated as to the medial consonant. In both words the medial consonant is a **flap** produced by rapid contact of the tip of the tongue against the gum ridge. We say that English / t / and / d /, which contrast in initial and final position, are "neutralized" in medial position. Thus, neutralization involves: (1) the suspension of contrast between two phonemes, and (2) the presence of a sound which differs from the realizations of the two neutralized phonemes in positions where they contrast.

In French, neutralization is found in the mid vowel system: the contrast between the high-mid vs. low-mid members of the pairs / e / vs. / ɛ /, / ø / vs. / œ /, and / o / vs. / ɔ / is generally suspended in medial (non-final) syllables. Consider the vowels / e / and / ɛ /. As shown in Table 6.1, in the orthoepic norm, they contrast in final free syllables. But since / e / does not occur in final checked syllables, no contrast is possible in that environment. The absence of / e / in the final checked syllables does not constitute an instance of neutralization, however, since the vowel that occurs in that environment is identical phonetically to the [ɛ] of *lait;* this is simply a case of limitation of distribution. In such phrases as *les nez* "the noses" and *l'aîné* "the eldest" there occurs in the first syllable a vowel intermediate in quality between [e] and [ɛ] which will be represented by [E]. The two criteria for neutralization apply here: / e / and / ɛ / do not contrast in this environment, and the vowel that appears, being neither [e] nor [ɛ], cannot be assigned to either of the phonemes in a non-arbitrary way. (In Chapter 10 it will be seen that at a higher level of the French phonological system, assignment of mid vowels occurring in medial position to the high-mid or low-mid member of each pair can be made by the use of different criteria.)

It will be remembered that phonemes may be viewed as constituted by sets of distinctive features. The distinctive features of / e / and / ɛ / are, respectively,

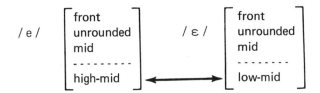

In medial position, the distinctive feature high-mid vs. low-mid which distinguishes / e / from / ɛ / is absent, and one may interpret neutralization as the occurrence of a unit subsuming both / e / and / ɛ / and characterized by the distinctive features they share, namely:

$$\begin{bmatrix} \text{front} \\ \text{unrounded} \\ \text{mid} \end{bmatrix}$$

In a formal, technical description of the French vowel system we would need to represent "neutralized" / e /:/ ɛ / with a different symbol and a different set of conventions (e.g., / / E / /), since it is a phonological unit different from a phoneme. In this introductory treatment, we will simply use / e / to represent instances where French speakers generally do not differentiate / e / and / ɛ /. In a sense, medial / e / is at the same time *both* and *neither* / e / and / ɛ /. It is both / e / and / ɛ /, since it contains the distinctive features which they share; it is neither / e / nor / ɛ /, since its phonetic realization differs from theirs. To state the notion of neutralization from a different point of view, for a French speaker the phonetic sequence [lEne] is ambiguous. It is impossible for him to recover *les nez* or *l'aîné* from the string of sounds on the basis of phonetic evidence alone; he must make use of higher-level—viz. grammatical and contextual—information. Dictionaries note the orthoepic pronunciation [lɛne] for *l'aîné.* Middle-class French speakers usually will use that pronunciation in monitored speech but will shift to the neutralized vowel [E] in spontaneous speech.

Neutralization affects the pairs / ø / vs. / œ / and / o / vs. / ɔ / in a parallel way. In non-final syllables / ø / and / œ / are realized by a short vowel with little lip rounding, [ə]. Such pairs as *jeudi* "Thursday" vs. *je dis* "I say" are not differentiated, and both would usually be pronounced [ʒədi]. Similarly, / o / and / ɔ / are, in non-final syllables, realized by a fronted rounded vowel [ɔ] intermediate in vowel quality between [ɔ] and [œ]. For example, both *fossé* "ditch" and *faussé* "falsified" are pronounced [fɔˤse], and a word such as *philosophie* is realized as [filoˤzɔˤfiˑ].

Since the realizations of neutralized [ɔˤ], subsuming / o / vs. / ɔ /, and [ə], subsuming / ø / vs. / œ /, are short, relatively front vowels produced with little lip rounding, there is a second-level neutralization which results in the suspension of such contrasts as *l'office* "the pantry" vs. *le fils* "the son." There is little phonetic difference between the [ɔˤ] of *l'office* and the [ə] of *le fils,* and French speakers would assign both [lɔˤfis] and [ləfis] to either *le fils* or *l'office* unless contextual cues were present to disambiguate the two words. As was the case with the front unrounded vowels, we shall use the symbols for the high-mid member (/ ø / and / o /) to represent the neutralized vowel in medial position. The various neutralizations in the mid-vowel system of French are summarized in Table 6.3.

Table 6.3 Neutralization in Mid Vowel System

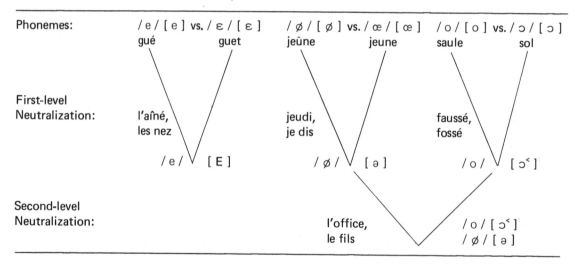

As a summary of this section, it might be useful to compare the neutralization of mid vowel contrasts on the part of middle-class Paris speakers and the reduction of contrasts in all positions according to the so-called *loi de position,* typical of Méridional speakers. The latter speakers, it will be recalled, produce six phonetically distinct mid vowels but have only three contrasts; Parisian speakers have six vowel contrasts but produce nine phonetically distinct vowels, three of which are the neutralized vowels [E], [ə], and [ɔˤ] which occur in medial position. Below we list a set of words containing mid vowels in medial and final position, and we compare their pronunciation by typical Méridional and Parisian speakers. First we provide the words in French spelling, then, in phonemic notation, the orthoepic norm (dictionary list pronunciation), then the Méridional and Parisian pronunciation in phonetic (rather than phonemic) notation:

Spelling	Orthoepic Norm (phonemic)	Méridional (phonetic)	Parisian (phonetic)
l'aîné	/ lɛne /	[lene]	[lEne]
collait	/ kɔlɛ /	[kole]	[kɔˤlɛ]
(il) dépose	/ depoz /	[depɔz]	[dEpoz]
heureuse	/ œrøz /	[ørœz]	[ərøz]
rester	/ rɛste /	[rɛs̩te]	[rEste]
poster	/ pɔste /	[pɔs̩te]	[pɔˤste]
Eustache	/ østaʃ /	[œs̩taʃ]	[əstaʃ]

In the last three items the dot indicates the syllable boundary. The first syllable is checked since it ends with / s / and determines the occurrence of the low-mid vowel in the Méridional pronunciation.

6.3   PEDAGOGICAL NORM

There are three attitudes that teachers can assume when faced with language variation. First, they may disregard it and adhere to the orthoepic norm; this attitude is the most prevalent one, and in addition requires one to castigate all deviations from the norm as "errors," "bad usage," "vulgar features," etc. Second, teachers may take a tolerant and non-authoritarian view about language variation but assume that the learner will acquire a "feel" for it without explicit statement and systematic teaching procedures. Third, teachers may set forth explicit pedagogical norms on the basis of accurate knowledge of the parameters of variation, particularly its sociolinguistic correlates. It is the latter view we espouse and that we will discuss in this section.

A pedagogical norm defines a type of pronunciation which is more uniform than that of natural speech, and as such, easier to learn. On the other hand it does not offend educated speakers of the language and will not inhibit the acquisition, ultimately, of the orthoepic norm or of the full range of variation displayed by educated native speakers.

The *loi de position* is a good starting point for the elaboration of a pedagogical norm for French mid vowels. It defines a very symmetric and simple system of distributing two phonetically distinct vowels: high-mid, tense, and non-glided vowel in free syllable; low-mid and laxer vowel in checked syllable. With regard to the pair [e] vs. [ɛ], it defines a type of pronunciation that is acceptable to educated Frenchmen. It also enables the teacher to eliminate drill in contrasting the two vowels in such minimal pairs as *gué* vs. *guet* and to concentrate instead on the production on the part of the English-speaking student of a non-glided [e] in final position—one of the most troublesome aspects of the French vowel system for English learners.

With regard to the rounded vowels, the *loi de position* states that only [o] and [ø] occur in free syllables, which is in accord with the orthoepic norm. But we have seen that the use of [œ] and [ø] instead of [ø] and [o] respectively in checked syllables produces unfavorable reactions on the part of educated speakers. To deal with this problem, we first need to ask how many French words end with a rounded high-mid vowel in a final checked syllable. Inspection of the *Français Fondamental* basic vocabulary list of 3124 words shows that there are only 36 words containing [ø] and 18 containing [o] in that environment. Of the 36 words containing [ø] in a final checked syllable, all end in / z /, and all are adjectives ending in the feminine suffix *-euse (heureuse, paresseuse,* etc.). Of the 18 occurrences of [o] in a final checked syllable the largest group also ends in / z /, but the list includes a variety of words (*côte, faute, haute, saute; fausse, grosse, sauce; sauf, chaude, chauve, pauvre, gauche,* and *jaune* vs. *cause, chose, dispose, propose, repose*). The problem is easily resolved by having students follow the *loi de position,* which permits them to predict the vowel quality of new words, e.g., *arrêt* [are] vs. *aubaine* [obɛn]. The small number of words which violate the *loi de position* are given as a set of idiosyncratic (exceptional) items. Note that a single statement needs to be made about occurrence of [ø] before / z /, which reduces the number of idiosyncratic items to 19 for the *Français Fondamental* list. It should be kept in mind, however, that the *loi de position* is not an accurate descriptive statement about the prestige accent of Standard French (Parisian middle-class Standard French) but a pedagogical norm which facilitates the acquisition of a fairly accurate and acceptable pronunciation on the part of beginning learners. Most teachers would agree, of course, that advanced learners should be led to control the maximum vowel system of French and to adhere to the orthoepic norm. This level of competence is reached by simply adding grammatical endings (e.g., *-ais, -ait*) or individual words (*jouet, lait*) to the list of items which violate the *loi de position.* It should also be noted that of the 18 items which violated the complementary nature of the distribution between [o] and [ɔ] posited by the pedagogical norm, 12 contained the graphic sequence *au;* of the remaining items where [o] is spelled *o,* five ended in / z /. Exceptions to the *loi de position* involving [o] can be handled by: (1) pointing out that *au* or *ô* followed by a consonant are pronounced [o], e.g., *aube, taupe, rôde, hôte;* (2) formulating the sub-rule that any *o*-type vowel followed by a / z / is pronounced [o]. It would be useful to present contrasts to emphasize these two points: (1) *lobe* vs. *l'aube, rode* vs. *rôde, sotte* vs. *saute;* (2) *gosse* vs. *gauze, rosse* vs. *rose.*

STUDY QUESTIONS

1.   Determine whether the following words contain free or checked syllables.

   a)   tort   <u>checked</u>   b)   lait   _____   c)   neutre   _____   d)   thé   _____

   e)   pose   _____   f)   pot   _____   g)   roc   _____   h)   boeuf   _____

2.   Determine whether the last syllable of the following words is free or checked.

   a)   paquet   <u>free</u>   b)   heureuse   _____   c)   j'achète   _____   d)   carotte   _____

   e)   l'épaule   _____   f)   épaisse   _____   g)   l'aveu   _____   h)   pareil   _____

3. Provide a minimal pair illustrating the following contrasts in orthoepic norm Standard French:
   a) / o / vs. / ɔ /   final syllable   _____
   b) / e / vs. / ɛ /   medial syllable   _____
   c) / ø / vs. / œ /   final syllable   _____
   d) / o / vs. / ɔ /   medial syllable   l'*au*tel vs. l'hôtel _____
   e) / ø / vs. / œ /   medial syllable   _____
   f) / e / vs. / ɛ /   final syllable   _____

4. Circle the orthoepic minimal pairs that would be pronounced alike by typical Méridional speakers.
   a) (fée vs. fait)   b) saule vs. sol
   c) veulent vs. veule   d) pour vs. pur
   e) pair vs. part   f) le fils vs. l'office
   g) coté vs. côté   h) pairie vs. péri

5. Indicate the vowel sound that would be pronounced by a typical Méridional speaker for each of the italicized vowels.
   a) joy*eu*se   œ_____   b) mauv*ai*s   _____
   c) eff*or*t   _____   d) ép*au*le   _____
   e) m*ai*son   _____   f) h*eu*reux   _____

6. Underline the vowels that would be neutralized by typical Parisian speakers of Standard French.
   a) év*é*nement   b) mon*é*taire   c) peureuse
   d) provoquer   e) économie   f) orthographe
   g) l'aumônier   h) Européen   i) élémentaire

7. Within the frame of reference of an introductory course in which the *loi de position* was adopted as a pedagogical norm, which of the following items (here transcribed phonetically according to the orthoepic norm) would constitute idiosyncrasies?
   a) porte [pɔrt]   b) voyelle [ʋwajɛl]   c) (rauque)[rok]
   d) balai [balɛ]   e) laitier [lɛtje]   f) morose [mɔˤroz]
   g) feutré [føtre]   h) postier [pɔˤstje]   i) horreur [ɔˤrœr]

7

REDUCTION OF THE FRENCH VOWEL SYSTEM

In Chapter 6 it was shown that in informal, spontaneous speech no French speakers differentiate six mid vowels in all environments. There are three other types of widespread variation in the number of vowel distinctions French speakers make, as well as in the exact pronunciation of certain vowel phonemes.

7.1   THE TWO a'S

In orthoepic norm Standard French a distinction is made between front [a] and back [ɑ], as evidenced by such minimal pairs as *la patte* [lapat] "the paw" vs. *la pâte* [lapɑt] "the dough" or *il est là* [ilɛla] "he's there" vs. *il est las* [ilɛlɑ] "he's tired." In addition, some words are listed in dictionaries with [ɑ], e.g., *sable,* and other similar words with [a], e.g., *table.* But many speakers in many parts of France do not as a rule differentiate two *a* vowels, or they will use variants ranging from [a] to [ɑ] interchangeably. In general, though, the front [a] is the most widely used variety, and one may produce a pedagogical norm containing a single / a / vowel, realized as [a]. The trend toward the reduction of the contrast / a / vs. / ɑ / seems to be a result of the small articulatory and acoustic difference between these two vowels, the low relative frequency of / ɑ / (see Table 7.1), and the relatively low differentiative function of the contrast: the number of minimal pairs such as *là* vs. *las, tache* vs. *tâche* is very small, and the members of each pair seldom co-occur in the same context. Many of the words which have an orthoepic norm pronunciation with / ɑ / occur infrequently and have been replaced in ordinary speech, e.g., *las* is rare in comparison to *fatigué, tâche* occurs much less frequently than *devoir, travail,* etc.

One of the features of *français populaire* spoken in the Paris region is the clear differentiation between front / a / and back / ɑ /. The former is pronounced more fronted with lower tongue

**Table 7.1 Relative Text Frequency
of French Vowels**

Vowel	Percentage
e	8.3
a	6.6
i	6.0
ɛ	4.5
œ	3.7
ã	3.5
u	2.4
õ	2.2
ɔ	1.9
y	1.8
ø	1.3
ẽ	1.2
o	1.1
ɑ	.5
œ̃	.5

position—[æ], as in English *pat.* The latter is produced with a more retracted and higher tongue position. For many Standard French speakers such pairs as *péri* "perished" vs. *Paris* pronounced with a *français populaire* accent would be undistinguishable since the fronted realization of / a /—[æ]—is too close to the realization of / ɛ /. Similarly, such pairs as *câline* "caressing" vs. *colline* "hill" would also be confused since the retracted realization of / ɑ / overlaps with those of / o /.

7.2   THE NASAL VOWEL / œ̃ /

Many Paris speakers no longer differentiate / ẽ / from / œ̃ / and have merged these two nasal vowels in the direction of the former. The low differentiative function of / œ̃ / accounts for its demise and, since differentiative function is an important factor in the equilibrium of a phonological system and in linguistic change, it is worthwhile to examine the loss of / œ̃ / in some detail.

The French nasal vowel system is characterized by two sets of distinctive features: front vs. back, and presence vs. absence of lip rounding.

/ ẽ / *in*	/ œ̃ / *un*	/ ã / *an*	/ õ / *on*
⌈ nasal ⌉	⌈ nasal ⌉	⌈ nasal ⌉	⌈ nasal ⌉
front	front	back	back
⌊ unrounded ⌋	⌊ rounded ⌋	⌊ unrounded ⌋	⌊ rounded ⌋

For nasal vowels, tongue height distinctions are not significant. Were lip rounding no longer distinctive, / ẽ / and / œ̃ / would merge as would / ã / and / õ /. This is precisely what is happening with regard to / ẽ / vs. / œ̃ /. But how can we account for the merger of *in* and *un* in the direction of the former, when the contrast *an* vs. *on* is preserved, particularly in view of the fact that the phonetic realizations of these two vowels are very close in some varieties of Paris speech? In these varieties / ã / is realized as [ɔ̃] and / õ / as [õ]. *Un* is among the two least frequent of the French vowels. Table 7.1 lists the relative frequency of occurrence of the vowels of French in a running text consisting of about 25,000 phonemes. The percentages given are in reference to the total phonemic inventory of the language (consonants plus vowels). *Un* also occurs in a small number of individual words. The *Petit Larousse* dictionary lists only twenty words containing *un*, excluding proper names. Many of these words are very rare, and the most frequent are compounds of the indefinite determiner *un: d'un, l'un, qu'un, chacun, aucun, quelqu'un.* Among the other frequent words in which *un* occurs are *commun, défunte, emprunt(er), humble, lundi, parfum.* The other three nasal vowels occur in such frequent inflectional and derivational affixes as *in-* (negative,) *-ant* (present participle), *-ons* (first person plural), and their potential lexical frequency would range in the thousands. Whereas *on* and *an* contrast in a large number of word length minimal pairs, only five can be found involving *in* vs. *un: brin* "bit" vs. *brun* "brown"; *Alain* "Alan" vs. *alun* "alum"; *empreint* "stamped with" vs. *emprunt* "loan"; *empreinte* "print" vs. *emprunte* "borrow" (third singular present). Few of these minimal pairs would occur in the same sentence. There are also minimal pairs involving adjectives containing the prefix *in-* and noun phrases with the indefinite determiner *un*, e.g., *involontaire* "involuntary" vs. *un volontaire* "a volunteer," but these items contrast only in sentences introduced by *c'est*, e.g., *c'est involontaire* vs. *c'est un volontaire.*

Little wonder then that many Paris speakers manage very well with only three nasal vowels. Some psycholinguistic experiments seem to suggest that, even for French speakers who consistently differentiate *un* from *in*, the former does not seem to function like the other vowels but is a function of particular lexical items. When a French speaker is given a nonsense word containing *in, an,* or *on* (say, **guinbe, *fanze, *ponbe*), he will correctly identify the vowels. But when he is given nonsense words containing *un* (say, **punde, *fungue,* or **tungle*) he will interpret them as nonsense words containing one of the other three nasal vowels (i.e., as **pinde, *fongue,* or **tangle*).

7.3   VOWEL LENGTH

Compare the length of the vowels in the words *pile, pelle, poule,* and *Paul* on the one hand, and *pâle* and *pôle* on the other. You will note that the vowels of the latter two words are considerably longer in duration. Now compare the duration of the vowels of the pairs *pelle* vs. *pèse, poche* vs. *port* or *vite* vs. *vive.* You will note that the second member of each pair contains a vowel that is longer than that of the first member. But in none of the examples given above is vowel length contrastive, that is, it does not by itself differentiate words. In fact the length (or shortness) of French vowels can be predicted in terms of three rules.

We start with the general principle that all French vowels are relatively short unless they are characterized by one of the following three rules:

1.   All nasal vowels are lengthened in final checked syllables, i.e., when they are followed by a final consonant; compare (phonetic length is noted by [:]):

fonte [fõ:t]	vs.	font [fõ]	
chante [ʃã:t]	vs.	chant [ʃã]	
cinq [sẽ:k]	vs.	saint [sẽ]	
emprunte [ãprœ̃:t]	vs.	emprunt [ãprœ̃]	

2. The vowels / ø /, / o /, and / ɑ / are lengthened in all final checked syllables:

rose [ro:z]	vs.	carreau [karo]
heureuse [œrø:z]	vs.	heureux [œrø]
pâte [pɑ:t]	vs.	pas [pɑ]

3. All vowels are lengthened in final checked syllables ending with the voiced fricatives / z /, / ʒ / and / v /, the resonant / r /, and the consonant cluster / vr / (these are termed "lengthening" consonants):

vise [vi:z]	vs.	vite [vit]
tige [ti:ʒ]	vs.	tic [tik]
lève [lɛ:v]	vs.	laisse [lɛs]
part [pa:r]	vs.	passe [pas]
lèvre [lɛ:vr]	vs.	lettre [lɛtr]

Some speakers lengthen all final vowels checked by the consonant / j / e.g., *travaille* [trava:j]. Still other speakers lengthen all final vowels checked by any voiced consonant, including the voiced stops / b d g /, e.g., *robe* [rɔ:b], *fade* [fa:d], *dogue* [dɔ:g].

In orthoepic norm Standard French, vowel length assumes a differentiative function when it occurs with / ɛ / in final syllable checked by non-lengthening consonants:

mettre [mɛtr] "to put"	vs.	maître [mɛ:tr] "master"		
lettre [lɛtr] "letter"	vs.	l'être [lɛ:tr] "the being"		
faites [fɛt] "(you) do"	vs.	fête [fɛ:t] "feast"		

Educated middle-class Paris speakers are likely to make such distinctions in monitored style, e.g., when they read. One such informant when asked by this author about her differentiation of *lettre* from *l'être* exclaimed: "Bien sûr que je fais une différence, l'accent circonflexe n'est pas là pour rien!" But even these speakers fail to differentiate [ɛ] from [ɛ:] in spontaneous speech.

Some speakers oppose short and long / a / in such pairs as

tache [taʃ] "stain"	vs.	tâche [ta:ʃ] "task"		
malle [mal] "trunk"	vs.	mâle [ma:l] "male"		
chasse [ʃas] "hunt"	vs.	châsse [ʃa:s] "frame"		
patte [pat] "paw"	vs.	pâte [pa:t] "paste"		

Most French speakers who make this contrast, however, realize it by opposing short [a] to long [ɑ:], in which case vowel length is no longer distinctive—the contrast is between / a / and / ɑ /, and the latter is lengthened by Rule 2 above.

In very formal style and in some Eastern dialects (Belgium, the French-speaking cantons of Switzerland) speakers oppose short and long vowels in final free syllables:

ami [ami] "friend, masc."   vs.   amie [ami:] "friend, fem."
roux [ru] "reddish"   vs.   roue [ru:] "wheel"

and the high vowels / i u y / in stressed checked syllables:

tous [tus] "all"   vs.   tousse [tu:s] "cough, imp."
sûr [syr] "sure, masc."   vs.   sûre [sy:r] "sure, fem."

7.4   SIMPLIFIED FRENCH VOWEL SYSTEM

The variations in the French vowel system we have discussed in the last two chapters suggest that, although learners of French should be taught to *discriminate*—to hear distinctions—sixteen vowel distinctions, they need to be taught to *differentiate*—to produce so that they are heard as distinct—only thirteen. This simplified system is presented in Table 7.2.

Note that although there are only three mid vowel contrasts, six vowel qualities must be distinguished: / e / is high-mid [e] in free syllables but low-mid [ɛ] in checked syllables; similarly, / ø / is high-mid [ø] in free syllables but low-mid [œ] in checked syllables; and / o / is high-mid [o] in free syllables but low-mid [ɔ] in checked syllables. This rule needs to be accompanied by a set of idiosyncratic items which contain a high-mid vowel in checked syllables, e.g., *gauche* and

Table 7.2 Simplified French Vowel System

	Front Unrounded	Front Rounded	Oral Back
High	i *ni*	y *nu*	u *nous*
Mid	[e] *fée*	[ø]*peu*	[o] *peau*
	e	ø	o
	[ɛ] *faire*	[œ]*peur*	[ɔ] *port*
Low		a *là* *las*	

	Front	Nasal Back
Rounded		õ *long*
Unrounded	ẽ *l'un* *lin*	ã *lent*

heureuse, or the low-mid vowel [ɛ] in free syllables, e.g., the imperfect and future endings, words written with the graphic sequence *-et,* etc. In the case of the latter, it is not necessary to have a list of idiosyncratic items containing [ɛ] instead of [e], since use of the latter in these items is not stigmatized.

STUDY QUESTIONS

1. Circle the contrasts that would not normally be made in the spontaneous speech of educated Paris speakers.
   a) emprunte/empreinte
   b) les malles/les mâles
   c) quelle sotte/qu'elle saute
   d) le maître/le mètre
   e) je ferai/je ferais
   f) veulent/veule

2. Provide one sentence length minimal pair for each of the following marginal vowel contrasts.
   a) / a / vs. / ɑ /   C'est une très grosse tache./C'est une très grosse tâche.
   b) / e / vs. / æ̃ /   _____
   c) / ɛ / vs. / ɛ: /   _____

3. Circle the words which contain a long vowel.
   a) pause
   b) bref
   c) feutre
   d) mauvaise
   e) blanche
   f) las
   g) blond
   h) sève

4. The last vowel of the following words is long. Group these words into three classes depending on which of the three rules specifying predictable vowel length applies to them.
   a) heureuse
   b) réalise
   c) diplôme
   d) ombrage
   e) enchante
   f) infâme
   g) autour
   h) emprunte
   i) horloge
   j) éteindre

   Rule 1—all nasal vowels are long in final checked syllables;
   enchante _____ _____ _____

   Rule 2—all high-mid vowels (except / e /) and / ɑ / are long in final checked syllables;
   heureuse _____ _____ _____

   Rule 3—all vowels followed by / z /, / v /, / ʒ /, and / r / are long.
   heureuse _____ _____ _____

5. Why can vowel length not be distinctive before / r /?

6.   State some of the factors that account for the merger of / ẽ / and / œ̃ / in the speech of many Paris speakers.

7.   Why is it inaccurate to say that Méridional speakers can produce only three phonetically distinct mid vowels?

8

SEMIVOWELS AND ASPIRATE h

8.1 PHONETIC CHARACTERISTICS

As their names indicate, semivowels are phonological units which share some of the characteristics of both vowels and consonants. French has three semivowel sounds, [j], [w] and [ɥ]. The first two sounds are found widely in languages of the world, but the last, [ɥ], is limited in its occurrence and is one of the phonetic features characteristic of French. From a phonetic point of view, the semivowels are best described with reference to the high vowels [i], [u], and [y], from which they differ by higher tongue position. In the production of the semivowels the tongue comes close to and even touches the roof of the mouth, and thus a constricted air channel results. Another important difference between the high vowels [i], [u], and [y] and their corresponding semivowel [j], [w], [ɥ] is that the former constitute syllables whereas the latter do not: compare the pronunciation of *pie* [pi] and *pied* [pje], *loup* [lu] and *loi* [lwa], and *nu* [ny] and *nuit* [nɥi]. In terms of distinctive features, semivowels differ from vowels by the feature [-syllabic], i.e., non-syllabic, versus [+syllabic] but from each other by the two sets of features—front versus back; unrounded versus rounded—which distinguish the three high vowels from each other:

	Unrounded		Rounded	
	+Syllabic	-Syllabic	+Syllabic	-Syllabic
Front	i	j	y	ɥ
Back			u	w

Evidence must now be offered that the three semivowels contrast with each other. Such evidence is available in the form of triads like *miette* [mjɛt] "crumb," *mouette* [mwɛt] "sea gull," and *muette* [mɥɛt] "dumb, adj., fem." Each of the semivowels may be considered as a set of distinctive features which differentiate it from the other two semivowels, from its corresponding high vowel, and from the other consonants of French, particularly the sonorants / l / and / r /:

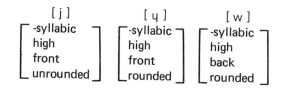

$$
\begin{array}{ccc}
[\,j\,] & [\,\mathrm{ɥ}\,] & [\,w\,] \\
\begin{bmatrix}
\text{-syllabic} \\ \text{high} \\ \text{front} \\ \text{unrounded}
\end{bmatrix} &
\begin{bmatrix}
\text{-syllabic} \\ \text{high} \\ \text{front} \\ \text{rounded}
\end{bmatrix} &
\begin{bmatrix}
\text{-syllabic} \\ \text{high} \\ \text{back} \\ \text{rounded}
\end{bmatrix}
\end{array}
$$

8.2   THE CONSONANT / j /

Like the sonorants / l / and / r /, the semivowels are produced with little local friction and turbulence and are inherently voiced. They differ from the sonorants primarily by their distribution with regard to word boundaries and neighboring vowels. From a distributional point of view semivowels may be defined as sound segments that occur before a vowel (—V) either: (1) at the beginning of a word (#), or (2) after one consonant (C—) or after certain consonants followed by / r / or / l /:

		[ɥ]	[w]	[j]
1.	# ____ V	huit	oui	iode
2.	C ____ V	puis	pois	pied
3.	C(r/l) ____ V	fruit	froid	

But the sound [j], unlike the other two semivowels, occurs in other positions, and thus from a distributional point of view behaves more like the sonorants / r / and / l /. Table 8.1 shows that it occurs also within a word between vowels, as in *griller* [grije], within a word and before a consonant,

Table 8.1. Distribution of Semivowels and Resonant Consonants

	ɥ	w	j₁	j₂	r	l
1. # __V	huit	oui	iode		reine	l'air
2. C __V	puis	pois	pied		près	plein
3. C (r or l) __ V	fruit	froid				
4. V __ V				griller	tirer	filer
5. V__ C				paillété	partout	palétot
6. V __ #				paille	par	pâle

as in *pailleté* [pajte], and at the end of a word, as in *paille* [paj]. In these environments [j] contrasts with the high front unrounded vowel / i /:

pays [pei] "country"   vs.   paye [pɛj] "pay"
abbaye [abbei] "abbey"   vs.   abeille [abɛj] "bee"
bailli [baji] "bailiff"   vs.   bail [baj] "lease"

Thus [j] behaves both like a semivowel and a consonant. Although we shall use the same symbol for both, we distinguish between the semivowel that occurs immediately preceding a vowel either after a consonant or at the beginning of a word (it is noted as j_1 in Table 8.1) and the consonant that occurs in medial position, before a consonant, and in final position (noted as j_2 in Table 8.1). Consonant and semivowel / j / have the same phonetic value but assume different functions in the language.

8.3   SEMIVOWELS AND HIGH VOWELS

Before we can attempt to provide a phonological interpretation of the semivowels, it is necessary to examine their relationships with their corresponding high vowels. These are particularly complex and differ for each semivowel and corresponding high vowel pair. We will start with the pair where the relationships are the simplest: [ɥ] and [y].

8.3.1   Syllabic and Non-Syllabic / y /

The semivowel [ɥ] occurs typically after a single consonant or consonant cluster consisting of a stop or / f / followed by / r / or / l / and before the vowel / i /, e.g., *suis, lui, bruit, fruit, pluie, fluide.* In these environments its corresponding high vowel [y] does not occur. On the other hand, only [y] but not [ɥ] is found after consonant clusters consisting of stop or / f / plus / r / or / l / and before a vowel other than / i /: *cruel, truelle, affluent.* In all other cases, either [y] or [ɥ] are permitted in the same word. Thus *muette* may be pronounced [myɛt] or [mɥɛt], *nuage* [nyaʒ] or [nɥaʒ], and *tuer* [tye] or [tɥe]. The substitution of two sounds for each other without a resulting change of meaning, such as that which is found in *muette, nuage* and *tuer* is termed **free variation.** Since whether a word contains the vowel [y] or the semivowel [ɥ] either is predictable from the environment or is not distinctive, no contrast / y / versus / ɥ / need be recognized. Accordingly, we will posit a single phoneme / y / which will be assigned the feature [+syllabic] when a high vowel or [-syllabic] when a semivowel on the basis of three simple rules stated in terms of the environment in which the phoneme finds itself:

Rule i: / y / ⟶ [ɥ] ———— i

Rule (i) states that / y / is realized as [ɥ] whenever it occurs before the vowel / i /. For example, *huit* is represented by / yit / and converted by Rule (i) to [ɥit]; similarly *lui* is / lyi /, *cuir* / kyir /, and *fruit* / fryi /.

Rule ii: / y / ⟶ [y] /KL——————

Rule (ii) states that / y / is realized as [y] whenever it is preceded by a consonant cluster consisting of a stop or / f / (symbolized by K) and / r / or / l / (symbolized by L). For example, *cruel* is represented by / kryɛl / and converted by Rule (ii) to [kryɛl]; similarly *affluent* is / aflyɑ̃ /.

Rule iii: / y / ⟶ [y] or [ɥ] / ——————— V_x

Rule (iii) states that / y / is realized as either [y] or [ɥ] when it is followed by a vowel other than / i /. For example, *muette* "dumb, fem." is represented as / myɛt / and is realized as [myɛt] or [mɥet]; *huer* "to boo" is represented as / ye / and is realized as [ye] or [ɥe].

Another solution, of course, is to note the particular sound that occurs in a particular word, so that words to which Rule (i) applies would always be represented with / ɥ /; words to which Rule (ii) applies would always be represented with / y /, and words to which Rule (iii) applies would be represented with / ɥ / or / y /, depending on the sound used by a speaker on a given occasion. But this solution would fail to reveal the fact that [+syllabic] [y] and [-syllabic] [ɥ] never contrast. It is interesting to note that French spelling conventions imply the solution adopted here: both [ɥ] and [y] are represented by the letter *u,* and it is assumed that the reader uses rules such as those formulated above in converting the spelling to sound.

8.3.2   Semivowel / w / and Vowel / u /

The occurrence of the semivowel [w] and its corresponding high vowel [u] is predictable in some environments, but the two sounds contrast in other environments so that the solution adopted for [ɥ] and [y] is inapplicable. The two sounds contrast before / a / or / ɑ /: *joie* [ʒwa] "joy" versus *joua* [ʒua] "he played" or *trois* [trwɑ] "three" versus *troua* [trua] "he punctured." These contrasts are somewhat peculiar in that, after a single consonant, the two words differ by the fact that one may be pronounced only with the semivowel whereas the other word may be pronounced with the semivowel or the vowel. For example, *joie* is always pronounced [ʒwa] whereas *joua* may be pronounced [ʒwa] or [ʒua]. Words in which [w] and [u] are in free variation contain a morpheme boundary between the variable segment and / a /. For instance, *joua* consists of the verb stem *jou-* followed by the past definite (*passé simple*) ending *-a.* We handle minimal pairs of the type *joie* vs. *joua* by assigning the member of the pair that may only be pronounced with [w] to the semivowel / w / and the one in which [w] and [u] are in free variation to the high vowel / u /; in other words, *joie* [ʒwa] is noted / ʒwa /, but *jou-a* [ʒwa] or [ʒua] is noted /ʒua /.

There are also instances of free variation between [w] and [u] before vowels other than / a / or / ɑ / and in which case no contrasts of the type presented above are possible: *jouet* "toy" [ʒuɛ] or [ʒwɛ]; *souhait* "wish" [suɛ] or [swɛ]; *mouette* "sea gull" [muɛt] or [mwɛt]. After groups of consonants consisting of stops or / f / plus / r / or / l /, / w / contrasts with / u /, and the latter can only be realized as the vowel [u] and never as the semivowel [w]. Compare *adroit* / adrwa /, which of course is converted to [adrwa], and *écrouer* / ekroue /, which is realized as [ekrue] only. Note that in the latter case [u] occurs before a grammatical boundary (*écrou-er*), as was the case for *trou-a.* To summarize the relationships between [w] and [u], words which in the conventional spelling contain the combination *oi* or *oin* are represented with / w / and are realized obligatorily with the semivowel [w]. Words which are spelled with *ou* are represented with / u /, and whether they are realized with / w / in free variation with / u / or obligatorily with [u] is determined by the environment and is amenable to statement in terms of the following rules:

Rule i: / u / ⟶ [u]/KL————

Rule (i) states that / u / is always realized as [u] when it is preceded by a consonant cluster consisting of stop or / f / plus / r / or / l /, for example, *écroua, brouette, prouesse.*

Rule ii: / u / ⟶ [u] or [w]/C————

Rule (ii) states that / u / may be realized as either [u] or [w] when it is preceded by a consonant, for example, *loua, louer, souhait, mouette, fouetter, fouet.*

Rule iii: / w / ⟶ [w]

Rule (iii) states that / w / is always realized as [w], for example, *foi, foin, toi, loin.*

8.3.3   Semivowel / j / and Vowel / i /

Analogous to contrast of the type *loi* [lwa] versus *loua* [lwa] or [lua] are contrasts such as *lion* "lion" [ljõ] versus *(nous) lions* "(we) bind" [ljõ] or [liʲõ]. Words in which the semivowel pronunciation is obligatory will be represented with / j /, for example, *lien* [ljẽ], *mieux* [mjø], *pied* [pje], *pion* [pjõ]. But words in which the semivowel and the vowel are in free variation will be represented with / i /. In these words, / i / is the last syllable of the stem: *li-er* [lje] or [lie] "to bind," *(vous) ri-ez* [rje] or [rie] "(you) laugh," *se fi-er* [fje] or [fie] "to trust."

Whenever / i / is preceded by a consonant group of the type KL, the syllabic pronunciation is required: *brioche* "brioche" [briʲɔʃ], *tablier* "apron" [tabliʲe], *cri-er* "to shout" [kriʲe]. The phonetic realization of / i / occurring before a vowel is determined by two rules:

Rule i: / i / ⟶ [iʲ]/KL————

Rule (i) states that where / i / is preceded by a KL consonant cluster, it is always pronounced [iʲ] e.g., *pli-er* is realized as [pliʲe];

Rule ii: / i / ⟶ [i] or [j]/C ————

Rule (ii) states that when it is preceded by a single consonant, / i / is pronounced [iʲ] or [j], e.g., *li-ons* / liõ / is realized as [ljõ] or [liʲõ].

It will be noted that in the phonetic representations of / i / followed by a vowel there appears a raised [j]. This symbol represents a short glide that is always present when [i] is followed by any other vowel. It must be distinguished from the full, consonantal [j] that appears in such words as *billet, cahier, briller, nettoyer, travailler* and that we have analyzed as / j$_2$ /. French speakers presumably hear a difference between *étriller* "to curry, comb (a horse)" [etrije] and *étrier* "stirrup"

[etriʲe]. It is likely the case that in rapid speech such a small phonetic distinction cannot be produced or perceived, but it is one that must be provided for in an overall phonological description of French. The words *étriller* and *étrier* are represented as / etrije / and / etrie / respectively, and Rule (ii), which applies to the latter to specify the syllabic pronunciation of / i /, introduces the short intervocalic glide [ʲ].

8.4   SEMIVOWELS AT THE BEGINNING OF A WORD

The vowels / i / and / u / and their corresponding semivowels / j / and / w / may also occur at the beginning of a word. In such cases the semivowels are of course realized obligatorily as [-syllabic] [j] and [w]: *iode* "iodine" / jɔd /, is always realized as [jɔd], *oiseau* "bird" / wazo / is realized as [wazo]. The vowels may be realized as either syllabic or [-syllabic]: *hier* "yesterday" / iɛr / is realized as [iɛr] or [jɛr]; *où est* "where is" / uɛ / is realized as [uɛ] or [wɛ].

The inherent relationships between the semivowels and the vowels is underscored by their behavior in *liaison.* As will be discussed in greater detail in Chapter 10, liaison involves the deletion or the retention of the final consonants of words in certain environments. Word final consonants are retained between vowels *and* semivowels—traditionally it is stated that word final consonants are "linked" (retained) in this environment. Thus there is no difference between such words as *ours* "bear" / urs / and *oiseau* "bird" / wazo / with regard to their behavior in liaison: *les ours, les oiseaux.* Vowels and semivowels also behave the same in **elision**, the deletion or retention of mute *e.* Mute *e* is always deleted before a vowel or a semivowel: *l'ours, l'oiseau,* and *l'île* "the island" (/ il /) and *l'iode* "iodine" (/ jɔd /).

But there are many words beginning with / j / and / w / before which consonants are deleted (not linked) and mute *e* retained (not elided): *les yaourts, le yaourt* (/ jaur / "yogurt"; *les whisky, le whisky* (/ wiski / "whiskey"). Most words beginning with a semivowel before which liaison consonants are deleted and mute *e* retained are relatively recent foreign loans and in fact show aspirate *h* behavior (see Section 8.6). Now, aspirate *h* may also occur before words beginning with a vowel, for example, *les homards, le homard* (/ ɔmar / "lobster"). The fact that they may also be preceded by aspirate *h* is added justification for considering semivowels inherently related to the high vowels / i / and / u /. There are also cases of free variation involving the presence or absence of aspirate *h.* The word *ouate* / wat / "wadding, cotton wool" has aspirate *h* when it occurs at the beginning of a phrase: *la ouate;* but it loses the aspirate *h* when it occurs within a phrase: *un tampon d'ouate* "a pad of cotton wool."

Since we have not posited an independent phoneme / ɥ /, how do we account for such cases as *le huit* [lǝɥi] *décembre* but *le dix-huit* / dizɥi / *décembre*? The numeral *huit* is represented as / yit / and occurs with aspirate *h* when it is used alone, but in the compound number *dix-huit,* it appears without aspirate *h* and the liaison consonant is retained. A phonological rule converts / y / to [ɥ] since it is followed by the vowel / i /.

8.5   SUMMARY OF SEMIVOWELS

The three semivowels recognized in traditional descriptions of French are considered inherently related to vowels rather than to the consonants. They are in fact high vowels which, however, cannot constitute syllables by themselves—they are [-syllabic]. In this regard they function as consonants do.

By considering the semivowels as basically vowels, we account for the extensive free variation between the high vowels and their corresponding semivowel and for the fact that the semivowels behave like vowels in liaison and elision and may be preceded by aspirate *h.* On the basis of the existence of contrasts such as *loi* vs. *loua* and *lion* vs. *lions,* it is necessary to posit two semivowel units / j / and / w /; but [ɥ] is best interpreted as a variant of / y / whose occurrence is determined by the environment in which it occurs.

The solution that we have adopted in the interpretation of the semivowels, although it was developed independently of orthographic considerations, is similar to that which is implicit in French spelling conventions. French spelling denotes semivowels with vowel symbols—*pied, fouet, tuer*—with the exception of semivowels occurring at the beginning of some words which are preceded by aspirate *h,* such as *yacht, watt.* French speakers have internalized rules which determine whether the vowel representation—*i, ou, u*—represents a semivowel sound, a high vowel, or whether the semivowel sound and the high vowel are in free variation. We also pointed out that in most cases where the semivowel sound and the high vowel are in free variation, there is a morpheme boundary after the variable segment.

With regard to words of the latter type, the learner is presented with a choice of variant: should he pronounce these words with the semivowel or the corresponding high vowel? That is, should *tuer* be pronounced [tye] or [tɥe]? One of the features of free variation is that both variants are acceptable to educated middle-class speakers, and, indeed, in the case at hand, French speakers would have difficulty stating which variant they used on a particular occasion and in perceiving the difference between the two variant forms. But since English learners are likely to insert a glide element after high vowels, it is preferable for them to use the variant with the semivowel. In other words, they should pronounce *lions* as [ljõ] rather than [liǰõ], since they are likely to pronounce the latter variant as [lⁱiǰjõ]. Another argument for selecting this variant in a pedagogical norm is the fact that the French spelling notes both / j / (where the semivowel is obligatory, e.g., *pied*) and / i / (where the semivowel and the high vowel are in free variation, e.g., *lions, rions*) the same way. If the learner pronounces variable items with the vowel, he is likely to generalize this pronunciation to items containing / i /, and he would produce wrong pronunciations in such words as *pied* *[piǰe], *fier* *[fiǰɛr].

8.6   ASPIRATE *h*

Some French words which begin with a vowel when pronounced in isolation behave as if they contained an initial consonant when they enter in construction with other words. In particular, they will condition the deletion of preceding final consonants and the retention of a preceding mute *e:*

	hache / aʃ / "ax"	la hache / laaʃ /
vs.	anche / ãʃ / "reed (music)"	l'anche / lãʃ /
	hêtre / ɛ:tr / "beech tree"	le hêtre / lØɛ:tr /
vs.	être / ɛtr / "being"	l'être / lɛtr /

Traditionally, words that begin with a vowel but behave in phrases as if they began with a consonant are said to begin with **aspirate** *h (h aspiré).* This term stems from the fact that many words which exhibit aspirate *h* behavior are in fact written with an initial *h*. But not all words that are written with an initial *h* contain aspirate *h*, and traditional descriptions oppose **mute** *h (h muet)* to aspirate *h:*

	horloge / orlɔʒ / "clock"	l'horloge / lorlɔʒ /
vs.	honte / ɔ̃t / "shame"	la honte / laɔ̃t /

In addition, some words which exhibit aspirate *h* behavior are not written with *h:*

Nous sommes *le onze* juin. / lǿɔ̃z / "Today's June 11."
Choisissez *le un.* / lǿœ̃ / "Choose number one."

To account for the difference in liaison and elision behavior between words that contain aspirate *h* and those that behave normally—that is, before which final consonants are retained and mute *e* is deleted—we must mark words that contain aspirate *h* as idiosyncratic. We follow the convention adopted by French dictionaries of representing aspirate *h* with an asterisk, e.g., **honte, *haut,* etc.

In some varieties of Standard French, for example Haitian Standard French, aspirate *h* manifests itself by some phonetic feature: some sort of glottal constriction or glottal catch or even the glottal aspirate [h] (which occurs in English *hen*). These various phonetic features may also occur in emphatic speech, e.g., *Je te hais!* [ʒətəhɛ] or [ʒətəʔɛ], where [ʔ] represents a glottal catch. But these phonetic features play no distinctive function in French; they are simply features that are within the range of permissible phonetic realization of word initial vowels in French. In sum, what characterizes aspirate *h* is not its overt phonetic features—which are usually totally absent—but its behavior with respect to liaison and elision, phenomena which are not, properly speaking, phonological (see Chapter 10).

Aspirate *h* is found mostly in words borrowed from Germanic dialects which in Old French did in fact begin with the glottal aspirate [h], and this explains why most words which exhibit aspirate *h* behavior are written with an initial *h*. In Modern French, aspirate *h*, whether it is represented by *h* or not, is a device by which the speaker is able to underscore certain words beginning with a vowel. It is, so to speak, a way of putting a word beginning with a vowel between quotation marks. The original stock of words which at one time were pronounced with [h] are thus marked as being somewhat unusual. Foreign loan words and proper names that begin with a vowel or a semivowel are introduced in French with an aspirate *h* as are many native proper names, titles of books and works of art, e.g.,

où est le yacht
l'article de André Tardieu
l'auteur de "il pleut bergère"
le quatrième volume de "A la recherche du temps perdu"
est-ce la Olifant
la fin de Hitler

As foreign loan words or proper names become "naturalized" or as native aspirate *h* words become more frequent, they lose their aspirate *h* and are treated as beginning with a normal vowel. Predictably, there is wide fluctuation in the pronunciation of such words. A person who uses a particular aspirate *h* word frequently will tend to treat it as a normal word, and it is not unusual to find even in the speech of educated speakers pronunciations like / dezariko / *des haricots* "some beans" for the more "correct" / deariko /. Quite revealing is the treatment of the proper name *Hitler.* When that infamous statesman first emerged into the limelight, newspaper editors and radio announcers treated his name as an unassimilated foreign word and always used it with aspirate *h: le dernier discours de Hitler, la jeunesse de Hitler.* Later the name was so widely used that it generated derivatives: *hitlerienne, hitlerisme,* all of which together with the base word were later given normal treatment: *la gardé hitlerienne, le danger de l'hitlerisme, la mort d'Hitler.*

As was stated in Section 8.4, aspirate *h* may also occur before word initial semivowels. Such contrasts as *l'oiseau* vs. *le watt* or *les oiseaux* vs. *les watts* are accounted for by marking *watt* as idiosyncratic—**watt* / **wat* /. Aspirate *h* occurs before all vowels (**hibou, *huche, *houille, *héros, *haine, *heuse, *heurt, *haute, *hors, *halte, *havre, *un, *onze, *hein, *hanche*), but it occurs most frequently before / a / and back vowels, e.g., **hache, *halte, *hareng, *haricot, *homard, *honte, *Hollande,* etc.

STUDY QUESTIONS

1. Indicate whether the segment represented by *u* is pronounced (1) as the vowel [y], (2) as the semivowel [ɥ], or (3) as either.

   a) truelle   [y]_____   e) cruauté _____

   b) bruine _____   f) fruit _____

   c) sueur _____   g) affluent _____

   d) gruau _____   h) fluide _____

2. Circle the items which may be pronounced with either a high vowel or a semivowel.

   a) nouer   e) hier

   b) nier   f) écroua

   c) tiers   g) adroit

   d) pois   h) lier

3. Indicate whether the following words contain the semivowel / j / or the consonant / j / by listing them under the appropriate column heading below.

   paille, Dieu, pion, cahier, nouille, appuyer, scier, yaourt

                 Semivowel   *Consonant*

4. List two words that belong to each of the following groups:

   a) beginning with / w /: oiseau_____ _____ _____

   b) beginning with / w / preceded by aspirate *h*: watt_____ _____ _____

   c) beginning with / j /: hier_____ _____ _____

   d) beginning with / j / preceded by aspirate *h*: hiéarchie_____ _____ _____

5. How would one show that *un, huit,* and *onze* sometimes contain an aspirate *h*?

6. Cite one minimal pair that supports setting up contrasts:
    a)   / u / vs. / w /
    b)   / i / vs. semivowel / j /

7. Cite one minimal or near-minimal pair that supports setting up a contrast / i / vs. consonant / j /.

8. Why can one not support the claim that [y] and [ɥ] must be established as two distinctive phonological units (phonemes)?

9. How would one account for: *la ouate* but *un tampon d'ouate?*

10. Transcribe the following *phonetically;* list all variant forms:
    a)   brioche   e)   iode
    b)   octroyer   f)   bruiter
    c)   il y a   g)   brouette
    d)   trois   h)   muette

9

STRESS AND RHYTHM

Utterances consist of more than a succession of vowels and consonants as neatly separated from each other as beads on a string. Vowels and consonants occur within a melody-rhythm matrix, the **prosodic contour,** and they are organized in successively larger units. In most languages the lowest-level unit of prosodic organization is the syllable which consists of a vocalic nucleus accompanied or not by consonantal material; the largest prosodic unit is the utterance which corresponds to the grammatical unit we call **sentence** or abbreviated and fragmentary realizations of the latter. The number of intermediate units between the syllable and the utterance that must be posited varies greatly from language to language, as does the nature of the prosodic contour. However the prosodic contour always consists of various hierarchical arrangements of the following elements: (1) **pitch,** the relative frequency of vibration of the vocal cords that underlies voiced sounds; (2) **stress,** the relative prominence placed on a given portion of a stretch of speech; (3) **rhythm,** tempo variations in the rate of production of the syllables or similar units of an utterance and their constituents.

Stress and rhythm are intimately linked, and we shall discuss them together in the present chapter.

9.1   STRESS

Stress refers to differences in prominence among the syllables of an utterance, but differences in the timing of successive syllables relative to each other also contribute to its phonetic characterization. In languages that have linguistically significant stress-level differences, so-called stressed syllables are not always produced with greater intensity—and are therefore not always louder—than so-called unstressed syllables. For this reason it might be preferable to speak of **accent** rather than stress, but we shall retain the traditional label.

Stress may play two distinct functions in a language: it may, like segmental material—vowels and consonants—differentiate utterances from each other; or it may serve essentially to signal the ordering of linguistic units and thus facilitate the analysis of the message. In the first instance we say that stress is **contrastive**; in the second instance we say that it is **demarcative**. Of course, stress may—and in fact often does—play these two roles simultaneously.

In French, stress is predictable and, hence, it is not contrastive; it serves mainly a demarcative function. It occurs automatically on the last syllable of a **phonemic phrase** and for that reason is termed **final stress**. Phonemic phrases are marked by a shift in pitch, either upward or downward, and sometimes corresponds to the syntactic grouping phrase. The length of phonemic phrases varies, but the range, on the average, is between three and four syllables:

J'ai *vu* Monsieur Du*rant* au ciné*ma* hier après-mi*di*. (2-4-3-5)
Qui vous l'a *dit*? —La conci*erge*. (4-3)
Répondez-*nous* dès que vous aurez re*çu* cette *lettre*. (3-5-2)

Phonetically, French final stress is characterized primarily by an increase in the duration of the vowel. In English, sentence stress is movable and can be used to underscore any part of a sentence, e.g.,

Jóhn leàves toníght. (sentence stress on *John*)
vs.   Jóhn leàves toníght. (normal pronunciation with sentence stress on *tonight*)

In French, final stress cannot be moved from the last syllable of a phonemic phrase. If one wishes to emphasize a word, the word must be permuted to that position through the use of an emphatic transformation:

Jean part ce *soir*. (normal: sentence stress on *soir*).
Jean, il part ce *soir*. (emphatic: sentence stress on *Jean*).
C'est *Jean* qui part ce *soir*. (emphatic: sentence stress on *Jean*).

In emphatic style it is possible to stress a non-phonemic phrase-final syllable by making it bear **emphatic stress** *(accent d'insistance)*. Emphatic stress, however, can only occur on the first syllable of the emphasized word; in the examples below, emphatic stress is represented by bold face.

un **ex**cellent étu*diant* "an excellent student"   vs.   un excellent étu*diant*
un **char**mant gar*çon* "a charming boy"   vs.   un charmant gar*çon*

The phonetic characteristics of emphatic stress are additional intensity, pitch rise, lengthening of the vowel, and increased force of articulation of the consonant. The sole occurrence of vowel length is sufficient to signal emphatic stress, but in that case the vowel is much longer than that of a syllable bearing final stress.

A variant of emphatic stress called **affective stress** *(accent d'insistance émotionelle)* occurs with a limited set of lexical items: pejoratives, superlatives, etc. This variant of emphatic stress occurs on the first syllable of a word which begins with a consonant:

> quel im*bécile*! "what a fool!"   but   quel *cochon*! "what a pig!"
> i*diot*! "idiot!"   *menteur*! "liar!"

In words that begin with a vowel but which occur immediately after a liaison consonant (see Chapter 10), the latter acts as an initial consonant and the emphatic stress falls on the first syllable:

> c'est‿*épatant*! / se **te** pa tã / "it's great!"
> il est‿*insupportable*! / i le **tẽ** sy pɔr *tabl* / "he's unbearable!"

9.2   LEARNING PROBLEMS

In English, stress is contrastive, and it differentiates such minimal pairs as *tránsport* (noun) vs. *transpórt* (verb) or *ínvalid* (person with permanent physical infirmities) vs. *inválid* (not valid). In fact several distinctive levels of stress must be posited for English. Pronounce the following two sentences aloud and note the differences in stress indicated by the three types of accent marks above the vowels:

> The óperàtor is síck.
> The òperátion is símple.

In these two sentences (˝) denotes loudest stress, (´) indicates the next stress level, and (`) represents the weakest perceptible level of stress; syllables which do not bear any accent mark are considered to have zero stress. Another important fact about differences in level of stress in English is that unstressed syllables (those that bear zero stress) contain the neutral vowel [ɨ]. Compare the italicized vowel in the following pairs:

> áble   a*bí*lity
> *à*pplicátion   applý

You will note that as stress shifts from the vowel of the first syllable, its quality changes to [ɨ].

It is to be anticipated that American learners may carry over the habit of correlating vowel quality and stress into French. Since in French the last syllable of a phonemic phrase is more prominent than all others, it will be heard by American learners as bearing a loud stress, and vowels that occur in the next-to-last position in a phonemic phrase will automatically be reduced to [ɨ]. This reduction of vowel quality has serious consequences in French, for the inflectional signals for gender and number are usually contained in noun markers that immediately precede the noun rather than in the last syllable of the noun itself. Also, two-syllable words that differ only with regard to the vowel of the first syllable will be confused. Consider the following paired items:

/ a / vs. / e /	ma sœur "my sister" salé "salty"	mes sœurs "my sisters" scellé "sealed"
/ œ / vs. / e /	le garçon "the boy" cela "this" ceux-là "those"	les garçons "the boys" c'est là "it's there"
/ i / vs. / e /	dix mois "ten months" il va "he goes" ils vont "they go" (masc.)	des mois "some months" elle va "she goes" elles vont "they go" (fem.)
/ u / vs. / o /	couler "to sink" couteau "knife"	coller "to paste" côteau "hill"
/ o / vs. / a /	volet "shutter"	valet "valet"

American speakers will pronounce the contrasting vowels of these pairs as [ɨ] and will therefore fail to maintain the contrast. Many of the vowel contrasts shown above and others like them may occur in identical sentences and contexts, and they are critical for accurate transmission of a message, e.g., *il est parti il y a dix mois* "he left ten months ago" vs. *il est parti il y a des mois* "he left some months ago" vs. *il est parti il y a deux mois* "he left two months ago."

Particularly persistent is interference involving cognate words which the learner may want to pronounce with the stress and vowel quality pattern of the English corresponding word:

English	*French*
bággage	bagage / ba *ga* ʒ /
Ápril	avril / a *vri*l /
máladỳ	maladie / ma la *di* /
èxplicátion	explication / eks pli ka *sjõ* /
èlectrícitỳ	electricité / e lek tri si *te* /

In English word boundaries are also demarcated by differences in the articulation of consonants depending on whether they are word initial or word final, etc. Consider, for example, the following minimal pairs distinguished solely by fine differences in the articulation of the italicized consonant:

it *s*wings / t+s /	it*s* wings / ts+ /
a *n*ice man / +n /	a*n* ice man / n+ /
the nigh*t* rate / t+r /	the ni*t*rate / tr /

These differences in articulation of consonants and vowels that occur mainly at word boundaries are called **word juncture.**

In French word juncture is not as clearly perceptible as it is in English. In monitored style, there are differences in the articulation of consonants which serve as word boundaries:

	trè*s* amis "very friendly"	/ z /
vs.	trei*ze* amis "thirteen friends"	/ z+ /
	un petit *t*orrent "a small torrent"	/ +t /
vs.	une peti*te* orange "a small orange"	/ t+ /
	trois petits *tr*ous "three small holes"	/ +tr /
vs.	trois peti*tes* roues "three small wheels"	/ t+r /
	à quel *c*oeur "to which heart"	/ +k /
vs.	à quel*que* heure "at some hour"	/ k+ /

The italicized consonant that occurs in the second member of each pair is produced with less articulatory tension than the corresponding consonant in the first member. To put it somewhat differently, the consonant of the first member of each pair is initial-like and is produced with more articulatory energy; the consonant of the second member is final-like and is produced with less articulatory energy. In other cases, word juncture is indicated by lengthening of a vowel:

	un signalement [siɲalmã̃] "a description"	
vs.	un signe allemand [si˳ɲalmã̃] "a German sign"	
	il est ouvert [tuvɛr] "it's open"	
vs.	il est tout vert [tu·vɛr] "it's all green"	
	un invalide [nɛ̃valid] "an invalid"	
vs.	un nain valide [nɛ̃·valid] "a worthy dwarf"	

But these fine articulatory differences are not readily perceptible to the average ear, and usually French speakers will mark word juncture by the insertion of final or emphatic stress or changes in intonation. For example, to differentiate *très amis* from *treize amis,* they will insert stress on the first syllable of *amis* and lengthen the liaison consonant in the first member of the pair—[trɛzzami̇́].

Liaison is sometimes explained by the fact that the French language does not permit the occurrence of two successive vowels and that a consonant sound is inserted for reasons of euphony. This explanation is easily refuted by citing some of the numerous cases of two, three, and even four successive vowels to be found in French:

au Havre / oavr / "at Le Havre"
du hareng / dyarã̃ / "some herring"
va à Orly / vaaorli / "go to Orly"
il va en haut aussi / ilvaã̃oosi / "he's also going upstairs"

In French, unlike English, vowel onset is smooth. Two successive vowels are not separated by a glottal catch or other transitional phenomenon. Glottal catches, represented by ʔ , occur in French only with phrase initial vowels marked by emphatic stress, e.g., *extraordinaire*! [ʔɛkstraordinɛr] "most unusual!".

The absence of word stress, of word juncture, and of transitional phenomena between successive vowels, particularly between vowels belonging to two different words, result in the fusion of individual words within phonemic phrases. Stress in French plays a demarcative role, but it demarcates phonemic phrases rather than words. Words are marked off from each other only in overcareful style characteristic of word-by-word reading where phonemic phrases correspond to individual words. Another feature that makes the demarcation of words difficult in French is that a consonant occurring within a phonemic phrase may have four different lexical sources: (1) it may be word medial, e.g., *entamé* / ãtame / "begun"; (2) it may be word initial, e.g., *ces tamis* / setami / "these sieves"; (3) it may be word final, e.g., *sept amis* / setami / "seven friends"; (4) it may be a liaison consonant, e.g., *cet ami* / setami / "this friend."

Thus in French, phonological structure does not clearly reflect grammatical and lexical organization. The sentence *Il en avait ici* is pronounced as a phonemic phrase consisting of six syllables, many of which do not correspond to the constituent words:

> / i   lã   na   ve   ti   si /
>   *Il*   *en*   *avait*   *ici.*

The second syllable is made up of part of the first and second lexical items, the third syllable of the second and third words, and the fifth syllable of part of the third and fourth words. This lack of clear demarcation of individual words, compounded by neutralization of mid vowel contrasts in phonemic, phrase medial position (see Chapter 6) gives rise to considerable ambiguity in the interpretation of messages and constitutes the greatest source of puns and humor. Consider the following riddle: *Quelles provinces de Grèce sortent d'un bourbier où sont tombés un athée et un abbé?* "What provinces of Greece emerge from a mud hole where have fallen an atheist and an abbot?" The answer, of course, is *La Thessalie et la Béotie* "Thessalia and Beotia." The humor resides in the two-way interpretation of the two phonemic phrases / latesali elabeosi /: (1) *l'athée sali et l'abbé aussi* "the atheist besmirched and the abbot too" or (2) *La Thessalie et la Béotie.*

9.3   SYLLABIFICATION

Because of the absence of word stress and word juncture, the syllable is the only phonological unit between individual vowels and consonants and the phonemic phrase. French is characterized by **open syllabification,** the peak of articulatory energy is generally on the vocalic center of a syllable rather than on the consonants that accompany the vowel. A French syllable is defined as a vowel which may or may not be preceded or followed by one or more consonants. Thus, a phonemic phrase contains as many syllables as it has vowels. Syllables may end with a vowel (free or open syllables) or with one or more consonants (checked or closed syllables). In any given sample of spoken French most syllables will be open. Recently reported statistical data on the composition of the syllables in random samples of French (Pierre Delattre, *Comparing the Phonetic Features of English, French, German, and Spanish,* p. 40) show that 76 per cent of 3,000 syllables were open (see Table 9.1); a comparable English corpus contained only 40 per cent open syllables.

Table 9.1 Relative Proportion of Syllable Types in a Random Sample of Spoken French

Syllable Type	Example	Frequency Percentage
CV	lait / lɛ /	55
CVC	sec / sɛk /	17
CCV	train / trɛ̃ /	14
V	où / u /	6
VC	art / a /	2
CCSV	proie / prwa /	1
CVCCC	muscle / myskl /	1

C is any initial consonant, S any semivowel, and V any vowel.

In English the existence of several levels of stress and of articulatory features that signal boundaries between words also serve to mark the boundaries between syllables, particularly when a single consonant or a consonant cluster occurs within a word. For example, in *nitrate,* prolongation of the first vowel marks the syllable boundary (*ni + trate*) and distinguishes it from *night rate* where the boundary occurs between the two consonants (*night + rate*). In French, as was pointed out in Section 9.2, there are no junctural features, and medial consonants or consonant clusters have to be assigned to the preceding or the following vowel on a different basis.

From a pedagogical point of view, it is important that English learners of French acquire the habit of open syllabification, ending most syllables with a vowel rather than with a consonant, as is the case for their native language. It is very useful to adopt a pedagogical norm for the division of syllables. The basic principle in this norm is to assign all single medial consonants to the following syllable and to anticipate the articulation of the vowel of the following syllable:

Il est arrivé. / i.le.ta.ri.ve /
Nos amis vous attendent. / no.za.mi.vu.za.tãd /

Note that all syllables end with a vowel except for the last one in the second utterance whose final syllable ends with / d /.

The division of utterances containing medial consonant clusters is more complex. For example, should the / tr / of *patrie* be assigned to both syllables or to the second? In other words should the word be divided as / pa.tri / or / pat.ri /? Similarly should *partie* be divided / pa.ti / or / par.ti /? It is important to note that there are no articulatory features that can guide our choice. The best guide in the division of medial consonant clusters is information about the type of consonant clusters that occur at the beginning of words. Table 9.2 shows the most frequent types of word initial consonant clusters in French. These consonant clusters fall into three types: (1) consonant + semivowel (these are not properly speaking consonant clusters, since semivowels are not true consonants); (2) K-type consonant (stop or / f / and / v /) + liquid (/ r / and / l /); (3) / s / + / p /, / t /, / k /, and / f / (see Table 9.2). We are now able to formulate a second general principle in syllabification: medial consonant clusters will

Table 9.2 Frequent Initial Consonant Clusters

C₁ \ C₂	w	j	ɥ	r	l	t	k	p	f
s	soir	sien	suer			stère	scandale	spécial	sphère
p	pois	pion	puer	prends	plan				
k	quoi	kiosque	cuit	cran	clan				
f	fois	fier	fuite	franc	flanc				
b	bois	biais	buisson	branche	blanc				
g	gouache			grand	gland				
t	toi	tien	tuile	tranche					
d	doigt	Dieu	duel	drap					
v	voix	vieux		vrai					
ʃ	choix	chien	chuinter						
ʒ	joie		juillet						
m	moi	mien	muet						
n	noix	nier	nuit						
l	loi	lien	lui						
r	roi	rien	ruine						

| Semivowels | Liquids | Obstruents |

be assigned to the following syllable if they constitute an occurring word initial cluster; otherwise, they will be divided between the two syllables. We apply this principle to sample two-syllable words:

après / a.prɛ /	but	arpège / ar.pɛʒ /
étui / e.tɥi /	but	amenons / am.nõ /
casquer / ka.ske /	but	traction / trak.sjõ /
actrice / ak.tris /		

Another principle may be invoked in the assignment of consonants constituting medial clusters. Consonants may be classified according to their relative force of articulation: stops such as / p t k b d g / are produced with the greatest force of articulation and resonants such as / r l / with the least. This classification also corresponds to one based on the relative closure or constriction of the air channel: stops involve the complete closure of the air channel, fricatives are produced with great constriction but resonants with a relatively open and unobstructed channel. Clusters consisting of a "strong" followed by a "weak" consonant form a single unit and are assigned to the following syllable: *après* / a.prɛ /, *établi* / e.ta.bli /, etc. Two strong consonants also form a single unit: *casquer* / ka.ske /, etc. On the other hand, weak consonants do not form closely knit units and are assigned to two different syllables: *parlons* / par.lõ /, etc. Combinations consisting of a weak followed by a strong consonant do not form clusters: *arpège* / ar.pɛʒ /, *caleçon* / kal.sõ /.

The use of these two principles for the division of medial consonant clusters does not always yield unambiguous results. Consider the case of the cluster / kspl / in *exploit.* The cluster / pl / occurs initially, as in *plein* or *plage,* and this suggests the division / ɛks.plwa /. But the combination / spl / is attested in three-consonant initial clusters: *splendide* / splãdid / and, while / pl / is an instance of a strong followed by a weak consonant and constitutes a unit assigned to the following syllable (/ ɛks.plwa /), / k /, / s / and / p / are all strong consonants and would need to be treated as a homogeneous group. This suggests a division / ɛ.ksplwa / which is counter-intuitive.

But note that the dilemma may be resolved if we consider only two-consonant initial clusters and if we also take into account occurring final two-consonant clusters. Thus, / ɛksplwa / is analyzed as / ɛks.plwa /, since / pl / occurs initially and / ks / finally: *axe* / aks /, *ellipse* / elips /.

9.4   GEMINATE CONSONANTS

Within words and phrases there are in French numerous instances of two-consonant clusters in which both consonants are identical; these are termed **geminate** consonants. When they occur within words, geminate consonants are the result of spelling pronunciations found especially in formal style, e.g., *immense* / immãs / or / imãs /, *illogique* / illoʒik / or / iloʒik /, *barrage* / barraʒ / or / baraʒ /. Within words, contrasts between a single and a geminate consonant occur only when the second consonant functions as an inflectional ending, e.g., *je mourais* / murɛ / "I was dying" vs. *je mourrais* / murrɛ / "would die," *nous travaillons* / travajõ / "we work" vs. *nous travaillions* / travajjõ / "we were working." Most of the instances of geminate consonants, and therefore most of the minimal pairs between single and geminate consonants, occur within phrases across word boundaries:

p	ne couds pas	vs.	ne coupe pas	"don't sew"	vs.	"don't cut"
t	cet art	vs.	cette tare	"this art"	vs.	"this blemish"
k	chaque an	vs.	chaque camp	"every year"	vs.	"every camp"
d	la dent	vs.	là-dedans	"the tooth"	vs.	"in there"
s	pas ça	vs.	passe ça	"not that"	vs.	"pass that"
m	tu mens	vs.	tu me mens	"you're lying"	vs.	"you're lying to me"
n	une oie	vs.	une noix	"a goose"	vs.	"a nut"
l	il a dit	vs.	il l'a dit	"he said"	vs.	"he said it"
r	il éclaira	vs.	il éclairera	"he lit"	vs.	"he'll light"

9.5   ASSIMILATION OF VOICING

We have defined voicing as vibration of the vocal cords and unvoicing as the absence of vibration (see Chapter 3). But in fact a variety of phonetic differences underlie this opposition which distinguishes / b d g v z ʒ / from / p t k f s ʃ /. In French, an important phonetic feature which accompanies voicing and unvoicing is articulatory tension, itself the product of a variety of physiological factors. Voiceless consonants are produced with more articulatory energy than voiced consonants; they are **fortis** whereas voiced consonants are **lenis**. Usually voicing and lenis articulation occur together as do unvoicing and fortis articulation, but there are also cases where the two sets of features become dissociated under the influence of a neighboring phoneme: fortis consonants acquire voicing and lenis consonants lose their voicing. This phenomenon is called **assimilation of voicing**. An assimilated / p / becomes voiced but does not lose its fortis character and is thus still differentiated from / b /. Conversely, an assimilated / b / becomes voiceless but retains its lenis character and still contrasts with / p /. Since / p / and / b /, like all paired-off obstruent consonants, continue to contrast when their voicing feature is assimilated to that of a following obstruent, the feature that distinguishes them from each other is in fact fortis vs. lentis. Voicing may be considered a redundant feature: fortis obstruents are voiceless and lenis consonants are voiced, except in environments where assimilation of voicing occurs.

9.5.1   Regressive Obstruent Assimilation

This type of assimilation of voicing involves the six pairs of obstruent consonants (distinguished by the contrast voiced/voiceless): / p b, t d, k g, f v, s z, ʃ ʒ /. The direction of the assimilation is from the second consonant to the first, whence the term **regressive**. A fortis voiceless consonant will become voiced when immediately followed by a consonant with the opposite set of features, namely, lenis voiced. Conversely, a lenis voiced consonant will become voiceless when immediately followed by a fortis voiceless consonant. Assimilation of voicing only takes place within a word or a phrase. In the examples below we shall use the subscript [.] to indicate loss of voicing and the subscript [˄] to indicate addition of voicing.

la jupe bleu	p̬b	la robe puce	b̥p
la robe bleue	bb	la jupe puce	pp
une patte de chien	t̬d	une grande tache	d̥t
une bec gracieux	k̬g	une vague claire	g̥k
une gaffe véritable	f̬v	une cave froide	v̥f
une vache jaune	ʃ̬ʒ	une page charmante	ʒ̥ʃ

Note that assimilation in the above pairs involves consonants which share all other features except voicing. Assimilation of voicing is not limited to such consonants but also extends to consonants which differ with regard to point or manner of articulation as well as voicing.

cette vache	t̬v	pas de chance	d̥ʃ
Cap Vert	p̬v	une robe comme ça	b̥k

Regressive assimilation of voicing does not completely reduce voiced vs. voiceless contrasts, but, since the contrast rests only on the features fortis vs. lenis, it is considerably weakened, particularly in normal style. Compare:

	je viens te parler	tp	"I've come to speak to you"
vs.	je viens de parler	d̥p	"I've just spoken"

or

	c'est acheté	ʃt	"it's bought"
vs.	c'est à jeter	ʒ̥t	"it's to throw away"

Foreign learners may have considerable difficulty in identifying assimilated obstruents and should be given intensive discrimination practice involving minimal pairs such as those above.

9.5.2   Progressive Assimilation

All non-obstruent consonants (/ m n ɲ l r)/ and the semivowels /(w ɥ j /) become partially voiceless when preceded immediately by a voiceless consonant in the same word or phrase:

le flanc	fl̥	palfrenier	lf̥
le cri	kr̥	la marquise	rk
l'héroïsme	sm̥	le hameçon	ms
passe-nous	sn̥	Annecy	ns
tiens	tj̥	pailleté	jt
pois	pw̥		
puis	pɥ̥		

Within a word, there is progressive assimilation of voicing involving the group / ʃv / e.g., *cheval* [ʃval̩], *cheveux* [ʃvø̩], *cheville* [ʃvij̩]. In normal style, the assimilation may be so strong that it may also involve the distinction fortis vs. lenis. In that case, / v / is replaced by / f /: *cheval* [ʃfal̩].

STUDY QUESTIONS

1.   Divide the following sentences into phonemic phrases and indicate the position of final stress.

Key

a)   _____   Pourqu*oi* avez-vous pr*is* la valise bleue?

b)   _____   Mon autre am*i* a un nouv*eau* bateau à v*oi*les.

c)   _____   Je ne sais p*as* ce qu'il a raconté.

d)   _____   Le troisième j*our* il a neig*é* toute la journée et
        pend*ant* la n*ui*t.

e)   _____   C'est un drôle de t*y*pe votre patr*on*.

2.   Provide two examples of phrases that, in careful style, might be distinguished by word juncture.
   a)   les sentiers/laisse entier _____
   b)   _____
   c)   _____

3.   Provide an example of each of the following word initial consonant clusters.
   a)   tr   train _____   c)   gl   _____
   b)   kr   _____   d)   fl   _____

e) vr _____   h) vj _____

f) pj _____   i) st _____

g) kw _____   j) sk _____

4.   Transcribe the following words on the basis of the orthoepic norm. Then divide each into syllables and give the reasons for the division you have chosen.

a)   réaction /re.ak.sjõ /   Reason: / ksj / is not an initial cluster, but / sj / is. Thus / k / is assigned to the first syllable and / sj / to the second.

b)   souffler

c)   africain

d)   salutation

e)   progression

f)   cultiver

g)   espièglerie

h)   européen

i)   exploitation

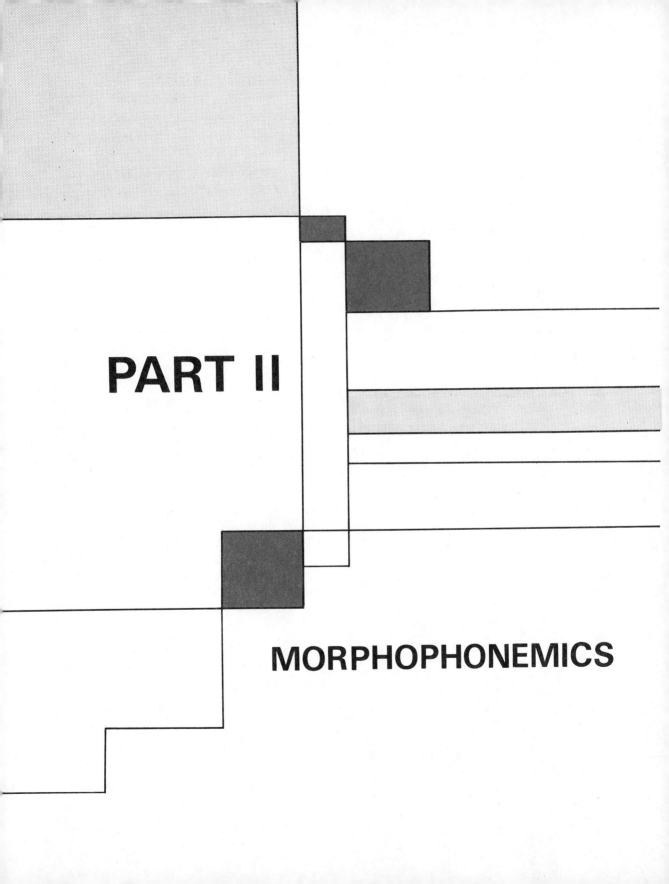

PART II

MORPHOPHONEMICS

10

LIAISON

The preceding seven chapters have presented a description of the pronunciation habits of French speakers: the number of phonological units that contrast with each other, the arrangement of these units relative to each other, and the realization of phonological units in terms of features of articulation. It was also pointed out that French speakers tolerate a fairly broad range of variation in pronunciation habits. Some of the variants, such as the number of mid vowel contrasts, are determined by geographical factors. Others, such as the particular articulation of /r/, correspond to social class membership. Finally, still others are features of style: the formality or the informality of the situation in which speech occurs or the relationship between the interlocutors. Whether a French speaker pronounces *pâte* as [pɑt] or [pat] or *ballet* as [balе] or [balɛ] does not affect communication of the message that is transmitted; at most, it influences the attitude of the listener toward the speaker. What we should like to emphasize at this juncture is that such regional pronunciations as [rɔz] instead of [roz] for *rose* or [nœtr] instead of [nøtr] for *neutre* are not ungrammatical or "incorrect."

There is in French another type of variation in the spoken form of words in which variant forms are each assigned an appropriate environment. Given a word with variants *x* and *y*, only *x* is appropriate in environment *A* and variant *y* in environment *B*. The use of *x* in environment *B* would be considered incorrect or ungrammatical by native speakers of the language. An example of this type of variation in English is the use of *a* or *an* before a following word. The shorter variant *a* is used before a word beginning with a vowel, e.g., *a pear* vs. *an apple*. The use of *a* before *apple* would be considered a grammatical rather than a pronunciation error.

French has two main types of variation in the form of words determined by the environment in which they appear, and to a certain degree by such factors as geographical provenience or social class membership of the speaker and stylistic considerations: **elision** and **liaison.** In this chapter we shall discuss liaison and various alternations in the final vowel of words which are associated with liaison.

10.1   LACK OF ISOMORPHISM

We generally expect that for every morpheme of a language there corresponds a single phonological representation. But perfect one-to-one correspondence between morphemes and their phonological representation (pronunciation) seldom exists. There are, of course, in French, as there are in English, words that have a single phonological representation: *voilà* / vwala /, *(la) dame* / dam /, *bateau* / bato /, *chou* / ʃu /. But lack of one-to-one correspondence between morphemes and their phonological representation is too widespread to be considered an idiosyncratic feature of a small number of words. There are two types of lack of isomorphism: **homophony** and **morphophonemic alternation.** Homophony is the representation of more than one word or minimum meaningful element (morpheme) by the same phonological form, e.g., in French / vɛr / represents seven different morphemes: *ver* "worm," *verre* "glass," *vert* "green," *vair* "grey and white," *vers* "toward," *vers* "verse." In this chapter we shall deal with morphophonemic alternation, the representation of one word by two or more phonological forms.

It is important to distinguish morphophonemic alternations that characterize a large number of morphemes and define what some linguists term the "phonetic genius" of a language from those that characterize a small set of morphemes only. Consider the variation in form of the regular plural morpheme in English.

That morpheme appears under three forms: / s /, / z /, and / əz /, e.g., *cat/cats, dog/dogs, horse/horses.* The choice among the three variant forms is determined by the phonological features of the final consonant of the noun: (1) / z / occurs after nouns ending in a vowel or voiced consonant (with the exception of the consonants listed under 3 below); (2) / s / occurs after voiceless consonants (again, with exceptions to be noted below); (3) / əz / occurs after consonants which share the sibilant nature of / s / or / z /, namely, / ʃ ʒ č ǰ /, as well as / s / and / z / themselves, e.g., *bush/bushes, garage/garages, church/churches, judge/judges.*

Having identified the three variant forms of the English plural suffix and stated the rules that determine their occurrence relative to the final segment of the noun, one may go on to discover the principle underlying the variation. Let us assume that / z / is the "underlying" form of the plural suffix. We need only explain why it does not occur after voiceless consonants and the sibilants. In English, suffixes must agree in voicing with the last segment of the stem to which they are affixed. That is, sequences such as / t / + / z / are not permitted; the voice feature of / z / is switched from [+voice] to [-voice] (that is, / z / is replaced by / s /), e.g., *cat/cats, lap/laps.* The occurrence of the variant / əz / after nouns ending in a sibilant is accounted for by the exclusion in English of sequences of consonants which share too many common phonological features. Such sequences, when they occur at morphological boundaries, are interrupted by the insertion of the neutral vowel / ə /.

Comparison of the variation in form of the preterite and the plural morpheme (as well as the third singular present and the possessive) in English shows that these various aspects of the morphophonemic structure of English are governed by the same underlying principles. The past tense morpheme has three surface realizations / t d əd / bearing the same relationships to each other as do / s z əz /. The three alternants of the preterite show the opposition of a voiced vs. a voiceless suffix (/ d / vs. / t /, e.g., *sag/sagged* vs. *sack/sacked* or *buzz/buzzed* vs. *pass/passed*) and the insertion of the neutral vowel / ə / before the voiced alternant / d /. The alternant / əd / occurs after verb stems ending in / t / and / d /, the two consonants which are too similar to the "underlying" form of the suffix / d /: *load/loaded, pit/pitted.* One obtains a more insightful description of English verb and noun inflections by positing for such morpehemes as plural of nouns and preterite of verbs a single underlying form (/ z / and / d /) and a common set of rules which, when applied to the underlying forms, derive all the attested surface regular forms.

There is in English another alternation in surface forms involving the plural of nouns. Before the plural suffix there is a shift of voicing of the final consonant of the noun: voiceless fricatives are voiced, e.g., *calf/calves, house/houses, wreath/wreathes.* Although this alternation affects a set of consonants sharing a set of phonological features (the set of voiceless fricatives), it does not characterize *all* voiceless fricatives, e.g., *cliff/cliffs* and not *cliff/*clives; pass/passes, myth/myths.* Thus, that alternation is idiosyncratic (irregular) and must be accounted for by marking each noun affected rather than postulating a general rule.

10.2   THE TRADITIONAL VIEW OF LIAISON

A proper analysis of liaison is fundamental for an adequate and insightful analysis of alternations in the form of French words that occur before inflectional endings such as those we find in adjective and verb forms. It is also essential for a proper understanding of the relationship between sound and letter in French.

One way to treat liaison would be simply to list the two variant forms for each French word that exhibits that phenomenon. For example, *on* would be listed as / õn / alternating with / õ /, *nous* as / nu / alternating with / nuz /, *petit* as / pti / alternating with / ptit /. It would also be necessary to state the environment in which each of the two variants occurred. Obviously, this is a rather clumsy and counter-intuitive solution which, particularly, fails to capture the obvious generalization that the form without the consonant occurs in isolation and before a consonant and the form with the consonant occurs before a vowel.

The traditional conception of liaison, and in fact the very term **liaison** ("linking") itself, implies a more elegant and insightful solution recently formalized by Sanford A. Schane. Although we shall attempt to show that it has serious weaknesses that force us to reject it for another solution that does not differ greatly from it, it will be worthwhile to examine the traditional view in some detail.

The traditional view assumes that all French words that are written with a final consonant letter have an underlying form that contains a final consonant sound:

Spelling	*Implied Underlying Form*
on	/ õn /
nous	/ nuz /
petit	/ ptit /

For the sake of convenience we use the term vowel to include also semivowels since liaison consonants are also pronounced before semivowels, e.g., *les oiseaux* / lez + wazo /. A general rule is applied to these underlying forms which (1) deletes the final consonant in isolation and before a consonant and (2) allows it to be pronounced or "linked" before a vowel. It is important to note that the deletion or the pronunciation of the final consonant is **obligatory** and that such mispronunciations as */ õa / for *on a* or */ õnva / for *on va* are ungrammatical and considered by native speakers as more serious errors than the use of wrong segments (e.g., * larus / for *la Russe*) or the transfer of articulatory features from the learner's native language (e.g., the use of glided [eʲ] for / e / in *bébé*).

Thus, from the traditional point of view liaison involves not so much the "linking" of final consonants present in the underlying form of words as their deletion or non-deletion under specified conditions. Depending on the environment in which they find themselves, words to which liaison applies—i.e., words that contain a final consonant in their underlying form—have a dual phonological output:

Underlying Form	Pre-Vowel	Pre-Consonant or Isolation
on / õn /	on a / õn + a /	on va / õ + va /
		on / õ /
nous / nuz /	nous avons / nuz + avõ /	nous savons / nu + savõ /
		nous / nu /
petit / ptit /	petit avion / ptit + avjõ /	petit navire / pti + navir /
		petit / pti /

In most interpretations of the traditional view of liaison it is assumed that any final consonant letter stands for a **liaison consonant**, i.e., one that is pronounced before a vowel but deleted otherwise. But in fact most final consonant letters are "silent" in that they do not represent consonants that are ever pronounced. In other cases they may represent consonants that are "potential" liaison consonants in the sense that they may be pronounced before a vowel under certain conditions that obtain infrequently. Consider for example, the words *et* and *enfant* and the ending *-ent*. *Et* constitutes a case of **liaison interdite** (absence of liaison) since no / t / is ever pronounced; its underlying form is / e / and the *t* is truly a useless silent letter. In the case of *enfant* the / t / is pronounced only in very formal styles, such as the recitation of poetry, and in an introductory treatment of French it is no doubt preferable to consider that its underlying form also does not contain a final / t /. In Chapter 17 we shall attempt to relate *enfant* to its derivatives *enfantin, enfantillage,* or *enfanter,* and we shall again debate the need to posit a / t / in its underlying form. For the present discussion, however, we limit ourselves to the deletion or pronunciation of liaison consonants across word boundaries and we do not take up the problem of their pronunciation within words across morpheme boundaries. In the case of the present tense third person plural ending, *-ent,* the letter *t* represents a / t / that is usually deleted in all environments but which may be pronounced before a vowel in careful style. (The final *t* of the ending *-ent* is pronounced obligatorily in constructions involving inversion, e.g., *parlent-ils* / parløtil /.) It constitutes a case of **liaison facultative** (optional liaison) which will be considered in Section 10.6 below.

Thus one weakness of the traditional view of liaison is that it fails to differentiate between silent letters (as in the case of *et*), potential liaison consonants which are rarely pronounced (e.g., *enfant*), instances of optional liaison (e.g., *-ent*) where the pronunciation of the liaison consonant is relatively infrequent in informal speech, and obligatory liaison (e.g., *nous, ils,* etc.). An indication of the relative frequency of the various types of phonological outputs of final consonant letters is provided by examining the 1000 most polyvalent words of the 3628 *Français Fondamental* basic vocabulary list. (Polyvalent words combine the most freely with other words, they are often used as synonyms for other words or appear in their definition, and generally exhibit lexicological and semantic characteristics that make them more useful than other words. See J.-G. Savard, *La Valence Lexicale.*

Paris/Montreal: Didier, 1970.) Of these, 160 ended with a potential or optional liaison consonant and only 22 with an obligatory liaison consonant.

Another weakness of the traditional view is that, in addition to the various types of liaison consonants, there are final consonants which are pronounced in all environments. These are the consonants that American learners of French recall by associating them with the word *careful,* i.e., / k /, / f /, / r / and / l /. In fact the most frequent final consonants that are always pronounced are / r /, / l /, and / j /, e.g., *sœur, seul, seuil.* In the sub-group of *Français Fondamental* basic words examined there were 21 instances of / r /, 29 of / l / and 7 of / j /. But in addition there were the following 10 words ending with a variety of other consonants:

/ s /	sens, fils
/ f /	chef, vif, boeuf
/ k /	sac, sec
/ t /	net, (but)
/ z /	gaz

According to the traditional view there are two main types of final consonant: those which are always pronounced, and various types of liaison consonants—consonants involved in forbidden liaison, optional liaison, and obligatory liaison. The former are accounted for by stating that the liquids / r /, / l /, and / j / (the latter is not properly speaking a liquid but does behave like one in many respects) can never be deleted and that the others constitute exceptions. In other words it is claimed that liquids cannot be liaison consonants. But this latter statement must be hedged by citing a set of exceptions such as the *-er* (infinitive ending) where the / r / is a liaison consonant; compare *Voulez-vous danser* / dãse / with *Voulez-vous danser avec moi* / dãse / or / dãser /, and the / l / of the pronouns *il* and *ils* which, in normal style, are deleted before a consonant: *il ne sait pas* / insepa / vs. *il a* / ila /; *ils partent* / ipart /, *ils ont* / izõ /. Note that in the case of *ils* the / l / is always deleted since, before a word beginning with a vowel, it will occur before liaison / z /.

10.3 LIAISON CONSONANTS AS "LATENT" CONSONANTS

To account for liaison we adopt a solution which, like the traditional view, provides each French lexical item (word or inflectional or derivational ending) with an underlying form. This underlying form is also an abstraction, unrelated to the written form, and must be "converted" into one or more phonological representations by the application of a general rule or lists of exceptions. We distinguish clearly between the morphophonemic level, which provides the underlying form of lexical items, and the phonological level, which specifies the pronunciation of lexical items in terms of strings of vowels and consonants and, ultimately, articulatory features. Generally, the units of the morphophonemic level (underlying forms) correspond one-to-one to units at the phonological level, e.g., **sali** → / sali /—we note underlying forms in bold face. But the morphophonemic level also contains **latent** consonants and the latent vowel **E** whose conversion to the phonological level requires a set of rules: liaison rules for latent consonants and elision rules for E. Liaison rules include the **liaison rule** proper and a set of less general rules associated with it.

French lexical items fall into four groups depending on the nature of their final segment:

1.   vowel, e.g., *joli, voilà, maison, enfant, nez;*
2.   consonant, e.g., *chef, sac, vif, sens, par, fil, pareil;*
3.   latent consonant, e.g., *mauvais, bon, commun, un, mon, nous, les, aux;*
4.   **E**, e.g., *fille, notre, patte, humide;* feminine ending, first and third person singular present ending.

As was the case with the traditional view, the liaison rule applies to underlying forms containing a final latent consonant. In the solution proposed here the liaison rule specifies that a latent consonant is deleted before a consonant or when the form occurs in isolation but realized as a consonant before a vowel. We summarize by applying our solution to the examples cited in 10.2:

Underlying Form	Pre-Vowel	Pre-Consonant and Final
on õ**N**	on a / õn + a /	on va / õ + va / on / õ /
nous nu**Z**	nous avons / nuz + avõ /	nous savons / nu + savõ / nous / nu /
petit pti**T**	petit avion / ptit + avjõ /	petit navire / pti + navir / petit / pti /

One of the striking features of French is the fact that many inflectional endings consist of only a latent consonant or mute *e*. Inflectional endings consisting only of a latent consonant generally involve optional liaison and will be discussed in Section 10.6 below. But it is possible to analyze the plural pronouns *nous, vous, ils, elles, eux* in terms of a nucleus referring to person and a plural ending -**Z**. The same analysis suggests itself for the determiners *mes, tes, ses, nos, vos, leurs, ces, des* and the fused forms *aux (à + les)* and *des (du + les)*.

How does the latent consonant solution for liaison account for the three types of liaison consonants of the traditional view illustrated by *et, enfant, -ent,* and *est*? In the case of *et,* the letter *t* is simply a feature of French spelling that bears no relationship to phonological features. The same interpretation extends to *enfant*—ãfã. The ending *-ent* will be shown to contain a latent **T** which is subject to optional rather than obligatory liaison. Finally, *est* contains a latent **T** subject to obligatory liaison.

Of course, words which contain a final consonant which is never deleted are in no way idiosyncratic; they end with a "real" or "stable" consonant, e.g., *sens* sãs, *vif* vif, *par* par, *bal* bal, *pareil* parεj. The infinitive ending *-er,* which, in the traditional view, had to be characterized as idiosyncratic because its final *r* functioned as a liaison consonant, is interpreted as containing a latent **R** in its underlying form—i.e., *trouver* is truve**R**.

10.4   LATENT AND STABLE CONSONANTS IN NUMERALS

French numerals display a variety of alternation of form involving their last segment. Straightforward liaison occurs with the numerals *un, deux, trois,* and *vingt:*

Underlying Form	Pre-Vowel	Pre-Consonant	Final
un œ̃N	un an / œ̃n + ã /	un franc / œ̃ + frã /	/ œ̃ /
deux døZ	deux ans / døz + ã /	deux francs / dø + frã /	/ dø /
trois trwaZ	trois ans / trwaz + ã /	trois francs / trwa + frã /	/ trwa /
vingt vẽT	vingt ans / vẽt + ã /	vingt francs / vẽ + frã /	/ vẽ /

The latent consonant of the underlying form is pronounced before a vowel but deleted before a consonant and when the numeral occurs in final position.

The numerals *sept* and *neuf* have underlying forms which end in stable consonants, i.e., consonants that are pronounced in all environments:

Underlying Form	Pre-Vowel	Pre-Consonant	Final
sept sɛt	sept ans / sɛt + ã /	sept francs / sɛt + frã /	/ sɛt /
neuf nœf	neuf hommes / nœf + ɔm /	neuf francs / nœf + frã /	/ nœf /

Neuf shows an idiosyncratic form / nœv / that occurs only before *ans* and *heures*. Note that this idiosyncratic form involves **voicing shift**—the replacement of / f / by its voiced correlate / v /.

Cinq and *huit* contain final consonants which behave both as stable and latent consonants. Predictably, the consonants are pronounced before a vowel, but they are also pronounced when the word occurs in final position. Like all latent consonants they are deleted before a consonant:

Underlying Form	Pre-Vowel	Pre-Consonant	Final
cinq sẽk/sẽK	cinq ans / sẽk + ã /	cinq francs / sẽ + frã /	/ sẽk /
huit ɥit/ɥiT	huit ans / ɥit + ã /	huit francs / ɥi + frã /	/ ɥit /

Six and *dix* pattern like *cinq* and *huit* in that their underlying form ends in a consonant that is both stable and latent. But in addition they show voicing shift. For these two numerals voicing shift has become generalized before all words beginning with a vowel. To put it differently, *six* and *dix* have underlying forms which contain a stable s that is replaced by latent Z: before a vowel, they have / z /; before a consonant, the latent consonant is deleted; in final position, they end with / s /:

Underlying Form	Pre-Vowel	Pre-Consonant	Final
six sis/siZ	six ans / siz + ã /	six francs / si + frã /	/ sis /
dix dis/diZ	dix ans / diz + ã /	dix francs / di + frã /	/ dis /

Voicing shift is not limited to the numeral system. It occurs also in adjective inflection and in derivation and accounts for such variations as *elle est grosse* / gros /, *il est gros* / gro /, *une grosse* / gros / *auto, un gros* / groz / *avion.*

10.5   OBLIGATORY AND OPTIONAL LIAISON

The point of view we have adopted in our discussion of liaison is that it rests on a morphophonemic feature of French, namely that in their underlying form certain lexical items contain a latent consonant which is obligatorily pronounced before words beginning with a vowel but deleted elsewhere. In order to provide the correct form of French words that show liaison, the learner need only memorize their underlying form and the general liaison rule. The number of words that show obligatory liaison is quite limited; examination of a list of frequently occurring and highly polyvalent basic words showed that there were only several dozen concrete words that contained a latent consonant. Thus the point of view we have adopted is more useful and practical than the traditional view according to which most French words end in a final consonant which is deleted most of the time in all environments, including before a vowel.

Most of the latent consonants found in informal conversational Standard French are involved in obligatory liaison. But there are nonetheless instances of latent consonants whose appearance before a vowel is optional:

Underlying Form	Pre-Vowel	Pre-Consonant	Final
sont sõT	Ils sont ici. / il + sõt + isi / or / il + sõ + isi /	Ils sont là. / il + sõ + la /	Ils sont / il sõ /

The number of lexical items involved in optional liaison is quite small and includes mostly grammatical endings, in particular, all verbal endings. As was the case for obligatory liaison, lexical items involved in optional liaison can simply be enumerated. Below we provide some examples of optional liaison:

Verb Endings	Je suis heureux.
	Nous sommes américains.
	Il devait aller au bureau.
	Vous pourriez inviter vos amis.
	Il peut envoyer sa secrétaire.
Noun + Plural Ending	Les enfants intelligents
	Nos amis étaient arrivés
	Les vieilles demeures antillaises
Function Words	Tout est en ordre
	Pendant un siècle
	Le livre dont il parle

If we compare the syntactic environments in which obligatory and optional liaison take place, we observe that the closer the syntactic link between the word containing a latent consonant and the following one, the more likely the occurrence of obligatory liaison. The sentence *Ils ont une voiture,* which may be pronounced / ilz+õt+yn+vwatyr / or / ilz+õ+yn+vwatyr /, contains two lexical items containing latent consonants *ils* ilZ and *ont* õT. Since we are dealing with two different grammatical endings—the plural suffix Z and the third person plural present suffix õT, the difference in their behavior may be accounted for by assigning them to two different classes. But note that the following contrast in liaison behavior cannot be handled in this manner: *les enfants allaient à l'école* / lez+ãfãz+alɛ / or / lez+ãfã+alɛ /. The determiner *les* and the noun *enfants* both contain the plural suffix **Z**. In order to account for the fact that **Z** is realized obligatorily in *les* but optionally when it occurs after the noun, it is necessary to provide syntactic information: the plural ending **Z** is realized when it occurs after a determiner but optionally when it occurs with a noun. There is also a syntactic difference between the constructions *les enfants* and *enfants allaient*. The first phrase constitutes a close-knit unit, a noun phrase (NP), which may function as a syntactic unit (subject, object, etc.). The second phrase cannot function as a syntactic unit because there is a major syntactic boundary between *enfants* and *allaient*. The syntactic structure of the sentence (S) *Les enfants allaient attendre ensemble* is:

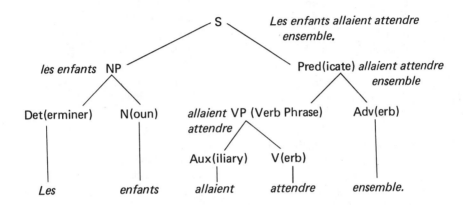

Obligatory liaison takes place within close-knit syntactic constructions such as NP's. Optional liaison takes place within constructions which constitute syntactic units, such as VP's (verb phrases), but which are not as close-knit as NP's. No liaison may take place between contiguous sentence elements which never participate in the same syntactic units such as nouns plus auxiliary verbs or between verbal elements plus determiners, e.g., *Ils ont écrit # une lettre* (where # represents a major syntactic break). These represent instances of the *liaison interdite* of traditional descriptions.

10.6   A PEDAGOGICAL NORM

Any optional feature is subject to variation, and indeed optional liaison is subject to extensive variation among French speakers. The factors which determine the pronunciation or deletion before a vowel of a latent consonant subject to optional liaison are very complex, but they are primarily sociolinguistic and stylistic. The more a speech sample is characteristic of *français populaire,* the fewer the instances of optional liaison. On the other hand, the more formal and deliberate the style, the more likely its appearance.

A learner of French should first be taught the relatively small list of lexical items that contain latent consonants subject to obligatory liaison. These should be introduced in sentences so that he also becomes familiar with the close-knit syntactic constructions in which these lexical items appear. A condensed list of these items and typical constructions in which they are used is offered below.

1. *Noun Phrases* (Modifier + Head Noun)
   Determiner + Noun   les enfants, cet animal, mes amis
   Numeral + Noun   deux amis, dix ans, neuf heures
   Adjective + Noun   un ancien ami, un petit enfant
   Determiner + Adjective   leurs anciens amis, mes autres enfants
   Adjective + Adjective   de vrais anciens documents
   Determiner + Pronoun   les uns, les autres

2. *Verb Phrases*
   Pronoun + Verb   vous allez, en avez-vous, les ont-ils
   Verb + Pronoun   ont-ils, allez-y, mettez-en
   Pronoun + Pronoun   vous y allez, ils en auront
   Pronoun + Pronoun in Imperative   donnez-en, donnez-nous-en
   c'est + NP   c'est évident, c'est un avocat
   il est (impersonal) + NP   il est évident, il était une fois

3. *Prepositional and Adverbial Phrases*
   Monosyllabic Preposition + NP   dans un an, sans amis, en été, sous un
                                          arbre, chez eux, dès aujourd'hui
   Monosyllabic Adverbs + NP   plus uni, trop aimable, pas utile,
                                          tout entier, bien étrange

4. *Bound Phrases* (illustrative list)
                                        rien à faire, un fait accompli,
                                        les Etats-Unis, les Champs-Elysées,
                                        un sous officier, avant-hier, tout à
                                        coup, Mesdames et Messieurs,
                                        comment allez-vous

The fact that liaison is both a feature of the morphophonemic composition of lexical items and of their syntactic function suggests that lexical items which contain them should be introduced and used in a variety of phonological and syntactic environments so that the learner may memorize their underlying form and their syntactic properties.

With regard to optional liaison, the principle we have adopted in all situations involving variation—namely, that variation be reduced as much as possible within the constraints imposed by attitudes of educated Standard French speakers towards variants—suggests that it be reduced as much as possible. All lexical items containing latent consonants whose realization before a vowel is not obligatory will be treated as if they did not contain the latent consonant, except for a small set of items where the realization of the consonant is frequent. For example, the verb endings *-ons* and *-ez* will be assumed to have the underlying forms õ and e rather than õZ and eZ respectively; the plural ending Z will not be added to nouns—i.e., the underlying form of *les enfants terribles* will be assumed to be leZ ãfã tɛriblE instead of leZ ãfãZ tɛriblEZ. In effect, the solution proposed eliminates the distinction between obligatory and optional liaison in the learner's productive inventory. He must add the following lexical items and syntactic constructions to the list of lexical items containing in their underlying form a latent consonant which must be realized before a vowel in the syntactic constructions indicated:

1. Present forms of *être*:
    je suis, il est, ils sont je suis américain, il est̲ ici, elles
                                                sont̲ en haut

2. *-ont* third person plural
    ending: font, ont, sont, vont elles vont̲ en France, ils font̲ un effort

10.7 LIAISON AND VOWEL ALTERNATION

In addition to voice shift (see Section 10.4), there are other alternations in the form of French words which are associated with liaison. These are changes in vowels which precede latent consonants falling into two main groups: (1) alternations between oral and nasal vowels and (2) mid vowel alternations.

10.7.1 Oral and Nasal Vowel Alternations

Compare the final vowel in the following two occurrences of the masculine form of the pre-nominal adjective *ancien: un ancien* / ãsjɛn / *ami* vs. *un ancien* / ãsjẽ / *camarade.* The adjective *ancien* has the underlying form **ãsjɛN** since it is realized with / n / when it occurs before a noun beginning with a vowel. However, if only liaison were involved in the determination of its two variant forms, its pre-consonant form would be */ ãsjɛ /. In addition to the deletion of the latent consonant, there is nasalization of the vowel or, if one prefers, its replacement by the corresponding nasal vowel. There are in French three alternations between oral vowels and corresponding nasal vowels associated with liaison. Only three of these are found between words, and all involve masculine forms of adjectives:

    1.   / in / alternating with / ẽ /   divin enfant/un moment divin
    2.   / ɛn / alternating with / ẽ /   ancien ami/ancien camarade
    3.   / ɔn / alternating with / õ /   bon ami/bon garçon

These three alternations also involve feminine and masculine (pre-consonant and final) forms of adjectives:

    1.   / in / alternating with / ẽ /   fine/fin; divine/divin
    2.   / ɛn / alternating with / ẽ /   saine/sain; italienne/italien
    3.   / ɔn / alternating with / õ /   bonne/bon

There are in addition two other predictable alternations between oral and nasal vowels in corresponding feminine and masculine nouns or feminine and masculine forms of adjectives:

    4.   / an / alternating with / ã /   paysanne/paysan
    5.   / yn / alternating with / œ̃ /   brune/brun

Alternation (2) is also found in the verb system: *ils viennent/il vient; ils tiennent/il tient.*

It should be emphasized that these alternations are predictable and, in this sense, regular rather than idiosyncratic. If we know that the last segment of the underlying form of a French lexical item is **N**, we can predict both the appearance and the precise quality of the nasal vowel. There are some cases of idiosyncratic alternations involving oral vowel plus **N** and nasal vowels. For example the alternation *ils prennent* / prɛn /: *il prend* / prã / is idiosyncratic since the nasal vowel is / ã / instead of the expected / ɛ̃ /. To account for the five alternations listed above, we postulate the application of a nasalization rule which nasalizes the vowel before any **N** that does not occur before a vowel. Nasalization is applied before liaison:

	Pre-Vowel	Pre-Consonant	Final
Underlying Form: bɔN	bon ami	bon copain	bon
Nasalization:	- - - - - -	bɔ̃N	bɔ̃N
Liaison:	bɔn	bɔ̃	bɔ̃
Phonological Output:	/ bɔn /	/ bɔ̃ /	/ bɔ̃ /

It will be shown in Chapter 14 that one of the effects of the addition of the feminine suffix **-E** is that it introduces a vowel which blocks nasalization and results in the presence of the final consonant in the feminine form of all adjectives containing **N** in their underlying form.

When nasalization is applied to underlying forms containing **i** and **y** + **N**, e.g., *divin* **diviN**, *brun* **bryN**, there are produced vowels ĩ and ỹ which have no corresponding surface nasal vowel phonemes. A rule is required, termed **nasal vowel adjustment**, which converts these two nonexistent vowels to the phonetically nearest surface vowels, / ɛ̃ / and / œ̃ / respectively. The derivation of the pre-consonant/ final forms of *divin* and *brun* is as follows:

Underlying Form:	*divin* **diviN**	*brun* **bryN**
Nasalization:	divĩN	brỹN
Nasal Vowel Adjustment:	divɛ̃N	brœ̃N
Liaison:	divɛ̃	brœ̃
Phonological Output:	/ divɛ̃ /	/ brœ̃ /

In the light of the regularity (predictability) of the alternation between forms containing an oral vowel + / n / and the corresponding nasal vowel without / n /, such forms as *un, mon, ton, son* or *bien* which are realized before a vowel by a nasalized vowel + / n / are idiosyncratic. In the case of *bien* *(bien étrange* / bjɛ̃n + etrãʒ /) we posit an underlying form **bjɛ̃N**, since the form */ bjɛn / is not attested. But for the other four lexical items we have evidence that the underlying form contains an oral vowel. The underlying form of *un* has to be **yN** because the feminine form of that determiner is / yn /. In the case of the singular possessive determiners *mon, ton, son,* some speakers use the fully regular forms / mɔn / *(mon ami)*, / tɔn /, and / sɔn /. The idiosyncratic behavior of / n / with regard to liaison of *un, mon, ton,* and *son* seems to stem from their syntactic property: determiners enter into a different syntactic construction with nouns than do adjectives. That the possessive determiners have a dual behavior is reflected by their intermediate status between determiners such as the definite and indefinite determiners *un* and *le* and adjectives (a distinction captured by the traditional label "possessive adjectives").

10.7.2 Mid Vowel Alternations

Compare the pronunciation of the adjective in the following utterances: *le premier* / prømjɛr / *étudiant* vs. *le premier* / prømje / *maître*. Adjectives whose underlying form ends in / ɛR / show a shift from / ɛ / to / e / in addition to the deletion of the consonant in the pre-consonant and final form. This change is predictable and affects a dozen adjectives, including *premier, dernier* and *léger*.

Related to the alternation / ɛ /:/ e / are parallel alternations involving the other two mid vowel pairs:

| / ɔ /:/ o / | sotte:sot; trop / trɔp / heureux:trop (/ tro /) fort |
| / œ /:/ ø / | ils veulent:il veut |

For both of these lexical items we must posit underlying forms containing a low-mid vowel and a latent consonant, sɔT and vœL respectively. For sɔT and vœL, a non-permissible form results after liaison is applied since low-mid rounded vowels do not occur in final free syllables (see Chapter 6). A mid vowel raising rule must be postulated which raises the low-mid vowel of the underlying form to the corresponding high-mid vowel:

		Pre-Vowel	*Pre-Consonant*	*Final*
Underlying Form:	sɔT	(sotte)	- - - - - -	(sot)
	vœL	(ils veulent)	- - - - - -	(il veut)
Liaison:		sɔt, vœl		*sɔ, *vœ
Mid Vowel Raising:		- - - - - -		so, vø
Phonological Output:		/ sɔt /, / voel /		/ so /, / vø /

The alternation / ɛ /:/ e / also characterizes the feminine and masculine (pre-consonant and final) forms of adjectives, e.g., *première/premier,* but it differs from those involving the rounded mid vowels in that / ɛ / is permitted in final free syllables, e.g., *guet, plaît, j'irais, j'avais.* Nonetheless, these alternations constitute evidence that the *loi de position* (see Chapter 6) which characterizes the distribution of mid vowels in certain accents of Standard French is deeply rooted in the morphophonemic structure of the language.

Morphophonemic alternations in the mid vowel system also provide support for an orthoepic norm for words containing mid vowels in medial position where, as has been shown in Chapter 6, the distinction high-mid vs. low-mid is neutralized. What is the "correct" vowel of *sauter* or *sottise*? In attempting to answer that question, in addition to the careful style pronunciation of educated Paris speakers, we can refer to the underlying form, which is itself based on all observed variant forms. Clearly the underlying form of *sottise* is sɔT-izE (where [-] stands for a morpheme boundary), since the masculine adjective *sot* is realized with a form showing mid vowel raising to produce / so / but the feminine form with the unchanged vowel / ɔ / (/ sɔt /). The underlying form of *sauter* is **soT-eR,** since we find only / o / in forms occurring before a consonant (*saute* / sot /) as well as in final position (*saut* / so /). *Saut* and *sot* have different underlying forms; their surface similarity results from the application of the mid vowel raising rule to the underlying form of *sot:*

		Pre-Vowel	Pre-Consonant or Final
Underlying Form:	saut **soT**	saut-er saut-e	saut
	sot **sɔT**	sott-ise sott-e	sot
Liaison:		sot-e sot	so
		sɔt-iz sɔt	*sɔ
Mid Vowel Raising:		- - - - - - -	- - -
		- - - - - - -	so
Phonological Output:		/ sote /, / sot /	/ so /
		/ sɔtiz /, / sɔt /	/ so /

The vowel / ɛ / is also involved in idiosyncratic alternations associated with liaison: *bel* and *nouvel* show a change / ɛ / to / o / when the underlying **L** is deleted, e.g., *un nouvel avion* vs. *un nouveau train; un bel homme* vs. *un beau garçon. Vieil* shows a change / ɛ / to / ø / when the **J** is deleted, e.g., *un vieil Indien* vs. *un vieux Chinois.* Finally, there is another idiosyncratic vowel change / ɔ / to / u / when **L** is deleted in *fol,* e.g., *un fol espoir* vs. *un vrai fou.*

10.8   LIAISON AND SPELLING

We have defined liaison as the realization of a relatively limited number of French lexical items with two pronounced forms differing by the presence versus the absence of a final consonant. The number of final consonants involved in this alternation is small: / t / *(il est* vs. *est-il),* / z / *(les enfants* vs. *les parents),* / n / *(un enfant* vs. *un fils),* / r / *(le premier étage* vs. *le premier rang),* / l / *(le nouvel an* vs. *le nouveau mois),* / j / *(un vieil homme* vs. *un vieux monsieur),* / p / *(trop heureux* vs. *trop triste),* / k / *(sang impur* vs. *sang pur),* but the presence or absence of all of these consonants is governed by the same phonological conditions (occurrence before a vowel versus before a consonant or in final position) and may be stated by the same rule. In addition liaison takes place between elements of a sentence that participate in lower-level (close-knit) constructions. To account for liaison we have assumed that certain French lexical items contain a latent consonant whose realization is either obligatory or optional. Thus, just as one must know that the word *calé* "intelligent" is composed of four segments, / k /, / a /, / l /, / e /, and differs from *collé* "struck" by the presence of / a / instead of / ɔ / as a second segment, so one must know that *sans* "without" differs from *sens* "direction sense" in that its final segment is latent whereas that of the latter is always realized: *sans argent* vs. *sans rien* vs. *sens interdit* vs. *sens normal.*

It is important to distinguish between liaison and the various types of variations described as part of the phonological structure of French. The free variation between [tye] and [tɥe] *(tuer)* is due to the fact that in French the sounds [y] and [ɥ] do not contrast. Both variants are grammatical. The variations between [le] and [lɛ] *(lait)* is due to the fact that, if we take the phonological habits of all French speakers, the distinction between / e / and / ɛ / is not crucial. Again, both forms are grammatical, and the choice of one or the other provides only information about the speaker's geographical provenience, the social class to which he belongs, or the degree of formality or informality attending the circumstances in which the word is produced. In all circumstances, the speaker has a certain amount of freedom to choose one or the other of the variants. But French speakers have no more freedom in choosing between / nu / and / nuz / for *nous* occurring before a vowel than they have for selecting / dwa / instead of / dwav / to express the present tense of the verb *devoir* that corresponds to *ils*. Only / nuz / and / dwav / are correct, and the choice of the other variant is ungrammatical. And just as one must know that *devoir* has a larger number of phonologically distinct forms in the present tense than does *parler* and one must be able to provide the appropriate form when one refers to a particular verbal person, so one must know that *nous* has two variants, whereas *tu* has only one, and one must be able to select the appropriate form depending on the phonological nature of the environment that follows.

Traditionally, French forms are described directly in terms of their spelling. As a result, any word ending with a consonant letter is assumed to have a latent consonant which will be deleted or pronounced according to liaison. But in the sentence *Les autres ouvriers # avaient ouvert # un ancien abri* only determiners and adjectives contain a latent consonant that is governed by obligatory liaison. So far as spoken French is concerned, the *s* of *ouvriers* and the *t* of *ouvert* do not correspond to any overt phonetic manifestations and do not contain latent consonants. The *t* of *avaient* corresponds to an optional / t / whose occurrence is rare in declarative sentences such as that provided as an example. It is however obligatory in inversion constructions: *Avaient-ils ouvert un ancien abri?* / avɛtiluvɛr /.

STUDY QUESTIONS

1. Which of the following words contain a latent consonant to which obligatory liaison applies?

    a) vous   f) sain
    b) orient   g) elles
    c) chef   h) français
    d) premier   i) (il) allait
    e) doux   j) très

2. Which of the following words contain a stable consonant?

    a) nid   f) vermeil
    b) amer   g) cerf
    c) mars   h) suif
    d) coq   i) vis (fem.)
    e) outil   j) net

3. List three words which contain each of the following latent consonants.

    a) **Z**   très   _____   _____   _____
    b) **T**   fort   _____   _____   _____
    c) **N**   commun _____   _____   _____
    d) **R**   dernier _____   _____   _____

4. List three words which each illustrate a latent consonant other than those listed in (3) above.

5. Give three examples of words ending with each of the following stable consonants.
   a)   k   sec   _____   _____   _____
   b)   f   vif   _____   _____   _____
   c)   s   ours   _____   _____   _____
   d)   t   est   _____   _____   _____
   e)   l   bal   _____   _____   _____
   f)   r   bar   _____   _____   _____

6. List three words that contain each a stable consonant different from those listed in (5) above.

7. List five endings involved in optional liaison.

8. Give the underlying form for the following words. Then indicate to which ones voicing shift applies.
   a)   grand **graD**; voicing shift, since *grand homme* / grᾶtɔm /
   b)   six   f)   sept
   c)   deux   g)   trois
   d)   neuf   h)   gros
   e)   huit   i)   mauvais

9. In the following phrases indicate obligatory liaison with a ligature (‿) and optional liaison with a slant line (/).
   Model: Les autres enfants/ arrivaient/ en autobus.
   a)   Rien est établi.
   b)   dès à présent
   c)   quand à moi
   d)   Je sais quand elle est arrivée.
   e)   après une heure
   f)   Prends-en un autre.
   g)   Mais il y en a beaucoup.
   h)   Quand est-il arrivé?
   i)   C'est en effet trop étroit.
   j)   Quel long hiver nous avons passé!

10. Provide one example for each of the following nasal/oral vowel alternations.
    a) / in / : / ẽ /
    b) / an / : / ã /
    c) / yn / : / œ̃ /
    d) / on / : / õ /
    e) / en / : / ẽ /

11. To which of the following words does mid vowel raising apply?
    a) sot   f) fermier
    b) léger   g) heureuse
    c) grosse   h) nouveau
    d) vieux   i) (il) veut
    e) danser   j) prêt

12. In what way are the following items idiosyncratic?
    a) un (in *un ami*)   b) ton (in *ton ami*)   c) beau

11

MUTE e

11.1   THE NOTION OF MUTE *e*

In the preceding chapter we have described liaison in terms of the inherent morphophonemic structure of certain French lexical items. These lexical items end in a latent consonant which is pronounced in certain circumstances but deleted in others. As a result, lexical items which contain a latent or liaison consonant have two distinct phonological representations. **Elision** is another morphophonemic phenomenon based on the inherent structure of certain French lexical items, namely, that they contain a vowel, **mute *e***, which may be pronounced or deleted depending on various sets of circumstances. There are two important differences between elision and liaison, however. First, latent consonants occur only at the end of lexical items, whereas mute *e* occurs at the end and in the middle of words. Second, the conditions under which latent consonants are pronounced or deleted may be stated relatively easily in terms of the following phonological environment or the syntactic structures in which the words containing latent consonants participate. Although there are instances of liaison determined by stylistic considerations (*liaison facultative*), the pronunciation or deletion of the latent consonant in given classes of lexical items (determiners, adjectives, monosyllabic prepositions, etc.) may be stated in terms of one simple and general rule. Elision, on the other hand, is subject to a variety of external factors (geographical provenience, social class membership, style) so that it is difficult to formulate a set of **categorical rules** about the pronunciation or deletion of mute *e* in classes of lexical items. Categorical rules state that a phenomenon does or does not occur. For instance, it is possible to make a categorical statement about the realization of latent consonants contained in determiners and adjectives since these are *always* pronounced before a word beginning with a vowel and *always* deleted elsewhere, e.g., *les autres enfants* vs. *les autres parents* vs. *les vrais érudits* vs. *les vrais savants.* But, in general, only **variable rules** can be formulated about the realization of mute *e*.

One can only state the relative probability of the pronunciation of the mute *e* of a given lexical item in a particular phonological and syntactic environment. This is another area of the structure of French in which it will be necessary to formulate a pedagogical norm which reduces the variation found in normal speech.

11.2 TRADITIONAL ELISION

Strictly speaking, elision is used in traditional description to refer to the obligatory deletion of mute *e* and the vowel of *la* (definite determiner) and *si* (conjunction) when these occur before a word beginning with a vowel:

le pont   l'immeuble
la maison   l'auberge
si tu veux   s'il veut

The traditional view of elision implies that the forms involved in liaison have underlying forms ending with a vowel and that this vowel is deleted when it occurs before another vowel across a word boundary, that is:

le immeuble   **lE imoebl**→/ l+imœbl /   l'immeuble
la auberge   **la obɛrʒ**→/l+obɛrʒ /   l'auberge
si il   **si il**→/s+il /   s'il

The deletion of the second of two successive vowels across word boundaries is explained in terms of euphony. It is claimed that the French abhor hiatus—the occurrence of two successive vowels—and that elision eliminates one of the successive vowels. This claim is easily refuted by the existence of numerous instances of two or more successive vowels across word boundaries in French, e.g., *si on dit* / si + õ + di /, *va à Arles* / va + a + arl /, *ou à Autun* / u + a + otõe /. It is preferable to limit the use of the term elision to the obligatory deletion of mute *e* before a word beginning with a vowel, whether or not it is reflected in the spelling by the use of the apostrophe. Underlying this view is the assumption that mute *e* is a latent vowel (hereafter represented by **E**) which is converted at the phonological level to either zero (deletion) or a vowel that ranges freely between the two front rounded vowels [ø] and [œ], but which is most usually realized as [ə].

Thus, **E** is not a phoneme since there are no cases of a three-way contrast between [ø], [œ] and [ə]. The phonetic entity [ə], as was pointed out in Chapter 6, is the realization of both / ø / and / œ / in medial position where that distinction is neutralized. Consider the potential minimal pairs *je dis* vs. *jeudi* and *jeune vaurien* "young good-for-nothing" vs. *je ne vaux rien* "I'm not worth anything." In normal style the members of these pairs are homophonous since the first vowel is realized as [ə]:

je dis [ʒədi]   jeudi [ʒədi]
je nə̸ vaux rien [ʒənvorjẽ]   jeune vaurien [ʒənvorjẽ]

If an educated middle-class Paris speaker tries consciously to differentiate the members of these two pairs, he will use [ø] in one and [œ] in the other:

je dis [ʒœdi]	jeudi [ʒødi]
jeune vaurien [ʒœnvorjẽ]	je nø vaux rien [ʒønvorjẽ]

(Of course, another way to differentiate the last two utterances would be to pronounce the E of *ne* in *je ne vaux rien:* [ʒənəvorjẽ]). Following the convention adopted in Chapter 6 of noting neutralized mid vowels with the high-mid phoneme, both *je dis* and *jeudi* would be represented / ʒødi / and both *je ne vaux rien* and *jeune vaurien* would be represented / ʒønvorjẽ / to indicate that in general the members of these two pairs are not differentiated from each other on the basis of pronunciation alone.

Elision is accounted for by a general rule which deletes E whenever it occurs before another vowel across word boundaries. By this interpretation, elision covers not only cases such as *l'oiseau* or *j'arrive,* where E is not represented by the spelling but replaced instead by the apostrophe, but also cases such as *notre école* or *une table étroite* where it is represented in spelling. For *notre* and *table* we posit underlying forms **notrE** and **tablE** which contain E as their final segment. The latent vowel is also posited as the feminine ending of adjectives and certain personal endings of verbs. Thus, the underlying form of *petite* is **pEtiT-E** and that of *(je) parle* **parl-E.** Note that while the E of *petite* corresponds to zero before both vowels and consonants (*une petite auberge, une petite maison*) it is realized as [ə] before words containing aspirate *h,* e.g., *une petite hutte* [yn+pətitə+yt]. The alternations *la/l'* and *si/s'* are best handled as idiosyncrasies. We cannot posit a latent **A,** since the only instance of an alternation / a / and zero is attested in the definite determiner feminine singular form. In all other cases *a* is never deleted, e.g., *Voilà un oiseau* / vwala+œ̃n+wazo /. The alternation / i / and zero is even more limited; it occurs only with *si* followed by the pronouns *il* and *ils.*

11.3   THE LINGUISTIC STATUS OF MUTE *e*

Some linguists claim that within a phonemic phrase (or a word) the vowel sound [ə]—the most neutral vowel of French from the point of view of articulation—is inserted to prevent the formation of non-permitted consonant clusters (see Chapter 9). In other words, they claim that [ə] is completely predictable. The inadequacy of this claim is easily demonstrated by the existence in French of consonant clusters that occur with or without the insertion of [ə]. Examples of words containing such clusters are given below:

pt	ptomaine "ptomaine"	[ptomɛn]
	petit "small"	[ptit] [pəti]
pn	pneu "tire"	[pnø]
	penaud "sheepish"	[pno] [pəno]
bl	blette "chard"	[blɛt]
	belette "weasel"	[blɛt] [bəlɛt]

kr	crête "comb"	[krɛt]	
	querelle "quarrel"	[krɛl]	[kərɛl]
fr	frais "cool"	[frɛ]	
	ferais "(I) would do"	[frɛ]	[fərɛ]
gn	gnome "gnome"	[gnɔm]	
	guenon "she-monkey"	[gnõ]	[gənõ]
sl	slave "Slav"	[slav]	
	cela "that"	[sla]	[səla]
sm	smoking "tuxedo"	[smoking]	
	semaine "week"	[smɛn]	[səmɛn]

The fact that *cela* may be pronounced with the consonant cluster [sl] or with [ə] intercalated between the consonants that constitute this cluster but that, on the other hand, *slave* may only be pronounced with the cluster, forces us to provide different underlying forms for the two words. We note these two words **sEla** and **slav**, respectively, to account for their different pronunciation potential just as we provide for the fact that *loua* may be pronounced [lwa] or [lua] but that *loi* may only be pronounced [lwa] by representing these two words differently at the underlying level—**lua** vs. **lwa**, respectively. To summarize the linguistic status of **E**, it is a feature of French morphemes which determines the potential presence in the phonological output of a vowel ranging in quality between [ø] and [œ]. Since it usually occurs in phonemic phrase-medial position, **E** is most frequently realized by the short centralized front rounded vowel [ə], the realization of both / ø / and / œ / in positions where the contrast between these two phonemes is neutralized. We now need to examine the conditions under which **E** is realized when it does not occur immediately before a vowel, an environment in which it is obligatorily deleted.

11.4   MUTE *e* IN FINAL POSITION AND BEFORE ASPIRATE *h*

Elision proper, defined in the preceding section as the obligatory deletion of **E** before an immediately following vowel, does not account for the pronunciation or deletion of **E** in other environments. We shall first consider the case of **E** occurring in phonemic phrase-final position and before aspirate *h*. Compare:

l'homme [lɔm]   le homard [ləɔmar]
l'oubliette [lublijɛt]   la houille [lauj]

The words in the right- and left-hand colums all begin with a vowel, but those in the right-hand column contain aspirate *h*. **E** is obligatorily pronounced, i.e., realized as [ə], before aspirate *h*. Now compare:

dis-le [dilø]   suis-je [sɥiʒ]
sur ce [syrsø]   est-elle [ɛtɛl]

All four morphemes (*le, ce, je,* and *elle*) have underlying forms containing a final **E**. This can be verified by using them before a word containing aspirate *h*, e.g., *elle hausse* [ɛləos] *les prix* "she's raising the prices." In addition all four phrases end with a pronoun. The deletion of **E** in *suis-je* and *est-elle* but its retention in *dis-le* and *sur ce* may be explained in terms of differences in the syntactic structure of these phrases. *Suis-je* and *est-elle* are the result of subject plus verb inversion, whereas *dis-le* is an instance of the sequence verb plus pronoun, more specifically, an instance of the combination imperative verb plus object pronoun where normal verb plus object order is preserved (compare *tu dis cela* vs. *tu le dis*). *Sur ce* "thereupon" is a fixed phrase representing a rare use of the indeterminate pronoun *ce* after a preposition. The fixed phrase *sur ce* and the combination of imperative verb plus object pronoun constitute special syntactic constructions which are converted to phonemic phrases containing a special boundary (symbolized by #). That is, *fais-le* is **fɛZ+lE #**, and *sur ce* is **syr+sE #**. When it occurs before #, **E** is obligatorily retained. Since it occurs in final position it is realized by the phoneme / ø /: *fais-le* **fɛZ+lE** / fɛlø /.

There is a case which constitutes a counter-example to the rule proposed for the pronunciation of **E** in final position: *mets-l'y* "put it there." We have proposed that the construction imperative plus object pronoun entails the presence of the boundary marker # before which **E** is obligatorily realized. Given the underlying representation **mɛTZ lE#i**, we would expect the phonetic realization [mɛləi] instead of the actually occurring [mɛli]. In order to prevent the former output we would need to specify that the boundary marker # may not be inserted within sequences of post-posed pronouns. That is, the underlying representation of *mets-l'y* is in fact **mɛ lE i**. It is noteworthy that the occurrence of *mets-l'y* is relatively rare; speakers usually say *mets-le là* [mɛləla] and thus avoid the sequence *le+y*.

The fact that the particular syntactic structure in which it occurs introduces the phonological boundary # after occurrences of **E** explains the differences in phonological output between such sentences as *Fais-le entrer* / fɛløɑ̃tre / and *Est-elle entrée* / ɛtɛlɑ̃tre /. But, except when it is immediately followed by #, **E** is obligatorily deleted at the end of a phonemic phrase. In the examples below, **E** (whose presence in the underlying form of the word given is attested by its occurrence before aspirate *h*) does not appear in final position:

Pre-aspirate h	*Final*
une petit*e* hutte	Elle est petit∅.
un modest*e* héros	Il est modest∅.
quatr*e* hangars	Il y en a quatr∅.
le simpl*e* hasard	C'est très simpl∅.

It is important to distinguish between the occurrence of a fully syllabic [ø] at the end of *dis-le* or *sur ce,* for instance, and that of **emphatic release** ([¨]) which is simply a phonetic variant of the release of final consonants in French. In Méridional Standard French, **E** may be realized as [ø] in final position even when it is not immediately followed by # . Compare the following three variant pronunciations of *Elle est grande.*

Méridional Accent:	[ɛ legrɑ̃dø]
Normal Style:	[ɛ legrɑ̃d]
Emphatic Style:	[ɛ legrɑ̃d¨]

The cases of pronunciation or deletion of **E** discussed so far are all determined by categorical rules. To summarize, these rules are:

1. **E** is pronounced when it is immediately followed by **#** , e.g., *fais-le* **#** *entrer, dis-le* **#** .
2. **E** is pronounced before aspirate *h,* e.g., *le homard, notre hutte.*
3. **E** is deleted when it occurs at the end of a phonemic phrase, e.g., *Elle est petite, C'est simple.*
4. **E** is deleted when it occurs before a vowel within a phonemic phrase, e.g., *l'amour, notre ami, une jolie étudiante.*

These rules may be simplified further by stating that **E** is obligatorily deleted in the immediate environment of a vowel or in phonemic-phrase final position *unless* it is immediately followed by (1) the boundary **#** or (2) aspirate *h.*

11.5   THE "LOI DES TROIS CONSONNES"

The pronunciation or deletion of mute *e* in word- or phonemic phrase-internal position is not subject to categorical but to variable rules. Variable rules are probabilistic: they state that in a particular environment and subject to particular conditions the chances of the pronunciation of **E** are such and such. The remaining mute *e* rules that will be presented are general factors that weigh toward the retention of **E**; when these factors are not present, **E** is deleted. In the next sections of this chapter we shall discuss these factors and then use them in the elaboration of a pedagogical norm.

In a handbook of French phonetics published early in this century Maurice Grammont (*Traité pratique de prononciation française.* Paris, 1911) formulated a general principle intended to cover all instances of **E** in word- or phonemic phrase-internal position: *"L'e caduc* [mute *e*] *se prononce seulement lorsqu'il est nécessaire pour éviter la rencontre de trois consonnes."* This principle, labelled inappropriately "la loi des trois consonnes," has since Grammont's formulation been proclaimed as a categorical rule. But Grammont himself stated numerous qualifications to the "principle" of three consonants, and we shall see that, on the one hand, there are in French numerous instances of three-consonant clusters uninterrupted by [ə] (*exploit* / ɛksplwa /, *c'est le principe* / selprɛ̃sip /), and on the other hand, certain sequences of two consonants that are usually interrupted by [ə] if an **E** is present in the underlying form of the words involved (*Que dit-il?* / kəditil / and not */ kdidil /, *Te trouves-tu ici?* / tətruvty isi / and not */ ttruvty isi /). Compare the following paired phrases:

l'ami dé Pierre	la soeur de Pierre
pas dé train	par le train
six pétites filles	sept petites filles

E is more likely to be deleted in the items in the left-hand column than in those in the right-hand column. Note that in the latter **E** is preceded by two pronounced consonants, whereas in those in the left-hand column it is preceded by only one consonant. In general, the fewer the number of consonants that occur before an internal **E**, the more likely it is to be deleted, and conversely. But it would be incorrect to say, as one would be forced to in interpreting the "loi des trois consonnes," that **E** *must* be pronounced if it is preceded by two or more consonants. Below are examples of the deletion of **E** preceded by two or more consonants, which results in the occurrence of three or more consonants:

une bell*e* statue b*ɛ*lE + staty / ynb*ɛ*lstaty /
on n*e s*e moque pas õ + nE + sE + mɔk pɑ / õ*n*sm*ɔ*kpɑ /
cette port*e* s*e* gondole pɔrtE + sE + gõdɔl / sɛtpɔ*rts*g̃õdɔl /
ce dép*art* s*e* présente mal depar + sE + prezãt mal / sdepa*rs*p*re*zãt mal /

It will be noted that the above clusters of three and four consonants all contain / s /.

Thus in assessing the probability of pronunciation or deletion of **E**, we must consider not only the number of consonants that precede **E**, but the nature of the cluster they form. Compare the following paired items:

un cambr*e*ment	un appart*é*ment
ampl*e*ment	quelqu*é*fois
notr*e* chambre	notr*e* port*é*-manteau
une tabl*e* ronde	une bours*é* vide

The **E** in the items in the right-hand column are more likely to be deleted than those in the left-hand column. In both sets of items, **E** is preceded by a two-consonant cluster. The consonant clusters differ, however, in that those in the left-hand column are permitted word initial clusters whereas those in the right-hand column are not. Consonant clusters of the type KL such as / br /, / tr /, / pl /, and / bl / constitute the most frequently occurring type of word initial consonant cluster in French and appear to favor the pronunciation of a following **E**. Note, too, that in a cluster consisting of a stop or / f / or / v / plus a liquid, the first consonant has greater articulatory force or as was pointed out in Chapter 9 (Section 9.3), a less open air channel. In a cluster such as / rt /, which consists of a liquid plus a stop or / f / or / v /, the first consonant has less articulatory force than the second.

The type of consonant cluster that follows **E** also plays a role in determining its retention or deletion. **E** is obligatorily retained when it is followed by a consonant cluster composed of a liquid (/ r / or / l /) and the semivowel / j /. Compare:

la chap*é*lure / laʃaplyr /	vs.	la chapelière / laʃapəljɛr /
nous chant*é*rons / nuʃãtrõ /	vs.	nous chanterions / nuʃãtərjõ /

Note that, unlike [j], the semivowels [w] and [ɥ] do not determine retention of **E**:

demand*é*-moi [dəmãdmwa]		
demand*é*-lui [dəmãdlɥi]	vs.	ne dit*e*s rien / nəditərjẽ /

Recall that [ɥ] has been analyzed as a predictable or free variant of the phoneme / y /. That is, / y / is predictably [-syllabic] ([ɥ]) when it occurs before the vowel / i / (see Chapter 8).

11.6   THE EFFECT OF PHONOLOGICAL BOUNDARIES ON THE PRONUNCIATION OF E

Compare the following paired utterances:

tenez	il faut tᵉnir
semez	il faut sᵉmer
cela	c'est cᵉla
levons-nous	nous nous lᵉvons
que dis-tu	c'est quᵉ tu pars
le garçon	c'est lᵉ garçon
je veux	c'est ce que jᵉ veux
ne pars pas	tu nᵉ pars pas

When a morpheme containing **E** occurs at the beginning of a phonemic phrase, **E** is more likely to be pronounced than when it occurs in the middle of the phonemic phrase. In both positions the probability of the pronunciation of **E** increases in direct proportion to the force of articulation of the consonant that precedes it. The smaller the aperture formed in the pronunciation of a consonant, the greater its force of articulation. Thus, stops are produced with the greatest force of articulation, then the fricatives, then the nasals, and finally the liquids.

But within a phonemic phrase the probability of pronunciation of **E** also varies. Compare the three items:

un appartᵉment vide
un portᵉ-manteau
une portᵉ manquée

The probability of the pronunciation of **E** decreases as we go down this list. These three items contain **E** preceded by the two-consonant cluster / rt / (which does not favor pronunciation of **E**) but differ with regard to the nature of the syntactic or morphological boundary present. In *appartement* there is no internal morphological or syntactic boundary. *Porte-manteau* is a compound which contains a low-level syntactic boundary. Finally, *porte manquée* is a phrase whose two constituent words are delimited by word boundaries. These facts lead us to formulate the following principle: the closer **E** is to a major syntactic boundary, the more probable is its deletion.

Such factors as rhythm or the length of the utterance in which it occurs also determine the probability of pronunciation of **E**. The following paired items contain instances of **E** preceded by a consonant cluster of the type liquid plus stop which, it will be recalled, favors its deletion. In addition, members of each pair have the same syntactic structure, although this fact is camouflaged by their spelling—some words are written with a hyphen, others are not. The members of the first pair are phrases consisting of noun plus adjective, the members of the second pair consist of a compound whose constituent elements are loosely joined, and the members of the third pair comprise compounds whose elements are closely knit. Note that *un ours blanc* is not "a white bear" (which is a phrase noun plus adjective) but "a Polar bear":

une arm∉ défensive	une arm*e* courte
un port∉-monnaie	un port*e*-balle
un arc-boutant / arkbutã /	un ours blanc [ursəblã]

The members of each pair differ only with regard to the number of syllables that the second element contains: two syllables for the first member versus one only for the second. If **E** is pronounced, both members of each pair have the same number of syllables.

Finally, compare the duration of the following phonemic phrases and of the [ə] produced when **E** is pronounced:

	Duration of phonemic phrase (in centiseconds)	Duration of [ə] (in centiseconds)
appart*e*ment	53	7
appart*e*ment vide	68	5
appart*e*ment vidé	81	3

The longer the duration of the phonemic phrase, the shorter the duration of [ə] and the higher the probability of its deletion.

11.7   E IN SEQUENCES OF MONOSYLLABIC MORPHEMES

E is often found in a set of monosyllabic morphemes (*je, me, te, le, se, ce, ne, de, que*), two or more of which may co-occur consecutively, e.g., *ce que, de ne, je ne te.* In these sequences the first **E** is pronounced and the second deleted unless the first consonant is a continuant (fricative or resonant) and the second a stop:

	First **E** *pronounced*	Second **E** *pronounced*
Continuant + Continuant	je n∉ sais pas	
	on s*e* l∉ pose	
	n*e* l∉ dites pas	
Stop + Continuant	t*e* l∉ dit-il	
	d*e* l∉ faire m'ennuie	
	qu*e* m∉ dites-vous	
Stop + Stop	qu*e* t∉ dit-il	
	d*e* t∉ dire	
Continuant + Stop		c∉ que je dis
		j∉ t*e* dirai tout

This principle does not seem to apply to *ne te* which is often pronounced / nət / rather than / ntə /. Thus, the pronunciation of **E** in a series of monosyllables is handled by a rule somewhat simpler than that stated above: in a sequence of two monosyllables containing **E**, the first **E** is pronounced and the second deleted except for the sequences *ce̸ que* and *je̸ te*.

This principle also extends to series of **E** in which the first is part of a monosyllabic morpheme and the second part of a following word:

le che̸val
ce se̸ra
le me̸nu
ne de̸mande rien
je se̸rai
de te̸nir
te le̸ver

This principle does not seem to have as much weight as that which favors the pronunciation of **E** in initial position and its deletion within phonemic phrases. For instance *Où est le̸ cheval?* is almost as frequent as *Où est le che̸val?*

In sequences of more than two monosyllables or in sequences of more than two **E**'s in consecutive syllables, the principle applies starting with the first monosyllable and progressing inward. Consider for instance the sentence *je ne te le redemande pas.* We apply the principle to the monosyllable sequence *je ne:*

je ne̸

Next we apply it to the second pair of monosyllables:

te le̸

Finally, we apply it to the successive sequence *rede-*:

rede̸

The pronunciation of the sentence is:

Je ne̸ *te* le̸ rede̸mande pas.

11.8   E AFTER WORD FINAL KL CLUSTERS

When it occurs at the end of a word, but within a phonemic phrase, preceded by a consonant cluster of the type KL (stop or / f / or / v / plus liquid), **E** undergoes two types of treatments. It may be pronounced:

notr*e* frère
la tabl*e* ronde

or it may be deleted, in which case the preceding liquid (/ r / or / l /) must also be deleted:

notre frère	vs.	not' frère
la table ronde	vs.	la tab' ronde
il ouvre la porte	vs.	il ouv' la porte
un souffre-douleur	vs.	un souff'-douleur

The deletion of **E** and the accompanying deletion of the liquid is characteristic of normal conversational style whereas its retention is typical of formal speech.

The deletion of **E** and a preceding liquid in word final KL clusters is affected by the deletion of the final / l / in the third person masculine subject pronouns *il* and *ils* and of the final / r / in the preposition *sur* when these words occur before a consonant:

	Normal Style	Formal Style
il dit	/ idi /	/ ildi /
Qu'est-ce qu'ils font?	/ kɛskifõ /	/ kɛskilfõ /
Il ne sait pas.	/ insɛpa /	/ ilnøsɛpa / [ilnəsɛpa]
sur le pont	/ sylpõ /	/ syrløpõ / [syrləpõ]

Before a vowel and in final position there is no difference in the forms that occur in normal and formal styles, e.g., *il a* / ila /, *ils arrivent* / ilzariv /, *sur un bateau* / syrœ̃bato /. The alternation between / i / and / il /, / i / and / ilz /, and / sy / and / syr / require that we posit two underlying forms for each of these three forms: **il** and **iL** for *il,* **ilZ** and **iLZ** for *ils,* and **syr** and **syR** for *sur.* The second of the two forms is used in normal style and the first in formal style. As may be seen from the examples given, the selection of one or the other of the two underlying forms influences the pronunciation or deletion of **E** contained in a following word. Consider the phonetic output of the phrase *Il ne sait pas.* In formal style, the underlying form is **il+nE+sɛT+paZ.** E is pronounced since it is preceded by two consonants: / ilnøsɛpa / [ilnəsɛpa]. The normal style underlying form is **iL+nE+sɛT+paZ.** The latent **L** is deleted since it occurs before a consonant: **i+nE.** E is deleted since it is now preceded by only one consonant: / insɛpa /.

Finally, there is the problem of the pronunciation of [ə] at the end of words that do not contain *-e* in the spelling, e.g., *un ours* / ursə / *blanc* "a Polar bear," *l'Arc* / larkə / *de Triomphe, un film* / filmə / *parlant* "a talking movie." The pronunciation of [ə] in these items is typical of informal rather than formal style and is even branded by some purists as "slipshod." These three compounds contain consonant clusters of the type liquid (/ r / or / l /) and small aperture ("strong") consonant plus small aperture consonant: / rs+bl /, / rk+d /; / lm+p /. Unlike clusters of the type KL (e.g., / tr /, / kl /, etc.) consonants of the type **L** plus small aperture consonant do not favor the retention of **E**. The pronunciation of these items with an intercalated [ə] is thus highly idiosyncratic.

11.9   A PEDAGOGICAL NORM

It is apparent from this introductory description that the prediction of the relative probability of the pronunciation or deletion of **E** in a given phonological and syntactic environment, by a given speaker, in a given situation, is quite complex. Samples of French speech occurring in a natural context can be expected to show wide variation. While the learner of French should be warned of the widely variable behavior of **E** and should be given training in noting its pronunciation or deletion in actual speech samples, he should be provided with a small set of rules which would enable him to handle **E** in a way that is neither too stilted nor unacceptable to educated middle-class Paris speakers. The following set of rules constitute a pedagogical norm that, we believe, meets these requirements.

Any **E** is *deleted* unless:

1.   It occurs before # or aspirate *h*, e.g., *dis-le, fais-le entrer; le haut, je le hais.*
2.   It occurs before the combination / rj / or / lj /, e.g., *chancelier, nous serions.*
3.   It occurs at the beginning of a sentence after a consonant or consonant cluster, particularly if that consonant is a stop, e.g., *Que dit-il? , Pesez ces tomates, Prenez-les; Je pars, Le train arrive.*
4.   It is preceded by two consonants, particularly if these constitute a KL consonant cluster, e.g., *Il me parle, le frère de Jean, autrement dit, l'appartement, on ne se moque pas, notre frère.*

In addition, in the sequences *ce que* and *je te*, the second rather than the first **E** is pronounced:

cé que je dis; jé te dis

STUDY QUESTIONS

1.   Give three examples of:
     a)   two consecutive vowels
     b)   three consecutive vowels

2.   If a French speaker differentiates *le rétour* vs. *leur tour* or *sur ce* vs. *sur ceux,* how would he pronounce them? Give a phonetic transcription.

     le rétour _____   leur tour _____

     sur ce _____   sur ceux _____

3.   Give three examples of:
     a)   **E** occurring before aspirate *h*:
          cette hache _____   _____   _____
     b)   **E** occurring before a consonant cluster of the type liquid + / j /:
          le chancelier _____   _____   _____

4.   Transcribe phonetically:
     mets-le en bas   _____
     fais-le entrer   _____

5.   In the pair of sentences below
     Marie ne part pas.   Emile ne part pas.
     E is more likely to be deleted in the item on the left. For each of the sentences below, provide a corresponding sentence differing by only one word and in which **E** is likely to be pronounced.
     a)   André né sait pas.   _____
     b)   Je ne dois pas.   _____
     c)   Elle veut le numéro.   _____

d)   Elle boit le café.   _____

e)   Il attend le facteur.   _____

f)   C'est un pot de lait.   _____

g)   J'aimerais le rencontrer.   _____

6. Provide three paired phrases which are analogous to those given below with regard to the behavior of **E**.   vous l'aimerez   vous l'aimeriez

7. Classify the following items in two groups on the basis of the nature of the consonant cluster preceding **E** and its role in determining its pronunciation or deletion.
    a)   proprement   e)   probablement
    b)   fortement   f)   ils récolteront
    c)   nous montrerons   g)   il encerclera
    d)   vous calmerez   h)   aigrement

8. Indicate which of the following **E**'s are more likely to be deleted. Insert a slash line through the appropriate *e*'s.
    a)   *Je n∉ le fais pas.*
    b)   Il veut que je le prenne.   f)   Je ne te le redemande pas.
    c)   Il se le demande.   g)   C'est ce qu'il ne te demande pas.
    d)   Tu ne me le donnes pas.   h)   Je ne te le redemande pas.
    e)   Je te le redemande.   i)   De ne pas se le reprocher est difficile.

9. What do the pairs
    c'est cela   vs.   C'est Slave   or   au frais   vs.   on ferait
    prove about the nature of **E**?

10. What is the "loi des trois consonnes"? Is it an accurate statement about the pronunciation or deletion of **E**? Use appropriate examples.

11. French writers often attempt to represent lower-class speech by showing deleted mute *e*'s, e.g., *Je n' veux pas qu' tu l' dises.* Is this an accurate portrayal of lower-class pronunciation habits?

12. How would one explain such contrasts as *suis-je* [sɥiʒ] vs. *dis-le* [dilø] or [dilœ]?

12

FRENCH SPELLING

12.1   THE NATURE OF FRENCH SPELLING

The playwright and wit George Bernard Shaw considered the conventional French spelling only slightly less whimsical and inadequate than the English spelling. To emphasize how inconsistent the latter is, Shaw is reported to have proposed that *fish* should really be spelled GHOTI: *gh* to represent / f /, as in *rough; o* to represent / i /, as in *women; ti* to represent / ʃ /, as in *nation.* The features of French spelling that Shaw and many would-be orthography reformers considered particularly inconsistent are the so-called "silent letters" and multiple representations of the same phonological units. One of the examples singled out by Shaw is the representation of / sã / as *sang, cent, sans, (je) sens,* and *(il) sent* by the use of two different combinations—*an* and *en*—followed by three different "silent" letters.

The ideal spelling system envisaged by Shaw and spelling reformers of the latter part of the nineteenth century and most of the present century is a phonological representation which provides perfect one-to-one correspondence between phonemes and letters. In that type of notation every phoneme would always be represented by the same letter and, conversely, a given letter would always stand for the same phoneme. For instance, the words *sang, cent, sans,* etc., which are pronounced alike and composed of two phonemes, would be represented identically by the use of two letters, one always noting / s / and the other / ã /. Conversely, the letter *s* would always represent / s / and would never stand for any other phoneme, and some graphic representation, say, *an,* would always represent / ã /.

The conventional French spelling clearly fails to meet this criterion for ideal spelling. But, in view of the existence of free variation among some French phonemes and of the morphophonemic phenomena of liaison and elision, French spelling in some ways provides a quite adequate representation of the language. Consider the so-called silent letters of *sans, cent, (je) sens, (il) sent,* and *sang,* for example. All of these words have at least two different phonological representations: / sã / *sans travail* vs. / sãz / *sans argent;* / sã / *cent francs* vs. / sãt / *cent ans;* / sã / *je me sens bien* vs. / sãz / *je me sens un peu fatigué;* / sã / *il se sent bien* vs. / sãt / *il se sent un peu fatigué;* / sã / *du sang* vs. / sãk / *qu'un sang impur abreuve nos sillons* ("La Marseillaise"). In these words the final consonant represents a latent consonant which is pronounced obligatorily before a vowel in *sans* and *cent* and optionally in the other words. In the case of *cent* and *sang* the final consonant letter also represents a consonant which appears in derivatives containing a suffix beginning with a vowel: *un centenaire* "a centenary," *sanguin* "sanguine, pertaining to blood" or *sanguinaire* "bloodthirsty." For these items and for all French words whose underlying form ends with a latent consonant that appears obligatorily or optionally, the spelling does not in fact represent directly their phonological realization but their underlying form. To convert the spelling to a phonological notation, it is necessary to apply the liaison rule and its associated rules such as mid vowel raising or nasalization. In other words, the graphic sequence *in* does not represent / ẽ / but both / in / and / ẽ /, depending on the environment. To correctly convert the spelling *divin,* the French reader must know that (1) that form is an adjective which will be involved in obligatory liaison if it precedes a noun beginning with a vowel within a NP and (2) when it is deleted the latent consonant **N** triggers the nasalization of the preceding vowel:

divin enfant	Obligatory Liaison:	/ divin /
breuvage divin	Nasalization:	/ divĩn /
	Nasal Vowel Adjustment:	/ divẽn /
	Deletion of **N**:	/ divẽ /

The letter *e* plays a role similar to that of certain final consonant letters. It represents the latent vowel **E** which is realized phonologically as either zero or a front rounded vowel depending on the nature of the following segment and a wide variety of factors (see Chapter 11). Thus, in *le Petit Chaperon Rouge* "little Red Riding Hood" the four *e*'s are not silent letters, for they may appear in some context (of course, it is true that the probability of realization of the **E**'s which these *e*'s represent decreases from nearly 100 per cent in the case of that of *le* to nearly 0 per cent in the case of that of *rouge*). Consider also the relationship between the letters *i, ou,* and *u* and their phonological manifestations. In order to convert these symbols to the appropriate sound, the reader needs to apply a set of rules since they represent both high vowels ([i], [u], and [y]) and semivowels ([j], [w], and [ɥ]), depending on the phonological environment. For example, when they occur followed by a consonant or in final position, these vowel letters represent a vowel sound, e.g., *si, vitesse; cou, rouler; nu, fumer.* But when they occur preceding another vowel, a set of rules (presented in Chapter 8) must be applied, since in that environment these vowel letters represent a high vowel, a semivowel, or free variation between the high vowel and the semivowel, e.g., *lien* / ljẽ /, *crier* / krie / [kriĵe], *(nous) li-ons* / ljõ / or / liõ /; *brouette* / bruɛt /, *lou-er* / lue / or / lwe /; *cruel* [kryɛl], *lui* [lɥi], *tu-er* [tye] or [tɥe]. It will be noted that the conversion of the letters *i* and *u* and the sequence *ou* to appropriate phonetic realizations requires consideration of the phonological environment (both that which follows and precedes) as well as the morphological structure in the case of *li-ons* and *lou-er.*

In summary, the conventional French spelling is not a phonetic or phonemic transcription but a **morphophonemic** representation. Given the widespread occurrence of liaison and elision, as well as free variation among certain French phonemes, it is a rather economical system of written representation, since it provides a single representation for two or more spoken forms. Because the rules of liaison and elision are very general, in the sense that they affect many French morphemes, it may be assumed that these have been internalized by French speakers, who would have little difficulty in converting the spelling to appropriate phonological representations.

12.2   HOW OPTIMAL IS THE CONVENTIONAL SPELLING FOR FRENCH SPEAKERS?

On the basis of the fact that it provides more or less an abstract underlying representation of French morphemes, the conventional spelling has been characterized as "optimal" by such linguists as Noam Chomsky. Implicit in Chomsky's claim that French spelling is optimal for its speakers is the contention that it corresponds to a level of representation that has some sort of psychological reality for speakers of French. In other words, he would claim that in their acquisition, storage, and use of the language, French speakers operate with underlying forms rather than their overt (surface) manifestations as strings of phonemes subsuming articulatory features. A discussion of Chomsky's claims would take us too far afield; instead, we shall limit ourselves to a discussion of the implications of these claims in evaluating the optimality of French spelling as a representation of the language for the average native speaker.

If French speakers operate directly with the underlying form of morphemes of their language, they extract these from the raw sound data in which they are embedded. They then match it with the other "surface" phonological form or forms and on that basis recover the underlying form. For example, when a French speaker hears *il a deux francs,* he extracts the surface / dø /, matches it with the other variant / døz / that contains the pronounced latent consonant / z /, and on that basis identifies the underlying form **døZ**. It should presumably be easy for him to learn to write it, not as *d + eu* on the basis of the sound (phoneme) correspondences / d /→d and / ø /→eu, but with an indication of the latent consonant, i.e., **Z**→x. It is quite reasonable to claim that even children at age five or six relate the surface forms of numerals, determiners, adjectives and the various morphemes involved in obligatory liaison. Thus, for them, learning to spell involves acquiring two sets of rules: (1) systematic phoneme to letter correspondences such as / p /→p, / ø / or / œ /→eu, etc.; (2) testing forms involved in obligatory liaison in various environments in order to identify the particular latent consonant they contain, and determining whether surface forms that contain a consonant cluster also have a variant in which that cluster is interrupted by a vowel in the [ø] to [œ] range to determine whether or not they contain **E**, e.g., *un petit garçon* compared to *un petit oiseau* and then / pti / and / ptit / pronounced as / pøti / or / pøtit /.

Proponents of spelling systems based on a phonemic notation, such as Shaw, would argue that to spell correctly such words as *petit* entails a complex process of relating overt phonic events to abstract representations. They would contend that it is much simpler for a child to write simply, say, *pti,* when he heard / pti / in *petit garçon,* and *ptit,* when he heard / ptit / in *petit oiseau.* They are no doubt right, but a phonetically based spelling system becomes unworkable for any language that shows wide geographical or social variation or extensive free variation unless one allows speakers considerable leeway in spelling. Indeed, in earlier times in England and France, the minority of literate speakers were very tolerant of each other's spelling idiosyncrasies, and there was no insistence on adherence to a strict norm. One spelled a word as one pronounced it or on the basis of the analogy of the moment. The only requirement was that the reader be able to decipher the writing on the basis of the context. For example, in the seventeenth century, the Maréchal de Saxe, one of Louis XV's most distinguished generals, wrote, upon being named a member of the Académie Française, that august body dedicated to maintaining the purity of the French language: "il veule me fere de la Cadémie; cela miret come une bage à un chas (ils veulent me faire de l'Académie; cela m'irait comme une bague à un chat)." With the democratization of education and the spread of literacy, orthographic laissez-faire was replaced with a rigid intolerance of deviations from a strict norm, and in general each word came to be assigned only one written representation. Within the constraints imposed by the modern normative attitude toward spelling, native speakers of French must learn that they cannot write words as they pronounce them.

Nonetheless, the conventional French spelling is hardly optimal for the average native speaker, and is even less so for the young child. In addition to the instances of obligatory liaison and alternations involving inflectionally related forms such as the masculine and feminine of adjectives, there are numerous cases of optional liaison which are generally not made by the majority of speakers in daily conversational speech. Also, the average speaker is not aware of derivationally related forms such as *sain/saine/santé/sanatorium, plein/pleine/plénitude, faim/affamé/famine,* or *fin/final* which would enable him to correctly differentiate the written representation of the base forms *sain, plein,* and *fin,* all of which contain the final nasal vowel / ẽ / in the surface form. Consider the following set of alternations:

fin	fine	finesse
plein / plɛn / vs. / plẽ /	pleine	plénitude remplir
sain	saine	sanitaire
faim		affamé
cinq / sẽk / vs. / sẽ /		

The only alternations the average speaker can be expected to be conscious of are the liaison variants of *plein* and *cinq* and the masculine and feminine forms of the adjectives *plein/pleine* and *sain/saine* which show the alternation / ɛn / vs. / ẽ / as opposed to those of *fin/fine* which shows the alternation / in / vs. / ẽ /. If French spelling were optimal we would expect these various forms to be represented:

fin	fine	finesse
plen	plèn	plénitude
sen	sèn	sanitaire
fin		afamé
cinq		

That is, the spelling would differentiate, on the one hand, forms where the basic form ends in / ẽ / and where there are no liaison or inflectional variants and those that show the alternation / in / vs. / ẽ / from those that show the alternation / ɛn / vs. / ẽ / on the other hand. When we consider the numerous inconsistencies in correspondences between phonemes and letters, such as the use of both *an* and *en* to represent / ã /, e.g., *l'an* vs. *lent,* or the use of *c* and *s* to represent / s / before the same vowels, it is clear that learning to spell is for French children a long and arduous process which requires the memorization of complex rules and long lists of idiosyncratic items. In this sense, it is far from an optimal written representation of the language, and efforts to reform it should be warmly welcomed by all those whose aim is to provide all French speakers with a tool that will permit them to communicate their thoughts by means of writing efficiently but which may be acquired by means of the smallest amount of training.

12.3   TEACHING FRENCH SPELLING TO FOREIGN LEARNERS

The teacher of French as a foreign language has no choice but to teach the French spelling as it now exists, for better or worse. It would be counter-productive for him to adopt the point of view that, in as much as it is far from optimal for the native speakers, it is completely unsystematic and can only be taught on a word-by-word basis. In order to teach it efficiently, he must concentrate on its systematic features, which, as we have seen in Section 12.1, are, fortunately, numerous.

Since French spelling is a morphophonemic notation, one can spell French words correctly only if one knows their underlying form. This knowledge is derived from the identification of the phonemes which constitute a given word as well as from information about the grammatical function it plays in the sentence in which it occurs and the derivational and inflectional series in which it participates. What are the pedagogical implications of the recognition that speech and writing are two partially dependent and partially autonomous expressions of a single abstract underlying reality and that no simple one-to-one correspondence obtains between them?

First, one needs to distinguish between learning to *read* and learning to *spell*. Reading aloud involves only converting sequences of letters into sequences of phonemes, and it is a skill acquired relatively easily provided one possesses the ability to produce French phonemes accurately and fluently. Because of its very nature, French spelling provides abundant information about the phonological mapping of words. From the point of view of the reader, the inconsistencies and vagaries of the conventional orthography are merely redundancies. For instance, of the eight different graphs for / ẽ / *(faim, tiens, plein, symbole, impasse, pain, examen)*, only *en* is ambiguous since it could also stand for / ã / *(lent* / lã /)*. Presented with any of the other seven graphs in any environment, the student would have no difficulty responding with / ẽ / rather than with any of the other three nasal vowels. Similarly, even though the consonant / k / is represented by seven different graphs *(qui, chaque, coq, acquis, kilo, chrétien, car)*, it is only when he is confronted with *ch* and *c* that the student might be likely to produce a consonant other than / k /, namely / ʃ / in *chrétien* and / s / in *car* on the analogy of *chez* and *celle* respectively. Traditional handbooks of phonetics have generally handled the problem of teaching reading (here narrowly defined as the ability to convert a sequence of letters to sound) adequately. Quite appropriately they have provided the learner with many-to-one lists of letter-to-sound correspondences, e.g., *om, on*→/ õ /; *au, o, eau*→/ o /; *f, ff, ph*→/ f /. Even such complex letter-to-sound relationships as the representation of / e / and / ɛ / by *e, é, è, ê, ai* plus or minus a multitude of "silent" consonant letters can be learned without much difficulty, since in all cases a single oral response is made to a variety of visual stimuli.

But, **spelling**, i.e., providing written representations for given spoken forms, is quite a different task. Most authors who have dealt with the question blithely proceeded as if the teaching of spelling could be handled by merely reversing the process of reading. But to say, for instance, that / k / is written *qu, que, q, cq, k, ch,* and *c,* is of no utility whatever to the student unless one provides him with information that will enable him to select one of the seven graphs in any given case, that is, to spell / ki / "who" with *qu (qui)* but / kar / "for" with *c (car)*. Presumably this information is available to literate French speakers who are more likely to write nonsense words like */ kim / and */ kag / as *quime* and *cague*, respectively, rather than **kime*, **cime,* or **kague*. In initial position, only *c* or *qu* are used with high frequency. The latter is used before *i* and *e* and the former before the other vowel representation. The letter *c* never has the value / k / before *i*. Thus, the spellings **kime*, **cime*, and **kague* would be excluded.

Any procedure to teach French spelling must take into account a fundamental aspect of the structure of French, namely, the absence of clear phonological signals for word boundaries. In French, final stress marks off units which are generally longer than words (phonemic phrases), and junctural phenomena of the type that differentiates English *nitrate* and *night rate* or *an aim* and *a name* do not occur consistently (see Chapter 9); word identification ultimately depends on grammatical or contextual cues. Since the student is expected to spell sentence length utterances rather than words lifted out of context, the first step in learning to spell in French is the segmentation of sentences into their constituent words by grammatical analysis and contextual inference.

After individual words have been isolated, to spell them correctly requires three sets of rules. First, there exists a large set of systematic correspondences between phonemes and their graphic representation, and rules can be formulated which specify that a given phoneme or a given phoneme in a particular environment is represented by a given letter or group of letters. Second, latent consonants and E are predictable on the basis of variants occurring in different phonological environments and on the basis of inflectional variants. In addition, there are systematic correspondences between grammatical endings, such as the personal endings of verbs, and graphic representations. Third, lists of items, such as *doigt, poids, scie, type,* or *cathédrale,* which contain idiosyncratic features not amenable to systematic statement in terms of the first two types of rules, need to be memorized. The fact that French spelling is a morphophonemic notation suggests that it cannot be taught to learners who have not acquired a certain knowledge of the grammatical structure of the language. The next sections of this chapter will present some of the three sets of rules required for a foreign learner to provide the correct spelling of French words. These rules will be labelled (1) **phonological**, (2) **grammatical**, and (3) **lexical**, respectively. It should be added that rules which convert written representations to phonological representations are necessarily much simpler.

12.4   PHONOLOGICAL RULES

Phonological rules must permit the student to predict with a high degree of success the exact representation of phonemes in specific phonological environments. Some of these rules take the form of simple correspondence lists, for example:

1.   phonemes represented by single letters: / a /→ *a,* / i /→ *i,* / y /→ *u,* / p /→ *p,* / b /→ *b,* / d /→ *d,* / f /→ *f,* / j /→ *y,* / m /→ *m,* / n /→ *n,* / l /→ *l,* / r /→ *r;*
2.   phonemes represented by letter combinations / ʃ /→ *ch,* / œ̃ /→ *un,* / ɲ /→ *gn,* / u /→ *ou;*
3.   fixed combinations of phonemes represented by letter combinations: / wa /→ *oi,* / wẽ / → *oin,* [ɥi] → *ui.*

Assuming that the student is able to isolate individual words, these rules make it possible for him to spell such short sentences as *Il a du foin* or *Loulou a soif.*

In the formulation of these rules, relatively rare spellings like *y* and *î* for / i / and *ph* and *ff* for / f / would not be considered and would be relegated to lists. Such misspellings as **sifler* for *siffler* or **stile* for *style* would not shock educated Frenchmen as much as those like **duze* for *douze* or **cashe* for *cache* which might result in the confusion of contrasting forms and which show the lack of assimilation of more general and fundamental spelling rules.

After Rules 1 to 3 inclusive have been applied, it must be specified that all final stable consonants are written with the appropriate consonant letter plus *e:*

4. final / C /→ C + e, e.g., / ful /→ *foule,* / brav /→ *brave;* / bul /→ *boule;* / tir /→ *tire;* / altityd /→ *altitude.*

There are many instances of stable consonants, particularly / l / and / r / written without *e,* e.g., *bal, bar, sec, vif, sens.* These items are considered idiosyncratic and must be memorized.

Where a one-to-one correspondence between phonemes and letters does not exist, more complicated rules need to be devised. These specify that a phoneme *X* is rewritten as *a* in environment *Q* but as *b* in environment *R.* We consider first the spelling of vowel phonemes.

5. / õ / is written *om* before / b / or / p / and *on* elsewhere, e.g., / bõ /→*bon* but / tõba /→*tomba.*

6. / œ̃ / is written *um* before / b / or / p / but *un* elsewhere, e.g., / lœ̃di /→*lundi* but / œ̃bl /→ **umble.* (The asterisk indicates that the spelling of this word, although it illustrates the proper application of the spelling rules given so far, is not yet fully correct since the "mute *h*" has not yet been provided for.)

The application of Rules 1 to 6 will generate the correct spelling of words composed of the phonemes involved in nearly ninety per cent of cases. Where the phonological rules do not generate correct spelling, additional grammatical or lexical rules will need to be provided. The lexical rules are generally idiosyncratic, that is, they only apply to individual items. Consider, for example, the spelling of *bonbon, humble* and *parfum.* Given the phoneme strings / bõbõ /, / œ̃bl /, / parfœ̃ /, after Rules 1-6 have been applied, we obtain the letter strings **bombon, *umble, *parfun.* Clearly Rules 5 and 6 are violated by these items. The incorrect spellings **bombon* and **umble* can be corrected by idiosyncratic lexical rules which provide the "irregular" and unpredictable *n* before / b / and "mute *h*." To deduce the graph *um* rather than *un* in *parfum,* one would need to know that *parfum* belonged to the derivational series *parfumer, parfumerie,* in other words that the underlying form of *parfum* is really **parfyM.**

Two phonemes *X* and *Y* may be represented by a single graph *a.* This will seldom present difficulties because in such cases the phonemes seldom contrast with each other.

7. Both / ø / and / œ / are written *eu* in all environments, e.g., / pø /→ *peu;* / sœl /→ *seule.*

8. Both / o / and / ɔ / are written *o* in most environments, e.g, / dɔmino /→*domino;* / parabɔl /→ *parabole;* / mɔd /→ *mode.*

Obviously Rules 7 and 8 are inadequate to generate all spelling of the vowels / ø /, / œ /, / o / and / ɔ /. In addition to *eu,* another graph (*oeu*) is used for both / ø / and / œ /, and there are graphs which note only / ø / and / o /, for instance, *eû* and *ô, au, eau* (plus or minus latent consonant representations) respectively, e.g., *voeu*→/ vø /; *boeuf*→/ bœf /; *jeûner*→/ ʒøne /; *vos, veau, vaux* or *vaut*→/ vo /; *côte*→/ kot /; *pause*→/ poz /. Yet despite superficial appearances to the contrary, the conventional spelling is fairly systematic, and Rules 7 and 8 probably generate about seventy-five per cent of the correct spellings of / ø /, / œ /, / o /, and / ɔ / even without the application of grammatical and lexical rules.

The case of the representation of two phonemes *X* and *Y* by a single graph *a* also applies to the spelling of the semivowels.

9.   The semivowels / j /, / w /, and [ɥ] are written *i, ou,* and *u* respectively, e.g., / mjɛt /→*miette;* / mwɛt /→*mouette;* / mɥɛt /→*muette;* (note that the presence of *tt* instead of *t* is not predictable from the rules we have given so far).

The spelling of / k /, / g / and / ʒ / illustrates a more complex relationship between phonemes and their graphic representations. It will be simpler here to state the environment in terms of vowel letters rather than vowel phonemes. This means that before converting / k /, / g /, and / ʒ / to correct graphic representations, the appropriate phonological, grammatical, and lexical rules which specify the spelling of vowels will need to be applied. We contrast sets of rules stated in terms of the phonological environment versus sets of rules stated in terms of the graphic environment by using the spelling of / k / as an illustration.

10a. / k / is spelled *qu* in final position and before the vowels / i /, / e /, / ɛ /, / ø /, / œ /, / ẽ /, e. g., / pik /→*pique* (note that Rule 4 which specifies that all final consonant phonemes are written with a consonant letter plus *e* must be applied at this point); / nyk /→*nuque;* / ki /→*qui;* / kerir / →*quérir;* / kɛt /→ *quête;* / kø /→ *queue;* / kẽt /→ *quinte;*
11a. / k / is spelled *c* elsewhere, that is, in consonant clusters and before the vowel phonemes / a /, / u /, / y /, / o /, / ɔ /, / õ /, / œ̃ / and the phoneme sequence / wẽ /, e.g., / kav /→*cave;* / kyv /→ *cuve;* / alkɔv /→*alcove;* / kot /→*côte;* / kõt /→*conte;* / kwẽ /→*coin;* / kɥit / [kɥit] →*cuite.*

If the environment which determines the proper graphic representation of / k / is stated in terms of following letters, that is, if vowel spelling rules are applied first, a simpler set of rules is obtained. The set of rules would be as follows:

10b. / k / is written *qu* before vowels written with *e* or *i* or any combination of these with *n,* accents or other vowels in digraphs, e.g., *eu;*
11b. / k / is written *c* in consonant clusters and before vowels written with *a, o, u,* or any combination of these with *n,* accents or other vowels in digraphs, e.g., *ou.*

For instance, the spelling of / kõt / and / kø / would be derived by the application of the following rules:

(a)   / kõt /:/ t /→*te* by Rule 4; / õ /→*on* by Rule 5; / k / before *o*→*c* by Rule 11b—*conte;*
(b)   / kø /:/ ø /→*eu* by Rule 7; / k / before *e* →*qu* by Rule 10b; -*e* added by a grammatical rule which applies to feminine nouns ending with a vowel phoneme—*queue.*

Both alternative sets of rules (10a, 11a; 10b, 11b) may be reversed to convert letters to phonemes. The correct sound can be retrieved from all graphs in the stated environments: *coincer* is unambiguously / kwẽse /, *cascade* is / kaskad /, *quelque* is / kɛlk /, etc.; either set of rules may lead to some wrong spellings of / ka /, which is represented by *qua* in about 60 words and by *ca* in more than 2000 words. Here there is no other recourse but to list the items in which the main rule does not apply. Similarly, final / k / is represented by *c* in some masculine nouns, e.g., *sac, bloc, bouc, bec*. All items with / kã / must be listed individually since about half of them are spelled with *c (camp, cantine, cancer)* and the other half with *qu (quand, cinquante, quantité)*. The conversion of the graph *qua* to sound is problematic since it may be / ka / in *quartier* or / kw / in *quatuor;* going in the other direction, / kwa / is spelled *coi* in *coiffe, quoi* in *quoi* and *quoique*, and *qua* in numerous items, e.g., *quadrangle*.

The rules that govern the spelling of / g / and / ʒ / do not differ appreciably from those we have described above. / g / is written:

12. *gu* before vowels spelled with *i* or *e*, e.g., / gitar /→*guitare;* / fig /→*figue;* / gœl /→*gueule;*
13. *g* in consonant clusters and before vowels spelled with *a, o, u*, e.g., / grãd /→ *grande;* / gõfl /→ *gonfle;* / gamin /→ *gamine*.

/ ʒ / is written:

14. *g* before vowels spelled with *i* or *e* except the combination *eu*, e.g., / ʒifl /→ *gifle;* / ʒerãt /→ *gérante;* / kaʒ /→ *cage;*
15. *j* before vowels spelled with *a, o, u*, and the combination *eu*, e.g., / biʒu /→*bijou;* / ʒoli /→*joli;* / ʒœ /→*jeu;* / ʒœn /→*jeune*.

The total predictability of rules 14 and 15 is reduced by two sets of problems: / ʒ / before / ã / is written *j* if the vowel is represented by *an* or *am (janséniste, jambe)*, but in the great majority of cases where / ã / is written *en* or *em (gendre, gingembre)*, Rule 14 applies; *j* is also used sporadically before / ɛ /, e.g., *jésuite, jersey, jette*. More troublesome for the learner is the introduction of an *e* before vowels usually spelled with *a, o, u* to trigger the application of Rule 14 and the preservation of the same graphic representation for / ʒ / in words belonging to the same derivational and inflectional set, e.g., *mange/mangeons, cage/cageot, village/villageois*.

As is shown below, the letters and letter combinations *c, qu, g, gu*, and *j* enter in a sort of complementary distribution in their representation of the consonants / k /, / s /, / g /, / ʒ /, and there is never any ambiguity in proceeding from the written to the spoken form. The environment is stated in terms of the representation of the vowel that follows the consonant, *i, e*, versus *a, o, u*.

Letter(s):		*c*	*qu*	*g*	*gu*	*j*
Environment:	*i, e*	/ s /	/ k /	/ ʒ /	/ g /	(rarely / ʒ /)
	a, o, u	/ k /	(rarely / k /)	/ g /	---	/ ʒ /

Thus *cinéma* is unambiguously / sinema / and *cou* / ku /; *liquide* is unambiguously / likid /; *gifle* is unambiguously / ʒifl / and *gamin* / gamẽ /; *guide* is unambiguously / gid /; *jardin* is unambiguously / ʒardẽ / and *jérémiade* / ʒeremjad /.

Instances of a phoneme *X* represented by several graphs in a single environment or by several graphs in overlapping environments cannot be effectively handled by phonological rules and appeal must be made to lists. Thus, in final position / ẽ / may be written *in, ein, ain, aim, en (fin, peint, pain, faim,* and *Agen)*, and / ã / may be written *en* and *an* in most positions *(sang, cent)*. The most complicated instance of this type of phoneme-graph relation is illustrated by / s / which is represented by *s, ss, c, ç, t* as follows:

	Initial	In Clusters	Before Semivowel / j /	Intervocalic	Final
s	sire, sa	slave, geste			
ss			(nous) passions	classer	fasse
				polisson	
c	cire		différencier	glacer	face
ç	ça			(nous) poliçons	
t			station		

There is also the rare graph *sc* which occurs in *scie, conscience,* etc. Note, however, that the conversion of these six graphs to / s / is unambiguous in every instance because, while *s, c,* and *t* also represent / z /, / k /, / t / respectively, there is complementary distribution. For example *s* stands for / z / in intervocalic and final position (*lisons, mise*) and for / s / in initial position (*sou*), after a nasal vowel (*pinson*) and in clusters as illustrated in the table above. This last consideration demonstrates again that an adequate notation need not attain perfect and bidirectional correspondence between phoneme and graphic symbol, provided that the conventions used result in a non-contradictory representation of sound features by the symbol used, as well as an unambiguous conversion of the symbols back into sound features.

12.5   PHONOLOGICAL PLUS GRAMMATICAL RULES

The spelling of some vowels and consonants can be specified with greater accuracy if some grammatical information is provided within the phonological rules sequence. Consider the spelling of the consonant / j / which is represented by *i, il, ile, ille, i,* and *y.* To enhance the student's chance of writing that phoneme with better than the 1/6 accuracy that this kind of statement permits, the following set of rules can be formulated.

16.   The consonant / j / is spelled *i* in initial position (we discard marginal items like *yaourt, yole*), e.g., / jɔd /→*iode.*

17.   In final position / j / is spelled:
   a)   *il,* in masculine nouns and adjectives, e.g., / sœj /→*seuil;* / travaj /→*travail;* / vjɛj /→*vieil;*
   b)   *ille,* in feminine nouns and adjectives and in verbs, except when it follows / i / in which case it is spelled *lle,* e.g., / fij /→*fille* but / taj /→*taille,* / travaj /→*travaille.*

18.   Between vowels / j / is spelled *il* when it follows / i / and *ill* elsewhere, e.g., / sijõ / → *sillon;* / bujõ /→*bouillon.*

19.   It is spelled *y* between vowels in words which alternate with forms in / wa / *oi* or [ɥi] *ui,* e.g., *vois/voyons, roi/royal, loi/loyal, fuis/fuyons.*

Since neither native speakers nor foreign learners can be expected to be intimately acquainted with the derivational patterns of the language, items covered by Rule 19, with the exception of verbs, are best furnished by lists. This also applies to the conversion of the various graphic representations to / j /, except that the graphic sequence *ille* stands for both / j / and / l /, e.g., *ville* / vil / but *bille* / bij /, and the pronunciation of each item so written must be memorized individually.

12.6   LATENT CONSONANTS

Many of the so-called final silent letters of French spelling are grammatical markers consisting of latent consonants involved in optional liaison and realized infrequently or an **E** which is often deleted. They can therefore be inferred only from constituents of syntactic units other than those to which they are affixed. Some of these grammatical endings are agreement and concord features which mark syntactic relationships and dependencies. Compare for example *un chapeau bleu* and *une chemise bleue.* The *-e* affixed to the adjective of the second NP does not correspond to any overt phonic signal, and it can only be predicted from the presence of a feminine noun in the NP. This is indicated at the surface level by the choice of the form of the determiner—*une* / yn / instead of *un* / œ̃ /. In order to spell correctly forms that contain such grammatical markers, the learner is required to identify overt phonic signals that often operate in a discontinuous fashion. Some of these are illustrated below:

/ legarsõ /	/ le /	= plural	les garçon*s*
/ ynvrɛfe /	/ yn /	= feminine	une vraie fé*e*
/ døptitpupe /	/ ptit / vs. / pti /	= feminine	petite poupé*e*
	/ dø /	= plural	deux petite*s* poupée*s*
/ ʒfini /	/ ʒ /	= 1st person sg.	je finis
/ ilfini /	/ il /	= 3rd person sg.	il fini*t*
/ ilzãplwa /	/ il /	= 3rd person	
	/ z /	= plural	ils emploi*ent*
/ tyãplwa /	/ ty /	= 2nd person sg.	tu emploi*es*

For example, in / døptitpupe / the choice of / ptit / instead of / pti / before a consonant indicates that the noun is feminine and that it is written with a final *-e.* The numeral / dø / signals plurality and guides the learner in affixing *-s* at the end of the adjective *petite* and the noun *poupée.*

Syntactic distribution also helps to resolve other spelling problems where concord or agreement are not involved. Five of the verb forms of *-er* verbs, which constitute the productive class of French verbs, end with the vowel / e /: *donné, donnez, donner, donnai, donnerai* (for many speakers must be added the forms *donnerais, donnerait,* and *donneraient*). Obviously phonological rules, no matter how sophisticated or detailed, would be of no avail. But the four verb endings *-é, -ez, -er, -ai* can be predicted and written correctly with complete success by inspection of the constructions in which they occur:

il a pass*é*	but	il va pass*er*
vous pass*ez*	but	vous all*ez* pass*er* or vous av*ez* pass*é*
je pass*ai*	but	j'ai pass*é* or je v*ais* pass*er*
je pass*ai*	but	je pass*erai*

The correct representation of the masculine form of adjectives requires knowledge of all liaison variants or, in the case of adjectives which do not occur before a noun (and these constitute by far the largest class), knowledge of the feminine form. Consider the masculine form of *mauvais* as compared to that of *vrai*. When they occur in final position or before a consonant both end with the vowel / ɛ /. But comparison with the pre-vowel form reveals the presence of an overt / z / *(un mauvais habit)* and indicates that a latent **Z**, which is written *-s* or *-x*, must be represented in the spelling. The choice of *-x* or *-s* is idiosyncratic, although *-x* is generally limited to adjectives ending in *-eu (joyeux, heureux).* Now consider the problem of the correct representation of the masculine form of *blanc, allemand,* and *intéressant,* all of which have surface forms ending in / ã / and all of which do not occur normally in pre-nominal position. Comparison with the respective feminine forms *blanche, allemande,* and *intéressante* enables the learner to determine that all three adjectives contain latent consonants and to note the particular latent consonant as *-c, -d,* and *-t* respectively.

In the case of final consonant letters which do not correspond to latent consonants that are realized with any significant frequency, such as those of *enfant, argent, champ* or *rang,* for example, lexical rules must be invoked which relate the base word to derivatives. Thus the *-t* of *argent* can be determined from *argenterie,* the *-p* of *champ* from *champêtre,* the *-g* of *rang* from *rangée* or *ranger.* But it is doubtful that most foreign learners have acquired a morphological system of French rich enough to enable them to make these associations. Like the average native speaker, they will need to memorize these words as idiosyncratic items. In other words, from a practical point of view, the final consonant letters of such words as *enfant, argent, champ,* and *rang* are indeed "useless silent letters."

Many of the genuinely silent consonant letters of French, which require native and foreign learners to memorize long lists of idiosyncratic items, are due to the differentiation of homophones for the "eye." As the Swiss linguist Henri Frei states: "C'est dans le besoin de clarté qu'il faut chercher la véritable raison des chinoiseries de l'orthographe." (*La Grammaire des Fautes.* Paris, 1929.) As a result of various changes in the French phonological and morphophonological systems, French words have lost a considerable part of their original substance (as compared to the form of their Latin etyma or corresponding forms in the other Romance languages). Many words which were formerly phonologically distinct have merged. To distinguish words with different meaning but identical surface form, scribes, grammarians, printers, and all persons who have influenced the development of the French conventional spelling have insisted that they be kept distinct in the orthography. This explains the proliferation of doublets such as *toit* "roof"/*toi* "you," *mur* "wall"/*mûr* "ripe," *conter* "to relate"/*compter* "to count," or triplets such as *foi* "faith"/*fois* "time"/*foie* "liver," *pain* "bread"/*pin* "pine"/*peint* "painted."

12.7   THE INFLUENCE OF FRENCH SPELLING ON PRONUNCIATION

In part because it can be codified and prevented from changing more easily than the spoken language, French spelling enjoys great prestige among French speakers. Most educated middle-class speakers consider the spelling the "real" language and daily speech a debased and corrupted version of it. And speakers who aspire to middle-class status and who are not intimately familiar with the orthoepic norm pronunciation of words subject to variation will often rely on the spelling. In this way, the spelling modifies speech habits and induces important changes in the structure of the language.

For example, the marginal mid vowel contrasts / o / vs. / ɔ / and / ø / vs. / œ / are to a certain degree maintained by orthographic differences, e.g., *fausser* vs. *fossé* and *jeûne* vs. *jeune.* In many cases the contrast between a high-mid and a low-mid rounded vowel corresponds to the presence vs. the absence of a circumflex accent in the spelling, e.g., *jeûne* vs. *jeune* and *côte* vs. *cote.* Spelling distinctions also account for the pronunciation of double consonants within such words as *annuel, illettré, immense, acquis.* Many words, some of which are used infrequently, have been reshaped by spelling pronunciations:

dompteur / dõtœr /→/ dõptœr / "tamer"
sculpteur / skyltœr /→/ skylptœr / "sculptor"
joug / ʒu /→/ ʒug / "yoke"
gageure / gaʒyr /→/ gaʒœr / "wager"
cheptel / ʃɛtɛl /→/ ʃɛptɛl / "cattle"
legs / lɛ /→/ lɛg / "donation"
aloyau / alwajo /→/ alɔjo / "sirloin"

Less widely known is the fact that the third person singular masculine subject pronoun is historically / i /, and that the presence of an / l / before a consonant or a grammatical boundary is a spelling pronunciation. The pervasive influence of the spelling and the attitude of middle-class speakers toward it is illustrated by the following anecdote.

At the turn of the century the famous Danish Romance linguist, Kr. Nyrop, was visiting the French phonetician, Paul Passy, at the home of the latter's father in the Paris suburbs. Passy had just explained the fact about the pronunciation of *il* we have presented above. Obviously displeased with such tolerance of slipshod pronunciation habits, M. Passy *père* interrupted: "Ne l'écoutez pas, Monsieur Nyrop, il ne sait pas ce qu'il dit / insepaskidi /! "

STUDY QUESTIONS

1. Show that the final consonant letter of the following words is not "useless."

   a) saint   Saint-Eustache_____   e) tout   _____

   b) cinq   _____   f) gant   _____

   c) plein   _____   g) fend   _____

   d) blond   _____   h) plus   _____

2. Which of the following vowel representations has multiple but systematic relationships to sound units? Give examples of the various sound values of these representations in contexts where they are fully predictable or unambiguous.

   a) *i*   _____   e) *e*   _____

   b) *u*   _____   f) *an*   _____

   c) *on*   _____   g) *en*   _____

   d) *ou*   _____   h) *in*   _____

3. Which of the following misspellings show nonetheless an awareness of French sound◄─►letter correspondences on the part of the learner?

a)   *jifler (gifler)   e)   *douse (douze)
b)   *lapen (lapin)   f)   *stile (style)
c)   *caneau (canot)   g)   *ventouz (ventouse)
d)   *phon (fond)   h)   *canadiaine (canadienne)

4. Comment on the pedagogical usefulness of the following statement:
"In French the phoneme / k / is spelled:

c colis   cq acquis
cc accord   k kilo
qu quand   ch chrétien
q coq   x oxyton

5. Which of the following spellings of / ʒ / can be considered idiosyncratic from the point of view of sound ◄─► letter correspondences of French?

a)   jeu   b)   jupe   c)   jars
d)   jonc   e)   jésuite   f)   jetée

6. In what way are the following graphic representations ambiguous?
a)   fille
b)   gens
c)   hier
d)   plus

7. Formulate a set of rules for representing / g /.

8. Formulate a set of rules for converting *en* to the appropriate sound(s) in particular environments.

9. What sort of morphophonemic information is required to correctly spell the following words?
   a) gris
   b) romps (je romps)
   c) huit
   d) rang
   e) pain
   f) plongeon
   g) camp
   h) sang

10. Identify the idiosyncratic orthographic features of the following words:
   a) temps
   b) théâtre
   c) siffler
   d) homme
   e) rayon
   f) gaiement

11. In the latest spelling reform project report, the following modifications were suggested: *quinsième, deusième.* What problems do these respellings raise?

12. Comment on the following reformed spelling proposals:
   a) les chous
   b) le caos
   c) l'ortografe
   d) l'aniversaire
   e) les travaus
   f) greques
   g) essencieles
   h) le sistème

PART III

MORPHOLOGY

13

GENDER AND NUMBER

In French, nouns are inflected for **number,** that is, they occur in the singular or the plural form. They are also assigned arbitrarily to one of two **gender** classes, masculine or feminine. Nouns occur usually in phrases accompanied by determiners and adjectives. The dependency of determiners and adjectives on the noun that functions as **head** of a noun phrase is marked by **agreement** in gender and number with the head noun. In other words, whereas nouns belong either to the masculine or the feminine class, determiners and adjectives are inflected for gender as well as for number; they potentially have different masculine and feminine forms. But in French, endings that mark gender and number are generally mute *e* and latent consonants respectively, and the overt realization of these endings is subject to the complex conditions that determine the pronunciation or deletion of latent segments. In this chapter we shall discuss the notion of arbitrariness of gender and the marking of gender and number primarily by means of variation in the form of determiners; in the next chapter, we take up the marking of gender by means of variation in the form of adjectives.

13.1   THE ARBITRARINESS OF GENDER

Beginning learners of French are often told on first contact with the language that there is no inherent semantic or formal feature of nouns that determines their assignment to the masculine or feminine class, and they are warned that it is only by brute memorization that one can learn to assign gender correctly to any particular noun. French grammarians also agree that gender assignment is arbitrary and that "Ce n'est que par l'usage que l'on apprend à reconnaître le genre des noms." Presumably, French children learn the gender of nouns from the presence of determiners or adjectives with different masculine and feminine forms, e.g., *la maison* vs. *le poison, une bonne boisson* vs. *un bon poisson.*

As we shall see in the next section of this chapter, differentiation in the form of determiners is partial only; in many cases determiners have the same form before masculine and feminine nouns. This means that French children are forced to memorize the gender of words on an individual basis, a procedure that is inefficient and, therefore, counter-intuitive. Might there not be some semantic and formal features of nouns that signal to French speakers membership to one or the other of the two gender classes?

In fact, there are some partial relationships between the gender and the meaning of nouns. Nouns that refer to human beings and to familiar animals are feminine if they refer to females but masculine if they refer to males:

Male *Reference*	*Female* *Reference*
le monsieur	la dame
le garçon	la fille
le taureau, le boeuf	la vache
le jars	l'oie

Admittedly, this correlation is only partial, for it does not extend to most animals whose denomination is arbitrary, some species designated with a masculine noun, e.g., *le rat, l'éléphant, le serpent,* and others by a feminine noun, e.g., *la souris, la panthère, la grenouille,* without apparent semantic motivation. Also, most of the nouns designating professions are masculine since these professions were until recently held exclusively by men. Thus Frenchmen are obliged to use such curious constructions as *Madame Dupont est un très bon professeur* or *Ecrivez cette lettre à Madame le Conseiller Municipal.* But that there is a correlation between gender and sex reference for human beings is demonstrated by recently coined feminine terms for traditional male professions, e.g., *un avocat/une avocate, un docteur/une doctoresse* and even *un chef/une chefesse.*

There are also some more limited correlations between the reference of nouns and their gender:

1. Terms that refer to most chemical elements and compounds are masculine: *le chlore, l'hydrogène, le mercure, le titane; le glucose, le maltose; le nitrate, l'acétate.*

2. Color terms used in the abstract are masculine: *le rouge, le noir.*

3. Names of languages are masculine: *le français, le chinois, le volapük.*

4. Names of trees are masculine: *un poirier, un hêtre, un conifère.*

5. Terms referring to geometric figures are masculine: *un hexagone, un octogone.*

There are other correlations involving both form and meaning. For example, any noun ending in / õ / and referring to a process is feminine, e.g., *la tension, la fusion;* any noun ending in *-té* and referring to an abstract concept is feminine, e.g., *la liberté, la parité, l'objectivité;* a noun ending in / œr / and referring either to an agent or a tool or instrument is masculine even if it designates a human female, e.g., *le docteur, l'opérateur, le condensateur, le radiateur.* On the other hand, any noun with the same reference but ending in / is / is feminine, e.g., *une opératrice, une motrice, une calculatrice.*

Recent research by a team of psycholinguists at McGill University in Montreal (André Rigault, "Les marques du genre," *Le Français dans le monde,* No. 57) suggests that French speakers assign gender to many nouns on the basis of phonological form. The final three segments of the more than 30,000 nouns of the 1962 edition of the *Petit Larousse* dictionary were examined and it was found that in many cases they served as a reliable indication of gender. Some of the results are reproduced in Tables 13.1 and 13.2.

Table 13.1 Gender Predictive Value of Last Segment of Nouns

Ending	No. of Fem. Words and Example		No. of Masc. Words and Example		Predictive Value Fem.	Masc.
œ̃	0		17	parfum		100 %
ã	14	dent	1949	camp		99.3
ẽ	9	fin	929	rein		99
ø	5	queue	184	feu		97.4
o	24	peau	841	bateau		97.2
ʒ	85	neige	1368	siège		94.2
m	114	lime	1292	problème		91.9
ε	61	raie	564	lait		90.2
z	551	brise	61	maltose	90%	

Table 13.1 shows the predictive value of some final segments. For example, / œ̃ /, which occurs in 17 masculine nouns, has a masculine predictive value of 100%. The consonant / z / has a feminine predictive value of 90%; it occurs in 551 feminine nouns but only 61 masculine nouns. This means that if a French speaker needs to use an unfamiliar word ending in / z /, his chances of using it with the correct form of determiners and adjectives are nine out of ten if he guesses feminine. If we take into consideration the fact that all nouns designating chemical compounds are masculine (e.g., *le glucose, le maltose*), his chances of guessing correctly increases if he has some vague knowledge of their referent. The longer the ending of a word, the more cues about its gender are available to the speaker. In Table 13.1 we note that a word ending in / r / is more likely to be masculine by a ratio of four to one (*le port* vs. *la peur*). If we know that the next-to-last segment is / œ /, the masculine predictive value increases to 94% *(le facteur* vs. *la peur).* The third from last segment increases the masculine predictive value to nearly 100%, e.g., *le raseur, le docteur, le sonneur, le chasseur.*

That French speakers assign gender, at least in part, on the basis of the phonological form of nouns was demonstrated by the fact that they assigned gender to nonsense words containing some of the final segments with high predictive value on the basis of the value which these segments have in actual words. For instance, a nonsense noun such as */ maso / would have been classed as masculine by most of the native speakers of French who participated in the McGill experiment, whereas */ raʒi / would have been classed as feminine. The reason for these choices is apparent from the data of Tables 13.1 and 13.2. More than 97% of nouns ending in / ʒi / are feminine. It is no doubt the case that French speakers use a combination of semantic and phonological information in correctly assigning gender to unfamiliar nouns. For example, the ending / œr / is strongly loaded for masculine

Table 13.2 Gender Predictive Value of Last Two Segments of Nouns

Ending	No. of Fem. Words and Example		No. of Masc. Words and Example		Predictive Value Fem.	Masc.
ro			117	bureau		100 %
sm			697	communisme		100
aʒ	10	nage	1277	présage		99.2
ɔm	8	pomme	445	homme		98.2
je	15	mariée	735	casier		98
if	3	digestif	128	récif		97.7
ys	4	puce	132	argus		97
st	33	peste	607	reste		94.8
œr	95	peur	1499	bonheur		94
az	72	base	7	vase	91.1%	
yd	43	solitude	4	sud	91.5	
jõ	1785	action	166	pion	92.6	
iz	84	franchise	7	sise	92.4	
te	924	jetée	73	pâté	92.5	
in	540	marine	29	babouine	94	
fi	112	graphie	7	défi	94.2	
ãs	453	chance	13	sens	97.3	
ʒi	246	bougie	5	logis	98	
øz	157	glaneuse			100	

(94% of actually occurring nouns ending with that sequence are masculine), but, in addition, many of them refer to human male agents or instruments and machines, e.g., *un tricheur, un lanceur, un transformateur.*

13.2   GENDER MARKERS

French nouns seldom occur independently in NP's. Except when used in the generic sense with certain prepositions, e.g., *une robe de soie* "a silk dress," *sans argent* "without money," *avec soin* "with care," and in certain verbal phrases, e.g., *chercher fortune* "to seek one's fortune," *demander pardon* "to beg forgiveness," *prendre garde* "to be careful," nouns are preceded by a determiner. In French the function of determiners is not only to express certain semantic attributes of the noun, e.g., definiteness, partitive, etc., but also to signal overtly its gender and whether it is used in the singular or in the plural. Consider the following contrasting sentences:

	(1)	La poste est en face.	"The post office is across the street."
vs.	(2)	Le poste est en face.	"The police station is across the street."
	(3)	Où est ma voile?	"Where is my sail?"
vs.	(4)	Où est mon voile?	"Where is my veil?"

Sentences (1) vs. (2) and (3) vs. (4) contain words with identical phonological form (and, in this instance, identical spelling) which differ in gender. The difference in gender, and ultimately the difference in meaning, are indicated by potential alternations in the vowel immediately preceding the noun: / a / vs. / ø / in the case of (1) vs. (2) and / a / vs. / õ / in the case of (3) vs. (4). Some grammars characterize words such as *la poste* and *le poste* or *une enseigne* "a sign" and *un enseigne* "an ensign" as nouns with dual gender ("noms à double genre"). It is more accurate to consider them simply as homophones (and homonyms, since they are spelled identically) which happen to differ in gender. From this point of view they do not differ from such homophone pairs as *la balle* "the ball" vs. *le bal* "the dance," *la mer* "the sea" or *la mère* "the mother" vs. *le maire* "the mayor," and *la paire* "the pair" vs. *le père* "the father" or *le pair* "the peer."

But clear gender marking is effected only in the singular when the determiner is immediately followed by a word (the head noun itself or an adjective preceding the head noun) beginning with a consonant or a word beginning with a vowel but containing aspirate *h*, e.g., *le garçon*, *le grand restaurant*, *le homard* vs. *la fille*, *la belle maison*, *la hache*. In the plural and in the singular when the determiner is immediately followed by a word beginning with a vowel, the gender distinction is

Table 13.3 Forms of Determiners

	Pre-Consonant		Pre-Vowel		Determiner
	Masculine	Feminine	Feminine	Masculine	
SINGULAR	le / lE /	la / la /	l' / l /		Definite
	mon / mõ /	ma / ma /	mon / mõn /[a]		Poss. 1 sg.
	ton / tõ /	ta / ta /	ton / tõn /		2 sg.
	son / sõ /	sa / sa /	son / sõn /		3 sg.
	notre / nɔtrE /		/ nɔtr /		1 pl.
	votre / vɔtrE /		/ vɔtr /		2 pl.
	leur / lœr /				3 pl.
	ce / sE /	cette / sɛtE /		cet / sɛt /	Demonstrative
	un / œ̃ /	une / ynE /		un / œ̃n /	Indefinite
PLURAL	/ le /	les	/ lez /		Definite
	/ me /	mes	/ mez /		Poss. 1 sg.
	/ te /	tes	/ tez /		2 sg.
	/ se /	ses	/ sez /		3 sg.
	/ no /	nos	/ noz /		1 pl.
	/ vo /	vos	/ voz /		2 pl.
	/ lœr /	leurs	/ lœrz /		3 pl.
	/ se /	ces	/ sez /		Demonstrative
	/ de /	des	/ dez /		Indefinite
	Pre-Consonant	Spelling	Pre-Vowel		

[a] / mõn / varies freely with / mɔn / where the vowel is not nasalized.

neutralized. Consider the classification of the definite, possessive, demonstrative, and indefinite determiners on the basis of their phonological form (Table 13.3).

Clear differentiation between masculine and feminine forms occurs only in the case of the indefinite determiner singular where the feminine form / ynE / contrasts with the masculine pre-vowel form / œ̃n / as well as the masculine pre-consonant form / œ̃ /. Despite the difference in spelling, the feminine form of the demonstrative determiner singular does not differ from that of the masculine pre-vowel form; both are pronounced / sɛt /.

One of the consequences of the neutralization of the distinction of gender in determiners is that there is some fluctuation in the assignment of gender of nouns beginning with a vowel. For example, *amour* is masculine when used in its most neutral sense, e.g., *De quel amour parlez-vous?* But it is feminine when it refers to transient passion, *les folles amours de sa jeunesse.* In fact, *amour* is a noun which is in the process of switching its gender affiliation from feminine to masculine. In the seventeenth century it was generally recognized as a feminine noun, as is shown by the following line from Corneille: *"Qu'avez-vous fait de cette amour?"* Other nouns that have variable gender are *orgue* "organ," which is usually used as masculine in the singular (e.g., *L'orgue de cette église est excellent.*) but as feminine in the plural (*Les orgues modernes sont très grandes.*); *hymne,* which is usually used as masculine when it means song or hymn but as feminine when it means specifically a religious hymn; *oeuvre,* which is used as feminine when it refers to a charitable endeavor (*faire de bonnes oeuvres*) or a specific literary work (*une oeuvre intéressante*) and as masculine when it refers to the totality of the work of an artist, composer or writer (*L'oeuvre de Pascal est très impressionnant.*) or to the foundations, unfinished walls and roof of a building (*le gros oeuvre*). Thus, it does not come as a surprise when one notices that educated speakers of French have difficulty in determining the gender of nouns which begin with a vowel that they use infrequently. A group of five French university students who were asked to provide the gender of a set of thirty words beginning with a vowel made the following wrong identifications (the number indicates the number of subjects who listed the wrong gender):

exode "exodus," m.	2	influenza "flu," f.	1
amitié "friendship," f.	1	oasis "oasis," f.	3
espace "space," m.	1	asile "asylum," m.	1
épisode "episode," m.	1	opprobre "opprobrium," m.	1
apogée "apogee," m.	3	acné "acne," f.	4
ongle "nail," m.	1	armada "armada," f.	1

It should be pointed out that in each case the subject knew the meaning of the noun to which the wrong gender was assigned; subjects were asked to provide an antonym or synonym of each of the thirty nouns on the list (see Study Questions) or to write a brief definition.

STUDY QUESTIONS

1. According to traditional grammars, how do French children learn the gender of nouns?

2. In English, nouns referring to animal species are replaced by *he, she* or *it*. This indicates that nouns referring to persons and animals have potential sex reference. For each of the English nouns below, provide its pronoun substitute and look up the French equivalent and its gender.

dog	he	le chien	cow		
cat	____	_____	horse	____	_____
goose	____	_____	duck	____	_____
mouse	____	_____	lion	____	_____
snake	____	_____	elephant	____	_____

3. Give examples of semantically determined classes of French nouns whose gender is predictable on the basis of their meaning.

    le pommier (all nouns referring to trees are masculine)

4. Provide the French equivalent of the following English nouns. What generalization can you make about the gender of the French nouns?

lemon tree	le citronnier	lemon	le citron	
pear tree	_____	pear	_____	
peach tree	_____	peach	_____	
almond tree	_____	almond	_____	
walnut tree	_____	walnut	_____	

5. Which of the following endings have predictive value for gender assignment? Provide two words belonging to the gender predicted and two which, belonging to the gender not predicted, may be considered exceptional.

    a) / o /   masculine predictive   le bateau   l'eau, une eau
                    value 97.4   le chapeau   la peau

    b) / ʒ /   _____   _____

    c) / ɛ /   _____   _____
                                               _____   _____

    d) / iz /   _____   _____
                                               _____   _____

    e) / te /   _____   _____
                                               _____   _____

    f) / k /   _____   _____
                                               _____   _____

6. How did the McGill research group prove that French speakers assign nouns ending in certain phonemes or groups of phonemes such as / õ /, / o /, / te /, etc. to the correct gender on the basis of phonological information only and not meaning?

7. List five words with identical pronunciation and spelling but belonging to different genders.

   a) la voile "sail" _____   le voile "veil" _____   d) _____ _____

   b) _____ _____   e) _____ _____

   c) _____ _____   f) _____ _____

8. Without referring to Table 13.3, fill in the slots of the following diagram with the appropriate spoken forms of the possessive determiner *son*. Then, provide similar diagrams for the definite, indefinite, and demonstrative determiners.

	Pre-Cons.		Pre-Vowel
	masc.	fem.	
Sg.	sõ	sa	sɔn
Pl.	se		sez

9. A guide on usage published in 1705 lists the following nouns whose gender assignment was controversial at that time:

   a) équivoque   d) anagramme
   b) épitaphe   e) oeuvre
   c) écho   f) amour

   Do you know their gender? Check the accuracy of your response by consulting a dictionary. Why would nouns beginning with a vowel sometimes have variable gender?

10. Ask fellow advanced students of French or native speakers of French, if these are available, to give the gender of the list of vowel initial nouns appearing on p. 149.

14

ADJECTIVE INFLECTION

14.1   GENDER INFLECTION

Traditional descriptions divide adjectives into two classes depending on whether they have distinct written forms for the masculine and feminine. *Invariable* adjectives have identical masculine and feminine forms; *variable* adjectives have distinct masculine and feminine forms. For the latter class, the feminine is derived from the masculine form by the addition of *-e;* variable adjectives whose two variant forms are not so related are considered irregular.

According to the traditional classification, there are six types depending on whether they show: (i) replacement of the final consonant of the basic masculine form, e.g., *vif/vive, heureux/heureuse;* (ii) addition of a grave accent to the vowel preceding the final consonant, e.g., *cher/chère, complet/complète;* (iii) doubling of the final consonant of the stem, e.g., *cruel/cruelle, gros/grosse;* (iv) various consonant and vowel changes, e.g., *blanc/blanche, frais/fraîche;* (v) a special masculine form occurring before a vowel, e.g., *fou/fol/folle, beau/bel/belle;* (vi) special contrasting masculine and feminine suffixes, e.g., *enchanteur/enchanteresse, créateur/créatrice.* But note that for the first three types this classification fails to distinguish adjectives which have a single spoken form *(cher, cruel)* from those that have two *(heureux/heureuse, complet/complète, gros/grosse).*

Table 14.1 offers a classification of French qualifying adjectives which takes into account variation in pronunciation as well as differences in spelling. The number of spoken forms and the relationship between the masculine and feminine forms define three major classes.

The first class comprises adjectives whose masculine and feminine forms are identical. It can be subdivided into adjectives with invariable orthographic forms and adjectives whose masculine and feminine forms are spelled differently. The second class groups adjectives whose masculine form is

Table 14.1 Classification of French Adjectives on the Basis of Their Spoken Forms

All adjectives except those preceded by an asterisk rank among the first 500 words in the *Français fondamental* list modified by utility and lexical valence indexes.

				PRE-NOMINAL	POST-NOMINAL
INVARIABLE	IDENTICAL ORTHOGRAPHIC FORMS			pauvre jeune	simple rouge
	VARIABLE ORTHOGRAPHIC FORMS	CONSONANT FINAL		seul/seule	clair/claire
		VOWEL FINAL		vrai/vraie	bleu/bleue
VARIABLE	**SUBTRACTIVE**	REGULAR	t	petit/petite	fort/forte
			z	mauvais/mauvaise	gris/grise
			d		froid/froide
			s		bas/basse
			ʃ		blanc/blanche
			g		long/longue
			j		*gentil/gentille
			l		*soûl/soûle
		IRREGULAR	d	grand/grande	
			s	gros/grosse	
			j	vieux/vieil/vieille	
			l	beau/bel/belle	
			n	bon/bonne	moyen/moyenne
			r	premier/première	léger/légère
	REPLACIVE	FINAL CONSONANT	f/v		vif/vive
			k/ʃ		sec/sèche
		SUFFIX	-eur/ -rice		*créateur/ créatrice
			-eur/ -euse		*trompeur/ trompeuse
			-eur/ -eresse		*enchanteur/ enchanteresse

derived from the feminine (this, of course, is the reverse of the traditional rule) by the deletion of the final consonant:

petite / ptit /→petit / pti /
froide / frwad /→froid / frwa /
mauvaise / movɛz /→mauvais / movɛ /

Adjectives, such as *petite/petit, froide/froid,* and *mauvaise/mauvais,* whose masculine is derived by deletion of the final consonant are regular. These adjectives are labelled **subtractive**. Irregularities for this type of adjective involve (1) special masculine pre-vowel forms (see Section 14.2 below) or (2) vowel changes in addition to the loss of the final consonant. The vowel alternation shown by adjectives ending in / n / such as *bonne* / bɔn / or *moyenne* / mwayɛn / involves nasalization and nasal vowel adjustment rules (see Section 10.7.1).

Feminine Form	Nasalization	Nasal Vowel Adjustment
bɔn	bɔ̃	
mwajɛn	mwajɛ̃	
fin	*fĩ	fɛ̃
bryn	*brỹ	brœ̃

Adjectives whose feminine form ends in / r / show the effect of the mid vowel raising rule (see Section 10.7.2) in addition to the loss of / r /: *légère* / leʒɛr /→*léger* / leʒe /. In adjectives whose feminine forms ends in / l / and in the adjective *vieille,* loss of the final consonant is accompanied by more idiosyncratic vowel changes:

bɛl	*bɛ	bo
fɔl	*fɔ	fu

Close inspection of the starred incorrect forms reveals that the actually occurring masculine forms are not in fact very idiosyncratic. These adjectives may be considered as a sub-class of those, like *léger/légère,* to which the mid vowel raising rule applies; the feminine form of all three adjectives contains a mid vowel pair member.

The third class is composed of adjectives whose masculine form contains a replacive final consonant (/ viv /→/ vif /; / sɛʃ /→/ sɛk /) or a different suffix. Except for *sec/sèche* and *frais/fraîche,* all replacive adjectives show replacement of / v / by / f /. In the case of adjectives containing variable suffixes, as in *trompeuse/trompeur* for example, both the feminine and the masculine forms consist of the base *tromp-* "to fool, to deceive" plus the feminine suffix *-euse* or the masculine suffix *-eur,* respectively.

In order to use regular variable adjectives correctly the learner of French needs to store only three pieces of information, as it were: (1) the fact that these adjectives have distinct feminine and masculine forms, for there are contrasting variable and invariable adjectives ending in the same consonant, e.g., *soûle/soûl* / sul / vs. / su / vs. *seule/seul* / sœl /; (2) the feminine form; (3) the rule that derives the masculine from the feminine by the deletion of the final consonant. If one attempted to derive the feminine form of these adjectives from the masculine, one would need to memorize for each individual adjective the consonant that is added:

pti + t → ptit
movɛ + z → movɛz
frwa + d → frwad

This is in fact tantamount to memorizing the masculine and the feminine for each individual adjective.

14.2 PRE-NOMINAL ADJECTIVES

The analysis of variable French adjectives in terms of a deletion rule is satisfactory so far as it goes, but it fails to take into account facts about the variation in form found in adjectives that may occur frequently before nouns. As shown in Table 14.2 the feminine form of regular variable adjectives is identical to the masculine pre-vowel form. Thus the form *petite* / ptit / is not strictly speaking the feminine form, and the pronunciation potential of the masculine form is not accounted for by the deletion rule. While it would be descriptively correct and adequate to state simply that variable adjectives that occur in pre-nominal position have a masculine pre-vowel form that is identical to the feminine form, we would require of a more complete analysis that it explain this identity as well as the difference in pronunciation between the masculine pre-consonantal and pre-vowel forms.

Table 14.2 Underlying and Spoken Forms of Regular Variable Adjectives

Underlying Form		Pronunciation	
		Pre-Vowel	*Pre-Consonant/Final*
petit **pEtiT**	Masc	ptit	pti
petite **PEtiT.E**	Fem		

To arrive at this explanation it is important to note that the feminine form of regular variable adjectives such as *petite/petit* has a variant form ending in mute *e* when it occurs before a word containing aspirate *h:* compare *une petite* / ptit / *maison* and *une petite* / ptitø / [ptitə] *hutte.* It would appear then that the feminine form of regular variable adjectives is morphologically complex: it consists of a base plus an inflectional ending, the latter being of course the latent vowel mute *e* **(E)**. The reason that the structural analysis of French adjective inflection (the analysis that postulates the derivation of the masculine form of variable adjectives of the replacive type by the deletion of the final consonant of the feminine form) fails to relate all actually occurring forms is that it operates directly with phonological manifestations rather than abstract underlying forms. The traditional formulation which derives the feminine from the masculine form is essentially correct if re-interpreted as follows: *The feminine form of all French adjectives is derived by the addition of the ending* **-E** *to the base (underlying form); the masculine form consists of the base plus a zero ending.* In order to derive actually occurring forms, liaison and elision rules must be applied.

Consider the adjectives *seule/seul* / sœl / and *petite* / ptit / vs. *petit* / pti /. How can one account for the fact that the first is invariable but that the second has distinct masculine and feminine forms and that, in addition, the masculine pre-vowel form is identical to the feminine form? Invariable adjectives have underlying forms ending in a stable segment (consonant or vowel, including mute *e*) whereas variable adjectives of the additive type have underlying forms ending in a latent consonant:

Adjective Class	Spelling	Underlying Form (Base)
Invariable		
final E	*simple*	sε̃plE
	rouge	ruʒ
final stable vowel	*vrai*	vrε
final stable consonant	*seul*	sœl
Variable		
final latent consonant	*petit*	pEtiT
replacive consonant	*sèche/sec*	seʃ/sεk
replacive suffix	*tromp- -eur/-euse*	trõp -œr/-øz

When the feminine ending **E** is added to the base of an invariable adjective, it is always deleted, except before aspirate *h*, and the actually occurring masculine and feminine forms are generally identical: *le seul train, la seule maison* (but *une seule hutte* [yn sœlə yt]). When it is added to a base ending in a latent consonant, however, the feminine ending **E** serves to protect the latent consonant from deletion before a consonant. Since the masculine form of variable adjectives consists of the bare base, the final latent consonant is not protected, and it is deleted when it occurs before a consonant or in final position, that is, at the end of a noun phrase or predicate. We illustrate the derivation of all the singular forms of regular variable adjectives with *petit* in Table 14.2.

If we take into consideration the total number of singular forms and the relationship between them, irregular variable adjectives of the subtractive type fall into three classes: (1) adjectives that show the effects of the nasalization or mid vowel raising rules in the masculine pre-consonant/final form: *bon, premier,* etc.; (2) adjectives that show voicing shift, *grand, gros;* (3) adjectives that show an idiosyncratic vowel change in the masculine pre-consonantal/final form such as *beau/bel, nouveau/nouvel, fou/fol, mou/mol,* and *vieux/vieil.*

The underlying form of *premier* is **prEmjεR**. All feminine forms contain the ending -**E**, and thus the latent **R** always appears in surface manifestation: *la première fois, la première histoire, elle est première.* In the masculine, **R** appears only in pre-nominal position before a vowel (*au premier étage*). In pre-nominal position before a consonant and in final position, the latent **R** is deleted and the mid-low vowel / ε / is raised to high-mid / e /: *le premier train, c'est le premier.* This is illustrated in Table 14.3. Adjectives such as *léger* and *sot* do not differ substantially from *dernier,* except that they rarely occur in pre-nominal position, and their potential masculine pre-vowel forms (/ leʒεr / and / sɔt /) are seldom attested. Note that the pre-consonant/final form / so / is also accounted for by the deletion of the latent consonant **T** from the base **sɔT** and the raising of the low-mid vowel / ɔ / to high-mid / o /.

Bon has the underlying form **bɔN**. The latent **N** is deleted in the masculine when it occurs before a consonant or in final position and the vowel is nasalized: *une bonne ouvrière, une bonne dactylo,*

Table 14.3 Underlying and Spoken Forms of Adjectives Like "Premier"

Underlying Form			Pronunciation	
			Pre-Vowel	Pre-Consonant/Final
premier **prEmjɛR**	Masc.			prəmje
première **prEmjɛR.E**	Fem.		prəmjɛr	

cette infirmière est très bonne, un bon étudiant / bɔn / vs. *un bon garçon, c'est bon* / bõ /. The determiners *un* and *aucun* pattern very much like *bon,* except that the vowel of the underlying form **yN** is nasalized in the masculine pre-vowel form as well as in the masculine pre-consonant form: *un* / œ̃n / *ami, un* / œ̃ / *camarade* (see Table 14.4).

Table 14.4 Underlying and Spoken Forms of Adjectives Like "Bon" ·

Underlying Form			Pronunciation	
			Pre-Vowel	Pre-Consonant/Final
bon **bɔN**	Masc.			bõ
bonne **bɔN.E**	Fem.		bɔn	

Adjectives that show the effect of the voicing shift rule, such as *grand* and *gros,* may also be viewed as showing a shift of the latent consonant in the masculine: **grãD→grãT, groS→groZ**. This is better motivated than the assumption that the change is the reverse, namely **grãT→grãD** or **groZ→groS**, since the consonant found in the feminine also occurs in derivatives: *grandeur, grosseur.* These adjectives have three different singular spoken forms since the masculine pre-vowel form differs from the feminine form by the change in consonant as well as from the masculine pre-consonant/final form by the presence vs. the absence of the stem-final consonant (see Table 14.5).

Table 14.5 Underlying and Spoken Forms of Voice Shift Adjectives

Underlying Form		Pronunciation	
		Pre-Vowel	Pre-Consonant/Final
grand **grãT**	Masc.	grãt	grã
gros **groZ**		groz	gro
grande **grãD.E**	Fem.	grãd	
grosse **groS.E**		gros	

Adjectives such as *beau/bel* which show an irregular vowel change in the masculine pre-consonant/final form have only two different spoken forms, for the masculine pre-vowel is the same as the feminine form. Note that the vowel change is a special form of mid vowel raising since in all cases the shifted vowel is high-mid or high (see Table 14.6).

Table 14.6 Underlying and Spoken Singular Forms of Irregular Adjectives Like "Beau/Bel"

Underlying Form		Pronunciation	
		Pre-Vowel	Pre-Consonant/Final
bel (beau) bɛL nouvel (nouveau) nuvɛL vieil (vieux) vjɛJ	Masc.		bo nuvo vjø
belle bɛL.E nouvelle nuvɛL.E vieille vjɛJ.E	Fem.	bɛl nuvɛl vjɛj	

Potentially, any French adjective may occur in pre-nominal position. This raises the problem of the underlying form present in the masculine form of such adjectives as *long* and *frais.* Recall that the feminine forms are, respectively, / lõg / and / frɛʃ /. The spellings *long* and *frais* suggest that the masculine underlying forms are lõK and frɛZ. The latter is in fact attested in the idiom *frais et pimpant* / frɛzepɛ̃pɑ̃ / "fresh and spruce," but *long* does not generally occur in pre-nominal position and speakers of French, when queried about the potential pronunciation of phrases such as *un long effort,* will permute the adjective to the post-nominal position to avoid saying / lõkəfɔr / or / lõefɔr /.

Invariable adjectives ending in **E** preceded by a group of consonants have two spoken forms. Before words ending with a vowel, **E** is deleted but it appears before a consonant: *un pauvre homme* / povr ɔm /, *une pauvre orpheline* / povr ɔrfəlin / but *un pauvre type* / povrə tip /, *une pauvre femme* / povrə fam /. In the case of **E** following consonant groups composed of a stop or / f / or / v / plus liquid (KL) and occurring before a consonant, in normal style, both **E** and the liquid member of the consonant group (/ r / or / l /) may be deleted / pov tip /, / pov fam / vs. *(à) juste titre* / ʒystə titr /.

14.3 PLURAL INFLECTION

Traditional grammars state that the plural of adjectives is formed by adding *-s* to the respective singular form. This statement is accurate provided that it is again kept in mind that *-s* is the written representation of **-Z** and that this ending is added to the underlying form of the base of the adjective. As was the case in the determination of the singular forms, elision and liaison rules operating on latent segments (here the plural ending **-Z** as well as the base-final latent consonant, if any, and the feminine ending **-E**) must then be applied.

Consider the consequences of adding **-Z** to an invariable adjective such as *joli.* The plural marker will only be realized phonetically when the adjective precedes a word beginning with a vowel, both in the masculine and in the feminine: *les jolis oiseaux* / ʒɔliz wazo /, *les jolies alouettes* / ʒɔliz alwɛt /. It will not be realized before a consonant or in final position: *les jolis moineaux* / ʒɔli mwano /, *les jolies perdrix, ils sont jolis* / ʒɔli /, *je les trouve jolies* / ʒɔli /. In invariable adjectives ending in **E** preceded by a consonant group of the type (KL), both **E** and **Z** are realized in the plural before a vowel (see Table 14.7).

Table 14.7 Underlying and Spoken Forms of Invariable Adjectives

Underlying Form	Pronunciation			
	Singular		Plural	
	Pre-V	Pre-C	Pre-C	Pre-V
pauvre **povrE** pauvres **povrE.Z**	povr	povrə/pov		povrəz/povz

In the case of variable adjectives whose base ends in a latent consonant, the adjunction of the plural ending **-Z** causes the latent consonant of the base never to be realized in the masculine plural since it is always followed by a consonant: *les petits garçons* **pEtit.Z garsõ.Z**→/ pti garsõ /, *les petits enfants* **pEtit.Z ãfã.Z**→/ ptiz ãfã /. Whereas the latent **T** of the base is deleted before **-Z**, the latter is realized when it occurs before a vowel. In the feminine plural, the **T** appears before both vowels and consonants, and the plural ending **-Z** appears before a vowel. Thus, while invariable adjectives like *joli* or *seul* have a total of two spoken forms, and invariable adjectives ending in a consonant group KL have three forms, regular variable adjectives have four (see Table 14.8).

Table 14.8 Underlying and Spoken Forms of Regular Variable Adjectives

Underlying Form			Pronunciation			
Singular	Plural		Singular		Plural	
			Pre-V	Pre-C	Pre-C	Pre-V
petit **pEtiT**	petits **pEtiT.Z**	Masc.		pti		ptiz
petite **pEtiT.E**	petites **pEtiT.E.Z**	Fem.	ptit			ptitz

It is important to note that although regular variable adjectives have four written and spoken forms, there is no isomorphy between the written and the spoken forms. For example, the pre-consonant form / pti / may only be characterized as masculine, for it is both singular and plural; the form / ptit / is masculine (pre-vowel) and feminine, singular and plural (feminine, pre-consonant). Only the forms in which the plural ending **-Z** is phonetically manifest (/ ptiz / and / ptitz /) are unambiguously feminine or masculine and marked for plural.

The masculine plural pre-vowel spoken form is in all variable adjectives derived from the masculine singular pre-consonant form by the addition of / z /; compare the spoken forms of adjectives of that type that occur in the various masculine environments:

	Singular Pre-Vowel	*Singular and Plural Pre-Consonant*	*Plural Pre-Vowel*
petit	ptit	pti	ptiz
grand	grãt	grã	grãz
gros	groz	gro	groz
bon	bɔn	bõ	bõz
beau/bel	bɛl	bo	boz
vieux	vjɛj	vjø	vjøz
dernier	dɛrnjɛr	dɛrnje	dɛrnjez

Thus, in the case of irregular adjectives characterized by various vowel changes (nasalization and mid vowel raising), the specially marked masculine plural form will reflect the change. In the case of *mauvais,* the masculine singular pre-vowel and plural pre-vowel forms will be identical with regard to pronunciation but not with regard to underlying form. The underlying form of that adjective ends in **Z** (**movɛZ**), and the / z / that appears in, say, *un mauvais appartement* / **movɛz** / is the realization of the latent consonant of the base. But the / z / that appears in *de mauvais appartements* is the plural ending **-Z.** The **Z** of the base is deleted in the plural; **movɛZ.Z→movɛ.Z,** and the plural ending **-Z** may then appear if the adjective occurs before a vowel.

Adjectives ending in *-al* fall into two classes. The smaller of the two classes is made up of invariable adjectives. Although they show four different written forms, e.g., *final, finale, finals, finales,* invariable *-al* adjectives have a single pronounced form, e.g., / final /. Other adjectives of this class include *fatal, glacial, idéal, jovial, natal, naval, théâtral.*

The second and larger group of adjectives ending in *-al* have an idiosyncratic masculine plural form ending in / o / *-aux,* e.g., *brutal/brutaux, général/généraux, normal/normaux, principal/ principaux,* etc. Thus these adjectives have two oral forms, although, like adjectives of the first group, they have four written forms. This second group of *-al* adjectives can best be accounted for by positing two different underlying forms. The regular underlying form ends in a stable **l,** but the underlying form for the masculine plural ends in latent **L** (see Table 14.9). In the masculine plural, when the plural ending **-Z** is added to the base, **L** is deleted: *brutal* + plural = **brytaL.Z→bryta.Z.** In

Table 14.9 Underlying and Spoken Forms of "-al" Adjectives Like "Brutal"

Underlying Form			*Pronunciation*	
Singular	*Plural*		*Singular*	*Plural*
brutal **brytal**	brutaux **brytaL.Z**	Masc.		bryto
brutale **brytal.E**	brutales **brytal.E.Z**	Fem.	brytal	

addition, when the **L** is deleted the **a** of the last syllable is changed to **o**: *brutaux* **bryto** / bryto /. Adjectives like *brutal* show two idiosyncratic features: (i) the presence of two different underlying bases; (ii) the replacement of **a** by **o** after the deletion of **L**. The feminine forms are underlain by the regular base ending in *-al.*

14.5   NOUNS WITH SPECIAL PLURAL FORMS

Except for a small group (e.g., *bal, carnaval, chacal, festival, récital,* etc.), nouns ending in *-al* (all of which are masculine) have a special plural form ending in *-aux.* Nouns ending in *-ail,* such as *travail,* behave like most nouns ending in *-al:*

Singular	*Plural*
journal **ʒurnal** / ʒurnal /	journaux **ʒurnaL.Z** / ʒurno /
mal **mal** / mal /	maux **maL.Z** / mo /
travail **travaj** / travaj /	travaux **travaJ.Z** / travo /

The differences in pronunciation (reflected by differences in spelling) are accounted for by positing an underlying form ending with a stable consonant in the singular and another ending with a latent consonant in the plural. After the deletion of the **L** before the plural ending **-Z**, **a** changes to **o**.

Differences in the spoken forms of the singular and plural forms also characterize a small group of masculine nouns. In addition to the loss of the final consonant before the plural ending these nouns also show various vowel changes:

Singular	*Plural*
ciel **sjɛl** / sjɛl /	cieux **sjɛL.Z** / sjø /
oeil **œj** / œj /	yeux **joeJ.Z** / jø /
oeuf **oef** / œf /	oeufs **oeF.Z** / ø /
os **ɔs** / ɔs /	os **ɔS.Z** / o /
aïeul **ajoel** / ajœl /	aïeux **ajoeL.Z** / ajø /

For these nouns, again, it is postulated that the singular and plural forms differ by the presence, as the final segment of their underlying form, of a stable versus a latent consonant, respectively. In all cases, except that of *oeil/yeux* and *ciel/cieux,* the vowel change involves mid vowel raising and is predictable. In *yeux* there is, in addition to the application of the mid vowel raising rule, the insertion of / j / at the beginning of the plural form. Two nouns, *cerf* and *ours,* have a variant plural form that shows the loss of the final consonant of the base before the plural ending **-Z**. For these variant pronunciations in which the singular and plural forms differ, we posit the following underlying forms:

Singular	*Plural*
cerf **sɛrf** / sɛrf /	cerfs **sɛrF.Z** / sɛr /
ours **urs** / urs /	ours **urS.Z** / ur /

The preferred variant form of the plural is identical to the singular form in pronunciation, that is,

Singular	*Plural*
cerf **serf** / sɛrf /	cerfs **serf.Z** / sɛrf /
ours **urs** / urs /	ours **urs.Z** / urs /

STUDY QUESTIONS

1. Give the underlying form and all attested singular forms of the following adjectives.

   a) vert   Underlying Form: **verT**

	Masc.		Fem.
	−C	−V	
	vɛr	vɛrt	

   b) doux

   c) brun

   d) mol/mou

   e) malheureux

2. List two adjectives that end with the following latent consonants (list the adjectives in the conventional spelling).

   a) T   _____   _____

   b) Z   _____   _____

   c) S   _____   _____

   d) N   _____   _____

   e) R   _____   _____

3. Classify the following adjectives into three classes as follows: (A) adjectives whose masculine form differs from the feminine by the loss of the final consonant of the stem only; (B) adjectives which, in addition, show a vowel change; (C) adjectives which, in addition, show a consonant change.

A	B	C

   grande, brune, saine, légère,
   grise, belle, heureuse, sotte,
   grosse, vieille, allemande, mauvaise

4. The following adjectives are listed as "irregular" in traditional grammars because their feminine written form shows doubling of the final consonant letter of the masculine:
   a) gros/grosse   c) cruel/cruelle   e) sot/sotte
   b) bon/bonne   d) pareil/pareille
   How would you classify these adjectives from the point of view of the variation in spoken form which they show?

5. In what way are *vif, sec, trompeur* idiosyncratic?

6. List five types of idiosyncrasies to be found in the derivation of singular and plural adjective forms. Provide an example for each type.

7. Provide *all* forms of the following adjectives and show the distribution of these forms with the aid of a diagram such as that given as model in (1) above.
   a) grande   b) nouvelle   c) grosse

8. Consider the following forms of *mauvais: un mauvais ami, deux mauvais amis.* Show how the final / z / that occurs in both these forms has a different source in the underlying form.

15

VERB INFLECTION: PRESENT STEM SYSTEM

15.1   GENERAL STRUCTURE OF THE FRENCH VERB

In French, the verb is the word class that shows the largest number of variant forms. Whereas adjectives have at most five different spoken forms (six if we take into consideration the form that occurs before feminine nouns beginning with aspirate *h*), the morphologically simplest class of verbs shows at least thirteen different spoken forms. For instance, disregarding the so-called literary tenses (preterite, *passé simple,* and imperfect subjunctive) and potential liaison forms, verbs belonging to the traditional *-er* class (here illustrated with *passer*) show the following actualized spoken forms:

Non-Finite/ Present	Present Subjunctive/ Imperfect	Imperfect	Future	Conditional
pasɑ̃	pasjõ	pasɛ	pasre	pasrɛ
pase			pasra	pasərjõ
	pasje			
pas			pasrõ	pasərje
pasõ				

In a spontaneous style of spoken French, the number of forms may be further reduced by the use of *on* instead of *nous* to express the first person plural; nonetheless, the total number of actualized spoken forms cannot be reduced below nine.

Variation in the form of French verbs is determined by two sets of deep-level categories: **person reference** and **tense-mood**. Tense-mood distinctions are expressed by several sets of tense-person endings as well as stem extensions. For example, the tense-person ending *-ions* signals either timeless (subjunctive) or past as well as first person plural reference: *nous chantions, il faut que nous chantions, nous chanterions, il fallait que nous chantassions.* In *-ions* one might choose to consider *-i-* as a stem extension signalling past or timeless and *-ons* as the first person plural (1 pl) ending, but for reasons that go beyond this introductory description we prefer to consider *-ions* as a single, albeit semantically complex, morphological unit. The most important stem extensions are the present stem extension *-is-* found in such verbs as *finir/ils finissent* and the future stem extensions *-er-, -ir-, -r-* of the regular verb classes exemplified by *chanter, finir* or *partir,* and *vendre* respectively. Person reference is expressed by tense-person endings or by alternations in the form of the stem. For instance, whereas 1 pl or 2 pl are always expressed by overt tense-person endings (*-ons, -ez, -ions, -iez; -mes, -tes*) the distinction between 3 sg and 3 pl is expressed in the present of many verb types by differences in the form of the stem, e.g., *il vend* / vã / vs. *ils vendent* / vãd /. In addition to the tense-person endings there are three non-finite endings characterizing three verb forms—the present participle, the infinitive, and the past participle—that may assume non-verbal functions such as subject or object of a sentence or adverbial and adjectival modification: *Boire un petit coup c'est agréable, Il est entré en chantant, Nous l'avons trouvée peinte en rouge.*

15.2 TENSE-PERSON ENDINGS

Most of the tense-person endings consist of latent consonants whose realization is only optional. Thus, except for those that are realized obligatorily in all environments, tense-person endings generally effect only potential differentiation between verb forms. These potential differentiations are usually not realized in spoken, spontaneous-style French.

Except in the present and the past perfect, all French verbs take the same sets of tense-person endings. There are three sets of these general tense-person endings.

Person Reference	Timeless	Future	Past Imperfect
1 sg	-E	-e	-ɛZ
2 sg	-EZ	-aZ	-ɛZ
3 sg	-E	-a	-ɛT
3 pl	-ET	-õT	-ɛT
2 pl	-jeZ	-eZ	-jeZ
1 pl	-jõZ	-õZ	-jõZ

There is considerable overlap in the form of tense-person endings from one set to another. For instance, the past imperfect and the timeless sets have identical 1 pl and 2 pl endings. Nonetheless, as a whole, each set of tense-person endings is distinct from all others. There are two sets of present tense-person endings. These define important verb classes and determine variation in the form of the present stem. These two sets of present tense-person endings differ only in the singular:

Person Reference	Set A		Set B
1 sg	-E		-Z
2 sg	-EZ		-Z
3 sg	-E		-T
3 pl		-ET	
2 pl		-eZ	
1 pl		-õZ	

There are also two sets of past perfect endings. The distribution of each set with respect to verb classes corresponds to that of the corresponding present set. Thus, Sets A of the present and past perfect endings are constituted by a zero form (∅); in the case of the 1 sg form there is also a vowel change (a→e), e.g., *je chantai* / ʃɑ̃te / vs. *il chanta*. A similar vowel change (a→ɛ) occurs preceding the 3 pl ending -rET:

Person Reference	Set A		Set B
1 sg	(a→ e) -∅		-Z
2 sg		-Z	
3 sg	-∅		-T
3 pl	(a → ɛ) -rET		-rET
2 pl		-tEZ	
1 pl		-mEZ	

15.3   STEM SYSTEMS

French verb **stems** are composed of a **base**, which carries the meaning of the verb, and a **stem extension**. There are three stems from which the various tenses—tense-mood (**finite forms**)—and the three non-finite forms are derived. Tenses are sets of six potentially distinct forms marked for person reference and tense-mood; the forms are termed **finite** forms.

Present Stem	Future Stem	Past Stem
Present Indicative	Future	
Imperfect	Conditional	Past perfect
Present subjunctive		(Imperfect subjunctive)
Present participle	Infinitive	Past participle

The past perfect and the imperfect subjunctive are not generally used in spoken French, and they will be left out of consideration in the remaining sections of our treatment of verb form variation.

Individual finite forms consist of one of the three stems plus one of the sets of tense-person endings:

Tense	Stem	Set of Endings
Present indicative	Present	Present
Imperfect	Present	Past (imperfect)
Present subjunctive	Present	Timeless
Future	Future	Future
Conditional	Future	Past (imperfect)

The present stem consists of the bare stem, except for verbs like *finir, remplir, rougir* which may be analyzed as composed of a base plus the stem extension *-iss-* / is /. Many of these verbs are derived from adjective bases (*rouge-rougir, pâle-pâlir, grand-aggrandir*) or nouns (*fin-finir, choix-choisir*), and the *-iss-* stem extension often has an **inchoative** meaning: "becoming X" or "causing something to become X." Thus the stem *finiss-*, which occurs in such verb forms as *ils finissent* or *nous finissions*, consists of the base *fin-* / fin / "end, finish" and the inchoative stem extension *-iss-*.

The future stem consists of the base plus, for regular verbs, one of three stem extensions: *—Er-*, *-ir-*, or *-r*, depending on the verb's class affiliation. The infinitive of all regular verbs may be viewed as the occurrence of the bare future stem. Differences between the future stem and the infinitive, such as the presence of the vowel / e / instead of mute *e* for *-er* verbs or of final mute *e* in *-re* verbs, may be accounted for in terms of morphophonemic changes that affect vowels occurring in stem final position.

The past stem is derived by the addition of a stem extension consisting of a vowel: *-a-* for *-er* verbs, *-i-* for *-ir* verbs, etc. Since the only form derived from the past stem which occurs frequently in spoken French is the past participle, we will attempt to account only for the derivation of the past participle rather than the entire past stem system.

15.4   PRESENT STEM SYSTEM VARIATION

Traditionally, French verbs are listed in dictionaries and classified on the basis of their infinitive. This is tantamount to classifying them on the basis of their future stem since it is on that stem that the infinitive is formed. As we will point out in Chapter 16, the classification of verbs on the basis of the future stem is very useful and has much to recommend it. But the traditional classification fails to distinguish verbs that have the same infinitive ending but whose behavior in the present system differs widely. For instance, while *cueillir* and *partir* both have infinitives ending in *-ir*, they take different sets of present endings: *je cueille* vs. *je pars*. In addition, *cueillir* has the single present stem / koej- /, whereas *partir* has variant long and short present stems: / part- / vs. / par /. Verbs with different infinitive endings may behave alike in the present system. Thus, *conclure, cueillir* and *donner* all have a single present stem.

The present stem system tenses have the highest relative frequency and include the present indicative, whose semantic range is the broadest in the sense that it may be used to refer to present (*Je pars maintenant*), past (*Hier j'ai vu Marie devant la poste; alors je lui dis . . .*) and future (*Je pars demain*) events. For this reason, a classification of French verb forms on the basis of their variation in form in the present system is more revealing of the morphological structure of verbs in spoken French and is more directly applicable to various pedagogical problems.

In addition to the choice of Set A versus Set B present endings, French verbs may be classified according to the number of present stems they show, the morphophonological relationship between variant stems, and the distribution of the variant stems within the present stem system. As will be demonstrated below, there is a direct relationship between the choice of set of present endings and stem variation.

15.5　ONE-STEM VERBS

One-stem verbs have the same stem in all present system forms. They show only three different present indicative forms in a spontaneous style of spoken French, e.g., *passer:*

	Singular	*Plural*
1		pasõ
2	pas	pase
3		

One-stem verbs include most *-er* verbs as well as a small group of *-ir* and *-re* verbs:

Infinitive	*3 sg Pres Ind*	*3 pl Pres Ind*	*3 Pres Subj*
ouvrir	ouvre	ouvrent	ouvre
cueillir	cueille	cueillent	cueille
courir	court	courent	coure
conclure	conclut	concluent	conclue

Most one-stem verbs take Set A present endings, although there are verbs, such as *courir* and *conclure* which take Set B.

One-stem verbs whose present stem ends with the high vowel **u** or **y** have an automatic alternation between the high vowel and its corresponding semivowel:

il tue / ty /　　　nous tuons [tɥõ] ~ / tyõ /
il loue / lu /　　　nous louons / lwõ / ~ / luõ /

Where it occurs in stem final position, the high vowel is realized as a syllabic, i.e., [y] or [u], but when it occurs in forms containing an ending beginning with a vowel, the high vowel is realized as a syllabic or a non-syllabic, i.e., [y] or [ɥ]; [u] or [w]. See Chapter 8 for a more detailed discussion of this type of free variation.

15.6   TWO-STEM VERBS

In our treatment of adjective gender inflection we pointed out that the shortened masculine form of subtractive variable adjectives resulted from the application of the liaison rule to a base ending in a latent consonant, i.e., **pEtiT #** →/ pti / and **pEtiT.garsõ**→/ pti / (as opposed to **pEtiT.otel**→/ ptit / and **pEtiT.E**→/ ptit /). In subtractive two-stem verbs the full present stem appears before tense-person endings which begin with a vowel, whereas the stem final consonant is lost before endings consisting only of a latent consonant. The variation in form of the present stem of these verbs can therefore best be accounted for if we assume that their present stem ends in a latent consonant. The underlying representation of the forms of *partir,* for example, are:

	Singular	Plural
1	parT.Z par.s	parT.õZ part.ons
2	parT.Z par.s	parT.eZ part.ez
3	parT.T par.t	parT.ET part.ent

When the liaison rule is applied to the singular forms, the stem final latent consonant is deleted since it occurs before another latent consonant; in the plural, the stem final latent consonant is protected by the vowel of the ending and always appears.

Thus the primary difference between single-stem and subtractive two-stem verbs is that the latter have a present stem ending in a latent consonant but the former have a present stem ending in a stable consonant or a vowel. Compare, for example, *bouillir* and *cueillir.* The latter has the underlying stem **koej-** and the former, **buJ-**; in addition these two verbs take different sets of present endings, but that difference is not determining:

bouillir Present Stem: *bouill-* **buJ**

	Underlying Form		Pronunciation	
	Singular	*Plural*	*Singular*	*Plural*
1	bou.s buJ.Z	buJ.õZ bouillons		bujõ
2	bou.s buJ.Z	buJ.eZ bouillez	bu	buje
3	bou.t buJ.T	buJ.ET bouillent		buj

cueillir Present Stem: *cueill-* **kœj**

	Underlying Form		Pronunciation	
	Singular	Plural	Singular	Plural
1	cueille kœj.E	cueillons kœj.ŏZ		kœjŏ
2	cueilles kœj.EZ	cueillez kœj.eZ	kœj	kœje
3	cueille kœj.E	cueillent kœj.ET		

One-stem verbs like *courir* and *conclure* also have a present stem ending in a stable consonant, although they take Set B endings: *il court* / kur / vs. *ils courent* / kur /; *il conclut* / kŏkly / vs. *ils concluent* / kŏkly /. The 3 pl form is identical to the singular forms since the stem final r is always realized regardless of whether it precedes a vowel or consonantal ending. Note that one-stem verbs which do not belong to the *-er* group have stems ending in **j-**, **r-** and clusters **KL-**; these types of final consonants are more generally stable than latent.

Haïr differs from regular subtractive two-stem verbs in that a vowel change accompanies the deletion of the stem final consonant: *ils haïssent* ai**S.ET** / ais / vs. *il hait* ε**S.T** / ε /.

The timeless and past tense-mood endings and the present participle ending all contain an initial vowel or mute *e*. Accordingly, the present subjunctive, imperfect, and present participle forms of two-stem verbs will always contain the full stem. Compare:

	Infinitive	3 sg Pres Subj	3 sg Impf	Pres Part
One-stem	passer cueillir courir	il passe il cueille il coure	il passait il cueillait il courait	passant cueillant courant
Two-stem	finir partir	il finisse il parte	il finissait il partait	finissant partant

The distribution of the variant stems of subtractive two-stem verbs is shown in Table 15.1.

Subtractive two-stem verbs show several patterns in the orthographic representation of the deleted latent consonant in present/indicative singular forms. The stem final latent consonant is never represented in *-ir* verbs: *je pars, il part, tu finis, il dort.* In *-re* verbs the stem final latent consonant ending is always represented in 1 sg and 2 sg forms: *je rends, tu bats, je romps, tu vaincs.* In *vaincre* and all *-dre* verbs the stem final latent consonant ending appears in the 1 sg and 2 sg but not the 3 sg: *il vainc, il vend, il descend.* Latent **-T** and the 3 sg ending **-T** coalesce into a single *t: il bat, il met;* finally, note *il rompt.* All *-er* verbs ending in **ʒ-**, represented by *g,* and *s,* represented by *c,* show

Table 15.1 Distribution of Variant Present Stems of Subtractive (above) and Vowel Replacive (below) Two-Stem Verbs.

Person-Reference	Present Ind.	Present Subj.	Imperfect	Pres. Part.
1 sg	- - - -	- - - -	- - - -	
2 sg	SHORT STEM	- - - -	- - - -	
3 sg	- - - -	- - - -	- - - -	
3 pl	- - - -	- - - -	- - - -	
	LONG (REGULAR) STEM			
2 pl	- - - -	- - - -	- - - -	
1 pl	- - - -	- - - -	- - - -	
Non-Finite				- - - -

Person-Reference	Present Ind.	Present Subj.	Imperfect	Pres. Part.
1 sg	- - - -	- - - -	- - - -	
	SHORT (CHANGED) STEM			
2 sg	- - - -	- - - -	- - - -	
3 sg	- - - -	- - - -	- - - -	
3 pl	- - - -	- - - -	- - - -	
	LONG (REGULAR) STEM			
2 pl	- - - -	- - - -	- - - -	
1 pl	- - - -	- - - -	- - - -	
Non-Finite				- - - -

predictable orthographic alternations. In Chapter 14 it was pointed out that in order to spell bases uniformly, *e* is added to *g* in environments where it would otherwise have the value / g / and a cedilla is added to *c* in environments where it would otherwise have the value / k /, namely, in the case of both letters, before vowels represented by *a, o, ou* or combinations in which these letters enter. Rather than *j, ge* is used to represent ʒ- before the endings *-ons, -ais, -ait, -aient* and *-ant* in such verbs as *nager* (*je nage* vs. *nous nageons);* similarly, s- is spelled *ç* before the same endings to avoid the alternation of *s* and *c*, e.g., *je commence* vs. *je commençais.*

15.7   VERBS WITH STEM FINAL "j"

Many verbs, mostly from the *-er* group, have two present stems differing by the presence and absence of / j /. These verbs are marked off from subtractive two-stem verbs by two features: (1) most take Set A endings; (2) the shorter stem occurs in the singular and 3 pl forms of the present indicative and present subjunctive as well as the three singular persons (see Table 15.1). Verbs of this type, like one-stem verbs, have only three different spoken forms in the present indicative, since the 3 pl and the singular forms are identical. This is illustrated with the verb *envoyer* whose full present stem is *envoy-* ãvwaj-:

	Singular	Plural
1		ãvwajõ
2	ãvwa	ãvwaje
3		

Members of this class of two-stem verbs include *-er* verbs whose present stem ends in *oy-* **waj-** (*employer, nettoyer, envoyer,* etc.), in *uy-* **yij-** (*ennuyer, appuyer,* etc.), and in *ay-* **εj-** (*payer, balayer,* etc.), as well as *voir, croire,* and *fuir.* Verbs with truncated stem final j- must be distinguished from one-stem verbs ending with a stable j- such as *réveiller, briller, aiguiller,* or *cueillir* on the one hand, and subtractive two-stem verbs ending in latent **J-** such as *bouillir,* on the other. In the case of *bouillir* the realization of **J-** before a vowel and its deletion before a latent consonant (*il bout* vs. *ils bouillent*) is quite straightforward. In the case of *réveiller, briller, aiguiller,* and *cueillir* the stem final j appears predictably in all present system forms. The deletion of j in the set of verbs under consideration cannot be accounted for in terms of general morphophonological rules of French and are idiosyncratic features of these verbs. The assumption that these verbs have stems ending in a vowel (i.e., *envoy-* **ãvwa-,** *ennuy-* **ãnyi-,** etc.) and that a / j / is inserted automatically when an ending beginning with a vowel follows immediately does not hold since we have verbs like *créer* in which vowel-to-vowel sequences do occur: *nous créons* / kreõ /.

There is a tendency in spontaneous style to treat verbs with a truncatable stem final j as if they were one-stem verbs with stem final j, such as *briller, réveiller,* or *cailler.* The stem final j appears in the singular and 3 pl of the present indicative and present subjunctive: *il paye* / il pεj /, *ils balayent* / balεj /.

Asseoir shows two patterns of variation in the present system. In *français populaire* it usually behaves like a two-stem verb with truncatable stem final j: *nous nous assoyons* / aswajõ / vs. *ils s'assoient, il s'assoit* / aswa /; *je m'assoyais* / aswajε /; *il faut que je m'assoie* / aswa /. In more formal style, generally, the present stem is not **aswaj-** but **asεj.** The stem final j is not truncated before endings that begin with **E** but only in the singular forms of the present indicative. In these forms the deletion of j is accompanied by a change of the vowel from / ε / to / je /:

1 pl Pres Ind	3 pl Pres Ind	3 sg Pres Ind
asseyons / asεjõ /	asseyent / asεj /	assied / asje /

(It would appear that / asje / may be accounted for by the transposition of / j / (/ asjε /) and the subsequent application of the mid vowel raising rule (/ asje /).)

15.8   VOWEL REPLACIVE TWO-STEM VERBS

A large number of *-er* verbs have two present stems whose distribution parallels that of truncated stem final **j** verbs and which differ from each other by their final vowel (see Table 15.1). These verbs take Set A endings and have only three spoken forms in the present indicative:

	Singular	Plural
1		mEnõ
2	mɛn	mEne
3		

(The symbol / E / is here used to indicate that the actual pronunciation of the stem is [mn], [mØn], [mœn], or [mən].) The variations in vowel quality shown by most verbs of this group are predictable from the phonological constitution of the stem. The first large group consists of verbs whose stem final vowel is **E.** That vowel cannot occur in word final checked (closed) syllables and is replaced by ɛ in all forms in which it would occur in that position, namely forms which end in latent segments (**E** + latent consonants):

Infinitive	*1 pl Pres Ind.*	*1 sg Pres Ind*
mener	menons **mEn.õZ**	mène **mEn.E** / mɛn /
jeter	jetons **ʒET.õZ**	jette **ʒEt.E** / ʒɛt /
feuilleter	feuilletons **fœjEt.õZ**	feuillette **fœjEt.E** / fœjɛt /

The second group of vowel replacive two-stem verbs contain stem final **e.** That vowel shifts to ɛ whenever it occurs in word final checked syllables. It will be recalled that the vowel / e / is excluded from final checked syllable (see Chapter 7), and the replacement of **e** by ɛ in verb stems is part of a general morphophonological process of French. Compare:

Infinitive	*1 pl Pres Ind*	*1 sg Pres Ind*
répéter	répétons **repet.õ** / repetõ /	répète **repet.E** / repɛt /
aérer	aérons **aer.õ** / aerõ /	aère **aer.E** / aɛr /
sécher	séchons **seʃ.õ** / seʃõ /	sèche **seʃ.E** / sɛʃ /

The distinction between / e / and / ɛ / is neutralized in non-final syllables so that many speakers use a vowel of intermediate quality in such forms as *nous répétons* or *vous séchez;* other speakers use a / ɛ / in these forms by analogy with the forms in which the stem final vowel shifts to / ɛ /, that is, they pronounce *répétons* as / repɛtõ /. On the other hand, speakers who always use / e / in open syllables will re-interpret verbs whose stem contains an underlying final ε as replacive vowel two-stem verbs. For example *fêter* has a present stem whose underlying form is **fɛt-**, and, according to the orthoepic norm, its 1 pl and 1 sg present indicative forms should be *nous fêtons* / fɛtõ / and *je fête* / fɛt /, respectively. But speakers for whom / e / and / ε / are in complementary distribution would pronounce these two forms instead as / fetõ / and / fɛt /.

There exist two orthographic conventions to represent verbs that show the replacement of **E** by ε. The changed vowel is represented by *è* (*il mène, il soulève, il épèle*) or by retaining *e* but doubling the following consonant letter (*il jette, il appelle, il ficelle*). This distinction is purely orthographic and in no way corresponds to differences in morphophonological behavior.

In subtractive two-stem verbs ending in the latent consonant **Ñ** the stem final vowel will automatically be nasalized in forms in which the stem final consonant is deleted:

Infinitive	*3 pl Pres Ind*	*3 sg Pres Ind*
craindre	craignent **krɛÑ.Et** / krɛɲ /	craint **krɛÑ.T** / krɛ̃ /
peindre	peignent **pɛÑ.ET** / pɛɲ /	peint **pɛÑ.T** / pɛ̃ /
joindre	joignent **ʒwaÑ.ET** / ʒwaɲ /	joint **ʒweÑ.T** / ʒwɛ̃ /

The symbol **Ñ** represents the latent consonant equivalent of ɲ. (In the singular present indicative forms of *joindre,* there is a non-predictable change *a→e* that accounts for the presence of / ɛ̃ / rather than / ã / in the phonetically manifest form.)

Finally, there are three verbs that show idiosyncratic vowel changes accompanying the deletion of the stem final latent consonant:

Infinitive	*3 pl Pres Ind*	*3 sg Pres Ind*
résoudre	résolvent **rezɔlV.ET** / rezɔlv /	résoud **rezɔlV.T** / rezu /
savoir	savent **saV.ET** / sav /	sait **saV.T** / sɛ /
valoir	valent **vaL.ET** / val /	vaut **vaL.T** / vo /

15.9   THREE-STEM VERBS

Three-stem verbs may be viewed as subtractive two-stem verbs with a replacive vowel in present system forms whose person endings do not contain an overt vowel (see Table 15.2).

In the case of *boire,* for example, the *regular* present stem *buv-* **byV-** is replaced by another stem that shows the vowel change *u→oi* (**y→wa**) in all forms containing an ending consisting of a latent consonant or mute *e* + a latent consonant. In addition, in the form consisting only of a latent consonant (the singular forms of the present indicative) the stem final latent consonant is predictably deleted. We speak of *regular* present stem when the phonetically manifest form is predictable from the underlying form, the adjunction of the appropriate set of tense-person endings, and the application of morphophonological and phonological rules. Consider the verb *finir.* The underlying form of the present stem is **finis-**. From that form and with the adjunction of endings containing a vowel (3 pl **-ET,**

Table 15.2 Distribution of Variant Present Stems of Three-Stem Verbs

Person-Reference	Present Ind.	Present Subj.	Imperfect	Pres. Part.
1 sg	- - - -	- - - -	- - - -	
	SHORT CHANGED	LONG CHANGED		
2 sg	- - - -	- - - -	- - - -	
	STEM	STEM		
3 sg	- - - -	- - - -	- - - -	
3 pl	- - - -	- - - -	- - - -	
2 pl	- - - -	- - - -	- - - -	
		LONG (REGULAR) STEM		
1 pl	- - - -	- - - -	- - - -	
Non-Finite				- - - -

2 pl **-eZ**, and 1 pl **-õZ**) are derived the present indicative forms containing / finis /: (/ il finis /, / vu finise /, / nu finisõ /). The adjunction of endings consisting only of a latent consonant (1 sg **-Z**, 2 sg **-Z**, 3 sg **-T**) and the subsequent application of the liaison rule produces the forms in which the final s of the underlying form of the stem is deleted: / ʒEfini /, / ty fini /, / il fini /. Present indicative forms are said to be "irregular" if they cannot be accounted for from the underlying form of the present stem, the adjunction of the appropriate set of present endings corresponding to the particular verb group, and the application of such morphophonological and phonological rules as liaison, mid vowel raising, etc. Irregularities are of two types: (1) a non-predictable change in the underlying form of the present stem, or (2) special endings. A form such as *je crains* / krẽ / is regular since it is predictable from the underlying form **krɛÑ-** with the 1 sg ending **-Z** and the required application of the nasalization rule followed by the liaison rule. On the other hand, such is not the case for *je joins* whose underlying form is ʒwaÑ-. In that case, the predictable form after adjunction of the ending **-Z** and nasalization followed by liaison would be / ʒwã /. We must therefore assume a change in the underlying form from ʒwaÑ- to ʒweÑ- or ʒwɛÑ-.

Like subtractive two-stem verbs, three-stem verbs show four spoken forms in the present indicative:

boire Present Stem: *buv-* **byV-**

	Underlying Form		Pronunciation	
	Singular	Plural	Singular	Plural
1	*boi.s* bwaV.Z	*buv.ons* byV.õz		byvõ
2	*boi.s* bwaV.Z	*buv.ez* byV.eZ	bwa	byve
3	*boi.t* bwaV.T	*boiv.ent* bwaV.ET		bwav

Two other verbs, *devoir* and *recevoir,* behave like *boire:*

Infinitive	1 pl Pres Ind	3 pl Pres Ind	3 sg Pres Ind
boire	buv.ons **byV.õZ**	boiv.ent **bwaV.ET** / bwav /	boi.t **bwaV.ET** / bwa /
devoir	dev.ons **dEV.õZ**	doiv.ent **dEV.ET** / dwav /	doi.t **dwaV.T** / dwa /
recevoir	recEv.ons **rEsEV.õZ**	reçoiv.ent **rEswaV.ET** / rEswav /	reçoi.t **rEswaV.T** / rEswa /

Four other three-stem verbs show an automatic vowel change (mid vowel raising or nasalization) in forms in which the stem final consonant is deleted: in *pouvoir* and *vouloir* / œ / is raised to / ø /; in *tenir* and *venir* / ɛ / is nasalized to / ẽ /:

Infinitive	1 pl Pres Ind	3 pl Pres Ind	3 sg Pres Ind
pouvoir	pouv.ons **puV.õZ**	peuv.ent **poeV.ET** / pœv /	peu.t **poeV.T** / pø /
vouloir	voul.ons **vuL.õZ**	veul.ent **voeL.ET** / vœl /	veu.t **voeL.T** / vø /
tenir	ten.ons **tEN.õZ**	tienn.ent **tjɛN.ET** / tjɛn /	tien.t **tjɛN.T** / tjẽ /
venir	ven.ons **vEN.õZ**	vienn.ent **vjɛN.ET** / vjɛn /	vien.t **vjɛN.T** / vjẽ /

In *prendre* the **E** of the regular present stem is replaced by ɛ: *nous prenons* **prEN.oZ** / prEnõ / *prennent* **prɛN.ET** / prɛn /. (Here, because of the preceding consonant cluster / pr /, / E / cannot be converted to zero; the phonetic realizations may only be [prənõ], [prørõ] or [prœnõ].) Then, when **N** is deleted in present indicative singular forms, there is a non-predictable change to ã: *il prend* / prã /. If this verb were a typical three-stem verb, we would expect to have / prẽ / on the basis of the underlying form **prɛN.T** and the application of the nasalization and liaison rules.

15.10   IRREGULAR TENSE-PERSON ENDINGS

A small number of verbs with high utility indexes and high relative frequency of occurrence show special tense-person endings: (1) *être* has the past perfect 1 pl ending *-mes* in the present indicative: *nous sommes* **sɔmEZ** / sɔm /; (2) *être, faire,* and *dire* show the past perfect 2 pl ending *-tes* in the present indicative: *vous êtes* **ɛ.tEZ** / ɛt /, *vous faites* **fɛtEZ** / fɛt /, *vous dites* **di.tEZ** / dit /; (3) *aller, avoir, être,* and *faire* take the future 3 pl ending *-ont* in the present indicative: *ils vont* **v.õt** / võ /, *ils ont* **.õT** / õ /, *ils sont* **s.õT** / sõ /, *ils font* **f.õT** / fõ /; (4) in *avoir* the present 3 sg ending appears in the present subjunctive: *il ait* **ɛ.T** / ɛ /, and in *être* the use of present endings applies to all singular forms of that tense: *je sois, tu sois, il soit* / swa /; (5) finally, *avoir* has a zero ending for the 1 sg form of the present indicative *ai* ɛ / ɛ /.

Etre, aller, avoir, and *faire* whose syntactic properties mark them off sharply from other verbs also have idiosyncratic morphophonological alternations in the present stem system. In particular the regular present stem appears only in the 1 pl and 2 pl forms: *all-* **al-**, *av-* **av-**, *fais-* **fEZ-** (for *être* it is in fact difficult to posit a single regular present stem). For *pouvoir,* there is a special 1 sg present indicative form *puis* used in formal style, particularly with inversion: *Puis-je vous aider?*

15.11 REPLACIVE STEMS IN PRESENT SUBJUNCTIVE

Faire, pouvoir, savoir, valoir, être, and *avoir* have a special replacive present stem that appears in all present subjunctive forms:

Infinitive	1 pl Pres Ind	3 pl Pres Subj	1 pl Pres Subj
faire	fais.ons	fass.ent / fas /	fass.ions / fasjõ /
pouvoir	pouv.ons	puiss.ent / pyis /	puiss.ions / pyisjõ /
savoir	sav.ons	sach.ent / saʃ /	sach.ions / saʃjõ /
valoir	val.ons	vaill.ent / vaj /	vall.ions / vajjõ /
être	sommes	soi.ent / swa /	soy.ons / swajõ /
avoir	av.ons	ai.ent / ɛ /	ay.ons / ɛjõ /

In the case of *être* and *avoir* differences in the spelling of the replacive stem do not reflect differences in underlying form and pronunciation. The replacive stems are, respectively, **swa** and **ɛ**. The alternation between *i* and *y* is due simply to the orthographic convention whereby the graphic sequence *oi* is replaced by *y: soi.ions→soyons, roi.ial→royal, loi.ier→loyer.* Recall also the irregular use of present rather than timeless endings in the following forms: *il ait, je sois, tu sois, il soit.*

In *aller* and *vouloir* the regular present stem occurs in the 1 pl and 2 pl of the present subjunctive and the replacive stem in the other persons:

Infinitive	1 pl Pres Ind	3 pl Pres Subj	1 pl Pres Subj
aller	all.ons	aill.ent / aj /	all.ions / aljõ /
vouloir	voul.ons	veuill.ent / vœj /	voul.ions / vuljõ /

Finally, the reader has no doubt observed that in our analysis of the verb the imperative is not considered a proper tense. So-called imperative forms are simply syntactic variants of corresponding present indicative forms derived by the deletion of the subject pronoun: *nous allons→allons! ; tu sors→sors! ; vous descendez→descendez!*

In the case of *avoir* and *être* present subjunctive forms are used instead of present indicative forms: *vous êtes gentil→soyez gentil! ; nous avons du tact→ayons du tact!* For *savoir* and *vouloir* the present subjunctive form is used in the 2 sg, but a special form differing from the present subjunctive by the use of the present endings is used in the 1 pl and 2 pl: *vous savez que je n'aime pas ça; sachez que je n'aime pas ça! ; vous voulez le faire; veuillez le faire!*

STUDY QUESTIONS

1. In addition to differences in the number of surface manifestations of present stems, what other differences do verbs like *passer* and *partir* show in the present system?

2. Provide the surface manifestation of all present stems for the following verbs:
   geler, remplir, dormir, ouvrir, tenir, vendre, vouloir

3. What underlying representation would you posit for the following verbs?
   (je) pars, (il) conduit, (tu) vends, (nous) lisons, (elles) mettent, (vous) écrivez

4. Although they all have present stems ending in / j /, *réveiller, bouillir,* and *ennuyer* differ in several respects in the present stem system. Discuss these differences.

5. List all actually occurring present indicative forms of:
   geler, répéter, mourir, acquérir, finir, sortir

6. Show how the following alternations in the final vowel of the present stem are predictable on the basis of the morphophonological structure of French:
   məne/mɛn; krɛɲ/krɛ̃; repete/repɛt

7. What is "irregular" about the derivation of the present stem forms of the following verbs?
   acquérir, résoudre, fuir, s'appuyer, savoir

8. What arguments can you provide for the analysis of *finiss-* as the base *fin-* "end" + the stem extension *-iss-?*

9. Give the underlying form and phonetic realization for:
   (je) sors, (il) veut, (elles) tiennent, (vous) venez

10. Give the regular and replacive present stems for:
    mourir, mener, sécher, valoir, pouvoir, venir, devoir, décevoir

11. List the irregularities in the present system of:
    dire, savoir, avoir, vouloir

12. Show the distribution of the following sets of present stem surface manifestations with respect to tense and person-reference:
    part-/par-; apEl-/apɛl-; ãvwaj-/ãvwa-; puv-/pœv-/pø-

13. Using the criteria of (1) choice of set of present endings, (2) number of variant present stem surface manifestations, and (3) nature of the relationship among variant stems, classify the following verbs:
    couvrir, courir, manger, employer, pouvoir, dire, prendre, pendre, servir, coudre, joindre, boire

16

PAST PARTICIPLE AND FUTURE STEM

16.1   VERB CLASSES

It was stated in the preceding chapter that traditional verb classes are based on the infinitive. In fact they are based on relations between the three verb stems. Since we are not taking into consideration the "literary" tenses (preterite and imperfect subjunctive), the past stem system is reduced to the past participle. Except for *-iss-* verbs whose present stem has been analyzed as base + stem extension (i.e., *finiss-* consists of the base **fiN-** plus the stem extension *-iss-*), the present stem of all French verbs is equivalent to the bare base. The future stem and the past participle are derived by the addition of the future stem extension and the past participle ending, respectively, to the present stem. The selection of particular future stem extensions and past participle endings defines three main classes of verbs which in fact correspond to the three traditional classes:

Traditional Label	Present Stem	Future Stem	Infinitive	Past Participle
-er	pass-	pass- er- (ER-)	pass- er (eR)	pass-é
-ir	part-	part- ir-	part- ir	part- i
	fin- -iss-	fin- ir-	fin- ir	fin- i
-re	vend-	vend- re- (rE-)	vend- re (rE)	vend- u

These three classes are defined as follows: (1) *-er* verbs have the future stem extension **-ER-** and the past participle ending **-e**; (2) *-ir* verbs have the future stem extension **-ir-** and the past participle ending **-i**; (3) *-re* verbs have the future stem extension **-rE-** and the past participle ending **-y**. The infinitive consists of the bare future stem extension, except for the *-er* and *-re* verbs where two generally predictable morphophonological changes take place. In the future stem, **-ER-** is unchanged since it occurs in non-final position because of the obligatory adjunction of an ending containing at least a vowel: *je passerai* **pas.ER.e** / pasre /, *nous passerions* **pas.Er.iõZ** / paserjõ /. But in the infinitive, since no ending is added to the future stem, **E** occurs in final position before a consonant, i.e., in a checked syllable. One of the more general deep-seated morphophonological principles of French is that **E** cannot be realized in final (stressed) checked syllables and must be replaced by some other vowel, often **e** or **ɛ**. This alternation between **E** and a front unrounded vowel also operates in determining the form of the present stem of such verbs as *jeter, mener,* or *prendre* (see Chapter 15). It might now be asked on what basis the latent **R** is posited. In monitored style / r / may appear in the infinitive of *-er* verbs: *Voulez-vous danser* / dãser / *avec moi? Nous aimerions déjeuner* / deʒœner / *à quatre heures.* The behavior of the future stem itself may be accounted for by positing either **r** or **R** since on the surface / r / always appears, but it is more economical to assume that it ends with the latter segment. When it occurs in final position, as in the infinitive, **R** is generally deleted; when it occurs before an ending beginning with a vowel, as is the case before all future and imperfect endings used to form the future and conditional tenses, it is realized obligatorily as / r /.

The stem final **E** of the future stem of *-re* verbs is obligatorily deleted when it occurs in the future stem proper (i.e., when it is used to form the future and the conditional tenses) but deleted or realized as [ə] according to mute *e* rules in the infinitive: *Il faut vendre* / vãdr /, *Il va attendre* / atãdr / *en face, On doit descendre* / desãdrə / *trois bouteilles.*

There is no justification for distinguishing between verbs like *partir* or *finir* on the basis of the derivation of their future stem and past participle from the base. For both types one adds the stem extension *-ir-* and the past participle ending *-i*. A distinction must be made between them, however, with regard to the derivation of the present stem from the base: in verbs like *finir* the present stem extension *-iss-* must be added to the base to derive the present stem. Stated differently, to derive the future stem from a form of the present system, such as *nous finissons,* one must first drop the present stem extension *-iss-* before proceeding with the adjunction of the future stem extension or the past participle ending.

It now becomes clear why the traditional classification of French verbs is a useful one. Since the infinitive is derived directly from the future stem, and since, further, past participle endings are distinct for the three main classes and in most cases consist of the vowel contained in or similar to the vowel of the future stem extension/infinitive ending, the latter enables one to derive all forms of a regular verb quite easily. We need to modify the traditional classification only slightly. First, we need to distinguish between verbs like *partir* and *finir* on the basis of the derivation of their present stem from their base. Second, in order to account for regular and predictable variations in the spoken form of the present stem of many verb types, we need to specify whether the base of verbs ends in a vowel, a stable consonant or a latent consonant. At the end of this chapter we will discuss the form of a descriptively adequate and pedagogically useful listing of French verbs and illustrate how the reader of such a listing would use the information given to derive all the forms of a verb. Here, we will simply classify a sample list of regular verbs according to the derivation of their present stem, future stem, and past participle from the base. (Note that in *conclu-u* the first *u* is deleted to give the past participle form *conclu*.)

Classification	Base	Present Stem	Future Stem	Past Participle
-er	pass- **pas-**	pass-	pass- er	pass- é
-er	men- **mEn-**	men-	men- er **mEn- ER**	men- é
-er	répét- **repet-**	répét-	répét- er	répét- é
-ir	part- **parT-**	part-	part- ir	part- i
-ir	cueill- **kœj-**	cueill-	cueill- ir	cueill- i
-ir/-iss-	fin- **fiN-**	fin iss-	fin- ir	fin- i
-re	vend- **vãD-**	vend-	vend- re	vend- u
-re	conclu- **kõkly-**	conclu-	conclu- re	conclu- u

16.2   FUTURE STEM IRREGULARITIES: FUTURE STEM ONLY

Within the framework of the analysis presented here, the derivation of the future stem or the infinitive other than by the adjunction of the stem extension appropriate to a given verb type would be considered an irregularity. Thus the future stem of *avoir* is irregular since it is not derived from the base *av-* but some replacive base *au.ɔ-*. The infinitive ending *-oir* **-war** is irregular by definition since, unlike the regular infinitive endings *-er* (**-ER**), *ir,* and *-re,* it is not identical to the future stem extension. In other words, adding *-oir* to the base does not yield the future stem. We describe first irregularities in the derivation of the future stem proper.

In verbs whose base contains **E** in the final syllable the future stem shows the change **E→ɛ** found in the present stem:

Infinitive	3 sg Pres Ind	3 sg Future
mener / mEne /	mène / mɛn /	mènera / mɛnra /
jeter / ʒEte /	jette / ʒɛt /	jettera / ʒɛtra /

But the change e→ɛ does not take place in the future stem of such verbs as *céder* or *répéter: répéter* / repete /, *il répète* / repɛt /, *il répétera* / repetra /. Some speakers, however, do use / ɛ / in future and conditional tense forms, although more frequently a vowel intermediate between e and ɛ is in fact used. This is as one would expect since the vowel in question occurs in medial position in future and conditional forms.

The truncatable base final **j** of verbs like *essayer, employer,* and *essuyer* also does not occur in forms derived from the future stem:

Infinitive	*3 sg Pres Ind*	*3 sg Future*	*1 pl Conditional*
essayer	essaie / esɛ /	essaiera / esɛra /	essaierions / esɛrjõ /
employer	emploie / ãplwa /	emploiera / ãplwara /	emploierions / ãplwarjõ /
essuyer	essuie / esyi /	essuiera / esyira /	essuierions / esyirjõ /

Balayer has one set of future and conditional tense forms in which the base final *-j* is truncated and another set in which it always appears: *il balaiera* / balɛra / or *il balayera* / balɛjra /. Note that in the 1 pl and 2 pl conditional the two alternate forms differ by a full syllable: *nous balaierions* / balɛrjõ / or *nous balayerions* / nu balɛjərjõ /. In *envoyer* the loss of / j / is also accompanied by a vowel change: *il envoie* / ãvwa / *nous envoyons* / ãvwajõ /, but *il enverra* / ãvɛra /, *nous enverrions* / avɛrjõ /.

In *acquérir* and *mourir*, *i* is deleted in the future stem: *il acquerra* / akɛrra /, *il mourra* / murra /. Note that in *acquerra* the presence of a following geminate *r* tends to open the vowel to / ɛ /.

Tenir and *venir* are marked by the insertion of **d** before the future stem extension as well as by the loss of the **i** from the stem extension itself. In addition, a replacive base identical to that used in the present stem system underlies the future stem finite forms. The underlying forms of the future stems for these two verbs are **tjɛNDr-** and **vjɛNdr-** respectively. The vowel of the base is nasalized when the base final **N** is deleted because of the adjacent presence of **d**: *il viendra,* / vjẽdra / *nous viendrions* / vjẽdriõ / [vjẽdrijõ]. Note that in the latter form a syllabic / i / (and the following automatic intervocalic glide [j]) is required because of the presence of the consonant group KL. Sequences / KL + j / such as the potential group / drj / of *vendrions* are not permitted and are prevented by the syllabic pronunciation of the **i** of the ending *-ions,* just as the realization of **E** prevents such combinations in *-er* verbs, e.g., *nous chanterions* / ʃãtərjõ / and not */ ʃatrjõ /. In both cases it would be improper to speak of the addition of some sound. Rather, the need to prevent non-permissible combinations leads to the realization of underlying segments present in the verb forms as vowels rather than the semivowel / j / or zero. The determining nature of the underlying segment is best illustrated by the contrast between the 1 pl conditional forms of *fondre* "to melt" and *fonder* "to found": *fondrions* **fõd-rE-iõZ** [fodriĭõ] vs. *fonderions* **fõd-ER-iõZ** [fõdərjõ].

A replacive future stem unrelated, for all practical purposes, to the base is found in *être, avoir,* and *faire: je serai, j'aurai, je ferai.* If we assume the bases to be, respectively, *êt-* **et-**, *av-* **av-**, and *fais-* **fEz-**, the derivation of the future stem from the base involves in all cases the deletion of the base final consonants, but the change of the vowel of the base is unpredictable in all three cases and is not determined by general morphophonological principles of French.

16.3 FUTURE STEM IRREGULARITY INCLUDING INFINITIVE

Most of the future stem irregularities affect the infinitive as well as the future and conditional tenses. The first type of irregularity involves the loss of the base final consonant and affects verbs with base final **-Z,** though not all verbs whose base ends in **-Z** show this irregularity:

Base (Present Stem)	1 pl Pres Ind	1 Future Stem	Infinitive
tradyiZ-	traduisons	tradyi rE	traduire
liZ-	lisons	li rE	lire
diZ-	disons	di rE	dire
plɛZ-	plaisons	plɛ rE	plaire

The deletion of -**Z** in these verbs stems no doubt from the fact that consonant combinations such as / zr / are not permitted in French. However the deletion of the base final consonants in *-re* verbs cannot always be explained on the basis of permissible consonant combinations. In *écrire* and its derivatives *décrire, souscrire,* etc., the stem final **V** is deleted but, on the other hand, that consonant appears in *suivre* and *vivre:*

Base (Present Stem)	1 pl Pres Ind	Future Stem	Infinitive
ekriV-	écrivons	ekri rE	écrire
syiV-	suivons	syiV rE	suivre
viV-	vivons	viV re	vivre

The second type of irregularity affecting all forms derived from the future stem involves the replacement rather than the loss of the base final consonant. All verbs affected belong to the *-re* group and have bases ending in -**S**, -**Z**, -**V**, -**Ñ**, and -**L**; the replacive consonants are in all cases **D** or **T**:

Base (Present Stem)	1 pl Pres Ind	Future Stem	Infinitive
nɛS-	naissons	nɛT rE	naître
konɛS-	connaissons	konɛT rE	connaître
parɛS-	paraissons	parɛT rE	paraître
kouZ-	cousons	kuD rE	coudre
rezoLV-	résolvons	rezuD rE	résoudre
krɛÑ-	craignons	krẽD rE	craindre
ʒwaÑ-	joignons	ʒwẽD rE	joindre
pɛN-	peignons	pẽD rE	peindre
vuL-	voulons	vuD rE	vouloir
faL-	(fallait)	foD rE	falloir
vaL-	valons	voD rE	valoir

Except for verbs with bases ending in **S** or **Z**, all these verbs show, in addition to the replacement of the base final consonant, various replacive changes in the final vowel. All verbs with stem final **L** show replacement with a high or high-mid vowel: *résolvons/résoudr-; vouloir/voudr-; valoir/vaudr-; falloir/faudr-.* In the last three verbs there are in fact two different irregularities in the derivation of future system forms: the replacive base final consonant and the irregular infinitive ending *-oir.* In the case of verbs with base final Ñ the replacement of that consonant by **D** is effected in two steps. First, **D** is added to the base (e.g., krɛÑ-→krɛÑD-), then the vowel is nasalized and Ñ is subsequently deleted: **krɛÑD- → krẽD-**.

In *résoudre* (**rezɔLV-**), *falloir* (**faL-**), and *valoir* (**vaL-**) the loss of **L** also entails the raising of the vowel to high or high-mid **o**. Since the base of *vouloir* (**vouL-**) already contains a high vowel, raising cannot take place. Finally, the irregular future stems of *tenir* and *venir* are also characterized by the insertion of **D** in the shifted base **tjɛN-** (rather than the regular base **tEN-** that appears in the infinitive) followed by the nasalization of the vowel and the accompanying deletion of **N**: **tjɛN rE → tjɛND rE→tjẽD rE**.

All the other *-oir* verbs, except *pleuvoir (pleuvra)*, show either replacement or loss of the base final consonant with or without vowel changes:

Base (Present Stem)	1 pl Pres Ind	Future Stem	Infinitive
plœV-		plœV rE-	pleuvoir
puV-	pouvons	pu rE-	pouvoir
saV-	savons	sɔ RE-	savoir
vwaj-	voyons	vɛ rE-	voir
asɛj-	asseyons	aswa RE-	asseoir
aswaj-	assoyons	asɛjE rE-	
byV-	buvons	bwa rE-	boire

16.4   IRREGULARITIES IN THE DERIVATION OF THE PAST PARTICIPLE

Irregularities in the derivation of the past participle involve either the use of an ending which is not characteristic of a given verb type—e.g., the use of the ending *-i* instead of *-u* for a *-re* verb—or various changes in the base. It will be recalled that the past participle is regularly formed by the adjunction of the past participle ending to the base: *pass- +é→passé; fin- + i→fini; vend- + -u→vendu.*

The first type of irregularity involves the switching of past participle ending. The following set of *-ir* verbs take *-u* instead of *-i:*

Base	Infinitive	Past Participle
cour-	courir	cour u
ten-	tenir	ten u
ven-	venir	ven u
vêt-	vêtir	vêt u

On the other hand, *suivre (suiv-)* takes *-i* instead of *-u: suivi. Etre* is a *-re* verb and should take the past participle ending *-u*, but instead *-é* is adjoined: *été.*

Another type of irregularity is the use of a zero past participle in verbs of the *-re* class whose stem ends in **y, i** or **j**:

Base	Infinitive	Past Participle
conclu-	conclure	conclu
ri-	rire	ri
fui- (**fyij-**)	fuir	fui

It will be recalled that **fyij-** contains a truncatable **j**: *il fuit* vs. *il fuyait.*

The third type of irregularity, which affects verbs of the *-re* class and verbs forming their infinitives irregularly by the adjunction of the infinitive ending *-oir,* consists of (1) the deletion of the base final consonant and (2) the deletion of the vowel of the last syllable of the base. The regular past participle ending *-u* is then added:

Base	Future	Infinitive	Past Participle
plais- **plɛZ-**	plair-	plaire	pl u
connais **konɛS-**	connaîtr-	connaître	conn u
paraiss- **parɛS-**	paraîtr-	paraître	par u
croiss- **krwaS-**	croîtr-	croître	cr û
lis- **liZ-**	lir-	lire	l u
croy- **krwaj-**	croir-	croire	cr u
voy- **vwaj-**	voir-	voir	v u
choy- **ʃwaj-**	cherr-	choir	ch u
dev- **dEV-**	devr-	devoir	d û
pouv- **puV-**	pourr-	pouvoir	p u
sav- **saV-**	saur-	savoir	s u
pleuv- **plœV-**	pleuvr-	pleuvoir	pl u
av- **aV-**	aur-	avoir	eu [y]

In the case of *crû* and *dû* the circonflex accent does not represent any difference in pronunciation. It is simply a device to permit a graphic differentiation of homophones: *il a cru (croire)* vs. *il a crû (croître); il a dû* vs. *du pain.* In the case of *résoudre,* whose base ends in a group of two latent consonants, there is only deletion of the second of the two consonants: *résolv-* **rez ɔLV-** and *résolu.*

The fact that verbs with infinitive in *-oir,* including *voir,* form their past participle by adjunction of *-u* supports assigning them to the *-re* group. It will be noted that verbs of that group whose base is not modified when the future stem extension **-re** is added (*devoir, pleuvoir*) behave like such regular *-re* verbs as *vendre* with regard to the derivation of the future stem: **VãD- + -rE→vãdr-,** and **dEv- + rE→dEvr-.** The derivation of their past participle differs from that of regular *-re* verbs only by extensive modifications of the base prior to the adjunction of the past participle ending.

Choir and its derivatives *déchoir* and *échoir* are used primarily in the past participle and it would be most economical perhaps to consider the past participles of these verbs as adjectives matching infinitives, for example: *les sommes à échoir* "sums to fall due," *les sommes échues* "sums that fell due."

The fourth type of irregularity involves the replacement of the base final consonant by a latent consonant. This replacement may also be accompanied by a change in the vowel of the final syllable of the base. In all cases, which affect mostly *-re* verbs, there is a zero past participle ending.

Base	Future Stem	Infinitive	Past Participle
dis- **diZ**-	dir-	dire	dit **diT**
fais- **fEZ**-	fer-	faire	fait **fɛT**
traduis- **tradyiZ**-	traduir-	traduire	traduit **tradyiT**
traiy- **trɛj**-	trair-	traire	trait **trɛT**
craign- **krɛÑ**-	craindr-	craindre	craint **krẽT**
peign- **pɛÑ**-	peindr-	peindre	peint **pẽT**
joign- **ʒwaÑ**-	joindr-	joindre	joint **ʒwẽT**
acquér- **aker**-	acquerr-	acquérir	acquis **akiZ**
assoy- **aswaj**-	assoir-	asseoir	assis **asiZ**
assey- **asɛj**-	assier-		
mett- **mɛT**-	mettr-	mettre	mis **miZ**
pren- **prEN**-	prendr-	prendre	pris **priZ**

In the case of *craindre* and other verbs with base final Ñ, a vowel change, brought about by the nasalization rule, automatically accompanies the deletion of the latent Ñ of the base, and thus the only irregularity shown by these verbs in the derivation of the past participle is the replacement of Ñ by T. The past participles of *mourir, couvrir* (and its derivatives), and *souffrir* are formed by the adjunction of latent T to the base without the deletion of the base final consonant. In addition, there are various vowel changes: a vowel addition with *couvrir* and *souffrir:* (couvr-→couvert; souffr-→souffert), and the replacement of **u** by **ɔ** in the case of *mourir (mour-→mort).* In the case of *clore* and its derivative *éclore,* the past participle is derived by adding a zero past participle ending and simply retaining the latent consonant of the stem: *clos-* **kloZ**-→*clos* **kloZ.**

The latent consonant found in some past participles is realized only in the feminine form. The latter is required only with verbs whose compound tenses are formed with *être: elle est morte;* with reflexive verbs: *elle s'est assise;* and with verbs whose compound tenses are formed with *avoir* in sentences in which the direct object precedes: *la lettre qu'il a traduite, cette robe, elle l'a mise.* In more spontaneous styles the agreement with the preceding direct object is not made, and the latent consonant does not appear in that syntactic context.

16.5   A CLASSIFICATION OF FRENCH VERBS

Traditional pedagogically oriented grammars of French classify French verbs in four regular classes (conjugations) on the basis, primarily, of their infinitive ending and provide a paradigm for a representative verb of each group. In addition, full paradigms are provided for so-called "irregular" verbs, verbs that fail to adhere fully to the rules of derivation of one of the four regular conjugations.

More recent structurally oriented classifications of French verbs have abandoned the infinitive ending as the primary classificatory criterion and use instead the number of variant present stems. We have pointed out that the traditional basis for classification of verbs is inherently sound, since, as the infinitive and the future stem are often identical, it rests in fact on the derivation of the future stem from the base. The infinitive ending (or, more exactly, the future stem extension) and the derivation of the present stem from the base will be used to classify regular verbs. Four classes (conjugations) are thus characterized: *-er, -ir, -ir/-iss-, -re.* It has been pointed out that except for the *-ir/-iss-* conjugation, the present stem is the same as the base, that is, the present stem extension is zero.

The infinitive ending may be viewed as an abbreviated classificatory notation which, together with the underlying form of the base and the various sets of tense-person endings, provides all the information required for the derivation of all the forms of regular verbs. Listing regular verbs in their infinitive form would be fully adequate, for example, *passer, partir, finir (-iss-), vendre.*

The base of all four verbs is derived by dropping the infinitive ending. Except for *finir,* where the present stem extension *-iss-* (*-is-*) must be added to the base, the base provides the present stem. Regular *-er* verbs take Set A present endings to form the present indicative, while the other three regular classes take Set B endings. Except for the "literary" tenses (past perfect and imperfect subjunctive), all the other sets of tense-person endings are common to all four verb conjugations. For *-ir* and *-ir (-iss-)* verbs the infinitive and the future stem are identical, but the future stem of *-er* and *-re* are also easily derivable from the infinitive. In the case of verbs of the latter group, one need only delete the final **E: vãdrE→vãdr-;** for *-er* verbs, the final e is replaced by **E: paseR→pasER-.** The past participles are derived by the addition of *-é, -i,* or *-u,* respectively, to the base.

Most irregular verbs contain some non-predictable feature in the derivation of one of the three stems, and less frequently, special replacive tense-person endings. But most of the forms of irregular verbs may be derived from the base and information about conjugation membership, the latter being provided by the infinitive ending; all one needs to list in addition are various replacive stems or other special features. Some verbs are more irregular than others, and, the more irregular a verb, the greater the number of special features that would need to be listed. It is never necessary, however, to provide the entire paradigm even of such an irregular verb as *être.* In the sample classification of irregular verbs presented here, which does not pretend to be exhaustive, verbs will be grouped according to their infinitive endings. In addition, the listing of irregular verbs will contain any stem or individual form which is not predictable from the underlying form of the base or the present stem and future extensions and past participle ending characteristic of the conjugation to which the particular verb belongs and signalled by the infinitive ending.

This additional information is analogous to the **principal parts** of traditional grammars, except that the principal parts of traditional grammars tended to be redundant. For example, such principal parts as:

passer	*je passe*	*je passerai*	*passé*
	je passais		
	il faut que je passe		

would be given for regular verbs. This information can be easily derived from the infinitive and a brief statement of the derivation rules and listing of tense-person endings for the four conjugations.

However, it is useful to provide some redundant information in pedagogically oriented classifications. Accordingly, in the sample listing below, redundant information consisting of full finite forms will be provided in addition to special replacive stems, past participles, or individual tense-person endings.

1.   *-er* verbs

   mener: men- **mEn-** *(je mène/nous menons)*; present stem *mèn-* **mɛn-**; future stem *mèner-* **mɛnEr-** *(je mènerai)*

   jetter: jet- **ʒEt-**; present stem *jett-* **ʒɛt** *(je jette);* future stem *jetter-* **ʒɛtER-** *(je jetterai)*

   Note that the distribution of the replacive present stem is fully predictable. Replacive present stems always occur in *stressed* present system forms, forms where the tense-person ending does not contain a stable vowel, namely, the singular and 3 pl forms of the present indicative and present subjunctive. It should be noted further that the replacement of **E** by **ɛ** is in fact predictable, since **E** never occurs in the final syllable of a stem. As there are two patterns in the orthographic representation of the replacive vowel, the particular orthographic pattern followed by a given verb would need to be listed.

   céder: céd- **sed-**; present stem *cèd-* **sɛd** *(je cède/nous cédons)*

   nettoyer: nettoy- **netwaj-**; present stem *nettoi-* **netwa-** *(je nettoie/nous nettoyous)*; future stem *nettoier-* **netwaEr-** *(je nettoierai)*

   ennuyer: ennuy- **ãnyij**; present stem *ennui-* **ãnyi-** *(nous ennuyons);* future stem *ennuier-* **ãnyiEr-** *(j'ennuierai)*

   payer: pay- **pɛj-**; alternate present stem *pai-* **pɛ** *(paye, paie/payons);* alternate future stem *paier-* **pɛEr-** *(payerai/paierai)*

   All *-er* verbs with bases ending in *oy* and *uy* have a truncatable base final **j** and lose the stem final **j** in the stressed present forms and in the future stem; all verbs with bases ending in *ay* (**ɛj**) have a replacive stem with truncated **j** alternating with the regular stem in the present and in the future. However, verbs with bases ending in *ey* (**ɛj**), e.g., *grasseyer,* are perfectly regular.

   aller: all- **al-**; present indicative forms *vais, vas, va, vont;* present subjunctive stem *aill-,* alternating with regular stem *all- (aille/allions)*; future stem *ir- (j'irai)*

2.   *-ir* verbs

Most *-ir* verbs *(dormir, mentir, servir, partir,* etc.) have bases ending in a latent consonant, e.g., *dorm-* **dɔrM-**. The latent consonant, which is also deleted in the singular present indicative forms (i.e., forms containing tense-person endings consisting of a latent consonant only), does not appear in the orthographic representation of these forms: *je pars, tu dors, il sert.* Another *-ir* verb that is fully regular is *bouillir* whose base is **buJ-** and not **buj-**. Accordingly, the latent consonant of the base is deleted in forms where the base is stressed: *je bous, ils bouent* vs. *nous bouillons*

   ouvrir (souffrir, etc.): *ouvr-* **uvr-**; Set A endings *(j'ouvre)*

   cueillir: cueill- **koej-**; Set A endings *(je cueille)*

   courir: cour- **kur-**; future stem *courr-* **kurr-** *(je courrai)*; past participle *couru*

   mourir: mour- **mur-**; present stem *meur-* *(je meurs/nous mourons)*; future stem *mourr-* *(je mourrais)*; past participle *mort*

   acquérir: acqér- **aker-**; present stem *acquier-* *(j'acquiers/nous acquérons)*; future stem *acquerr-* *(j'acquerrai)*; past participle *acquis*

   vêtir: vêt- **vɛT**; past participle *vêtu*

fuir: fuy- **fyij-**; truncatable **j** in present stem *(je fuis/nous fuyons);* future stem *fuir- (je fuirai);* past participle *fui*

tenir: ten- **tEn-**; present stem *tienn-* **tjɛN-** *(je tiens, ils tiennent/nous tenons);* future stem *tiendr- (je tiendrai);* past participle *tenu*

venir: ven- **vEN-**; present stem *vîenn-* **vjɛN** *(je viens, ils viennent/il vient);* future stem *viendr-;* past participle *venu*

Note that for both *tenir* and *venir* the singular forms of the present indicative show predictable nasalization of the vowel of the base accompanied by the deletion of the base final latent **N**.

3. *-ir (-iss-)* verbs

haïr: haï- **ai-**; present stem *hai-* **ɛ-** *(je hais/nous haïssons)*

4. *-re* verbs

All *-re* verbs have bases ending in a latent consonant and will show predictably a shortened present stem in singular present indicative forms: *je bats* / ba / vs. *ils battent* / bat /. In addition, all *-re* verbs with bases ending in a stop (*battre* **baT-**, *vendre* **vãD-**, *vaincre* **vɛ̆K-**, etc.) show orthographic particularities in the present indicative forms. These particularities are not idiosyncratic and can be covered by two general statements: (1) the deleted latent consonant is always represented in the singular present indicative forms—*je bats, tu vends-, il rompt*; (2) the 3 sg ending *-t* (**T**) fuses with the base final **T** and **D**—*il bat, il vend* (vs. *il rompt*). The spelling of the 3 sg present indicative of *vaincre, il vainc,* is a true irregularity. However, in pedagogically oriented classifications one might want to list as idiosyncratic the information on spelling subsumed by these two general statements.

vendre: vend- **vãD-**; orthographic representation of present stem *je vends, il vend*

battre: batt- **baT-**; *je bats, il bat*

rompre: romp- **rõP-**; spelling: *je romps, il rompt*

vaincre: vainqu- **vɛ̆K-**; spelling: *je vaincs, il vainc; vaincu*

mettre: mis- **miZ-**; past participle *mis*

craindre: craign- **krɛÑ-**; nasalization *(je crains/ils craignent);* future stem *craindr- (je craindrai);* past participle *craint*

The present stem behavior of verbs in *-indre (joindre, peindre,* etc.) is fully predictable from the presence of the latent **Ñ** at the end of their base. When the **Ñ** is deleted before a consonant, the vowel is also nasalized.

coudre: cous- **kuZ-**; future stem *coudr- (je coudrai)*

lire: lis- **liZ-**; future stem *lir- (je lirai);* past participle *lu*

dire: dir- **diZ-**; present indicative special form *vous dites;* future stem *dir- (je dirai);* past participle *dit*

croître: croiss- **krwaS-**; present stem spelling *croî- (je croîs);* future stem *croîtr- (je croîtrai);* past participle *crû*

plaire: plais- **plɛZ-**; present stem orthographic *il plaît;* future stem, *plair- (je plairai);* past participle *plu*

connaître: connaiss- **konɛS-**; present stem orthographic *il connaît;* future stem *connaîtr- (je connaîtrai);* past participle *connu*

naître: naiss- **nɛS-**; present stem orthographic *il naît;* future stem *naîtr- (je naîtrai);* past participle *né*

conduire: conduis- **kõdyiZ-**; future stem *conduir- (je conduirai)*; past participle *conduit*

suivre: suiv- **syiV-**; future stem *suivr- (je suivrai)*; past participle *suivi*

vivre: viv- **viV-**; future stem *vivr- (je vivrai)*; past participle *vécu*

résoudre: résolv- **rezɔLV-**; future stem *résoudr- (je résoudrai)*; past participle *résolu*

prendre: prenn- **prEN-**; present stem *prenn-* **prɛN-***/prend-* **prã-** *(ils prennent/je prends/nous prenons); (je prendrai)*; past participle *pris*

boire: buv- **byV-**; present stem *boiv-* **bwaV-** *(ils boivent/nous buvons)*; future stem *boir- (je boirai)*; past participle *bu*

rire: ri- **ri-**; present stem: intercalation of [j] before a vowel *(je ris/nous rions* [riᴊõ]*)*; past participle *ri*

conclure: conclu- **kõkly-**; past participle *conclu*

croire: croy- **krwaj-**; present stem *croi-* **krwa-** *(je crois/nous croyons)*; future stem *croir- (je croirai)*; past participle *cru*

voir: voy- **vwaj-**; present stem *voi-* **vwa-** *(je vois/nous voyons)*; future stem *verr-* **vɛr-** *(je verrai)*; past participle *vu*

devoir: dev- **dEV-**; present stem *doiv-* **dwaV-** *(ils doivent/nous devons)*; past participle *dû*

Note that the future stem of *devoir* is fully predictable.

Devoir is a -re verb with special infinitive ending *-oir.* Its future stem is formed by adding *-re* **(-rE)** to the base *dev-*: **dEv- + -rE→dEvr-.** For all *-oir* verbs, including *voir,* one should state that the infinitive ending is irregular, but inasmuch as the proposed listing would contain at least the infinitive and the base of all verbs, that irregular feature is already provided by the listing and a statement in the body of the listing would only be redundant.

recevoir: recev- **resEV-**; present stem *reçoiv* **reswaV-** *(ils reçoivent/nous recevons)*; past participle *reçu*

pouvoir: pouv- **puV-**; present stem *peuv-* **pœV-** with mid vowel raising *(ils peuvent/je peux/nous pouvons)*; spelling: *je peux, tu peux*; special present indicative 1 sg alternative form *puis*; special present subjunctive stem *puiss- (je puisse)*; future stem *pourr- (je pourrai)*; past participle *pu*

vouloir: voul- **vuL-**; present stem *veul-* with mid vowel raising *(ils veulent/je veux/nous voulons)*; spelling *je veux, tu veux*; special alternating present subjunctive stem *veuill- (je veuille/nous voulions)*; special 2 pl imperative form *veuilles*; future stem *voudr- (je voudrai)*; past participle *voulu*

pleuvoir: pleuv- **pløV-** used in 3 sg only; past participle *plu*

émouvoir: émeuv- **emœV-**; present stem mid vowel raising *(ils émeuvent/j'émeus)*; future stem *émouvr- (j'émouvrai)*; past participle *ému*

savoir: sav- **saV-**; present stem *sai-* **sɛ-** *(je sais/ils savent)*; special imperative forms *sache, sachons, sachez*; special subjunctive stem *sach- (je sache/nous sachions)*; future stem *saur-* **sɔr-** *(je saurai)*; past participle *su*

valoir: val- **vaL-**; present stem *vau-* **vo-** *(je vaux/ils valent)*; special alternating subjunctive stem *vaill- (je vaille/nous valions)*; future stem *vaudr- (je vaudrai)*; past participle *valu*

falloir: fall- **faL-**; used in 3 sg only; present stem *fau- (il faut/il fallait)*; special subjunctive stem *faill-; (il faudra)*; past participle *fallu*

asseoir: assey- **asɛj-**/*assoy-* **aswaj-**; alternating paradigms in present and future system; present stems *assied-* **asje-** and *assoir-* **aswa-** *(je m'assieds/nous nous asseyons)*; future stem *asseyer-* (regular) **asɛjEr-** *assiér-* **asjer-** and *assoir-* **aswar-** *(je m'asseyerai, je m'assiérai,* or *je m'assoirai)*; past participle *assis* *avoir: av-* **aV-**; present stem: special present indicative forms *j'ai, tu as, il a, ils ont;* special present subjunctive stem *ai- (j'aie, nous ayons);* future stem *aur-* **ɔr-** *(j'aurai);* past participle *eu* **y**

faire: fais- **fEz-**; special present indicative forms *ils font, vous faites,* present stem *fai-* **fɛ-** *(je fais/nous faisons);* special present subjunctive stem *fass- (je fasse, nous fassions);* future stem *fer-* **fEr-** *(je ferai);* past participle *fait*

être: ét- **eT-**; special present indicative forms *je suis, nous sommes, ils sont; tu es, il est, vous êtes; (étais);* special present subjunctive stem *soi-* **swa-** *(je sois/nous soyons);* past participle *été*

STUDY QUESTIONS

1. How are the following future stems irregular?

   tiendr-, ir-, fer-, verr-, voudr-, achèter-

2. For some verbs, such as *partir* and *vendre,* the future stem can be readily derived from the infinitive. For which of the following verbs listed in their 1 pl present indicative form is that the case?

   connaissons, revêtons, savons, résolvons, craignons, valons, concluons, conduisons, haïssons

3. A pedagogically oriented description of French proposes a rule according to which the 1 sg future form may be derived from the spoken form of the 1 sg present indicative by the addition of / re /, e.g., *je passe* / pas /→*je passerai* / pasre /. Which verbs classified as regular in the classification proposed here would be "irregular" on the basis of this rule?

4. Show how the following past participle forms are irregular:

   pu, su, suivi, écrit, conduit, fait, mis, vêtu, conclu, ri

5. On the basis of the rule: past participle = base + -*u*, which of the following -*re* verbs are irregular?

   vendre, dire, traduire, plaire, vaincre, croire, rompre, faire, descendre, connaître

6. List the underlying and actually occurring spoken form of the present and future stems and the past participle for each of the following verbs:

   porter, jeter, nettoyer, choisir, servir, cueillir, dire, taire, pouvoir

7. How are the following -*ir* verbs irregular?

   cueillir, souffrir, ouvrir, fuir

8. On what basis are the following present stem alternations predictable?

   ils craignent/il craint
   ils viennent/il vient
   ils peuvent/il peut
   ils jettent/nous jetons

   List three sets of present stem alternations involving differences in the last vowel of the stem which are *not* predictable on the basis of morphophonological principles of French.

9. Discuss the validity of the traditional system of four regular conjugations, in particular:

   a) How do the -*er* verbs differ from the other three types;

   b) How do the two -*ir* verb types illustrated by *finir* and *partir* differ?

10. Verbs characterized in the analysis presented in this book as containing a "truncatable" base final **j** may be described differently. One might posit that their base ends in -**wa** rather than **waj**-, e.g., *nettoyer* **netwa**- and that a **j** is inserted whenever stem extensions and endings beginning with a full vowel (excluding **E**) is affixed. How would this analysis affect rules of derivation of the present and future stem and the past participle of such verbs as *payer, bégayer, grasseyer, nettoyer, envoyer, essuyer, appuyer, croire, voir*?

17

DERIVATION AND DEEP-LEVEL MORPHOPHONEMIC ALTERNATIONS

17.1   LATENT CONSONANTS AND DERIVATION

The phenomenon of liaison, one of the striking features of French morphophonology, has been accounted for by the postulation of a set of latent consonants that are distinguished from stable consonants by the fact that they are realized only under certain phonological and syntactic conditions (see Chapter 10). Specifically, latent consonants are realized as corresponding stable consonant phonemes when (i) they are followed by a vowel and (ii) the word in which they occur is in close syntactic link with the word that follows immediately. It was shown in preceding chapters (10, 14-16) that latent consonants occur in a relatively small number of words (determiners and adjectives found normally in pre-nominal position, pronouns, certain monosyllabic forms of frequently used verbs such as *être,* and monosyllabic prepositions and adverbs, as well as in inflectional endings: plural of nouns, adjectives, and determiners; verbal person-tense endings. It was also pointed out that the number of frequently occurring latent consonants is quite limited: **Z, T, N,** and **R.** Other latent consonants are found in a very restricted number of forms: **G** in the adjective *long;* **D** in the adjective *grand;* **J** in the adjectives *vieil* and *gentil;* **S** in the adjectives *gros* and *faux.*

However, if we take into consideration bases that do not occur as isolated words but are always followed by some inflectional ending, the number of forms that contain latent consonants increases, as does the number of different latent consonants. Thus, the range is extended to all variable adjectives and multi-stem verbs of the subtractive type such as *française/français* **frãsɛZ-**, *suivre* **syiV-**, *dormir* **dɔrM-**, and *rompre* **rõP-**. In these bases the latent consonant appears only when it is immediately followed by a vowel. For adjective bases, this condition is met in the feminine where they are immediately followed by the feminine ending **-E**: *française* **frãsɛZ.E** / frãsɛz / vs. the masculine form *français* **frãsɛZ** / frãsɛ /. For verbs, the latent consonant is realized when it is followed by an ending beginning with a vowel, as is the case for the 1 pl and 3 pl present, for instance: *ils dorment* **dɔrM.ET** / dɔrm / vs. *il dort* **dɔrM.T** / dɔr /; *nous suivons* **syiV.õZ** / syivõ / vs. *je suis* **syiV.Z** / syi /.

The number of bases for which we must posit final latent consonants greatly increases when we take derivational processes into account. **Derivation** involves the addition of affixes to bases. While the addition of inflectional endings does not change the part of speech affiliation of a base (the addition of the ending -*ons* to the verb base *part*- results in the formation of a verb form *partons*), the addition of derivational affixes, particularly suffixes, usually produces a derivative whose part of speech affiliation differs from that of the base. For instance, the addition of the suffix -*ie* to the verb base *sort*- results in the formation of a noun, *la sortie*. Another major difference between inflectional and derivational suffixes is that. the latter, unlike the former, do not "close" the form. After the inflectional suffix -*ons* is added to *sort*-, further expansions are no longer possible but the addition of the noun-forming derivational suffix -*ie* may be followed by that of the plural ending: *sort.ie.s.* Consider the various levels of derivation in:

> util- (adjective base)
> util.is- (verb-forming suffix -*is*)
> util.is.able (adjective-forming suffix -*able*)
> in.util.is.able (negative prefix)
> in.util.is.able.s (plural suffix)

In Chapter 10 it was stated that to analyze liaison across word boundaries it is simpler to consider that such words as the noun *enfant* do not contain any latent consonant. In other words, the underlying form was assumed to be *ãfã* instead of *ãfãT,* for when it occurs as a simple form (i.e., not followed by the plural suffix -**Z**), it is never in close syntactic link with a following word: *un enfant/anxieux*. But derivatives of *enfant* such as *enfanter* "to give birth," *enfantin* "childish," and *enfantillage* "childishness" all show a manifest / t / , and it is necessary to posit the base *ãfãT*- underlying these derivatives and the simple form *enfant*. Similarly, latent consonants must be posited for the following singular nouns: *départ (partir), rang (ranger), sang, (sanguin), banc (banquise, banquier)*, etc.

The increase in the number of forms for which latent consonants must be posited and in the number of different latent consonants which results when both inflectional and derivational processes are considered forces us to reconsider the choice we made between the two alternative interpretations of liaison. In Chapter 10 we opted for the latent consonant morphophoneme theory according to which a distinction is made between stable consonants mapped directly into consonant phonemes and latent consonants that must be converted into zero or corresponding consonant phonemes by the liaison rule. This theory requires the establishment of two sets of consonants appearing in underlying forms, for, except for **b**, every stable consonant is matched by a corresponding latent consonant morphophoneme:

Stable Consonants			*Latent Consonants*		
cap	net	sac	romp-	bat-	vainqu-
tomb-	vid-	tangu-	- - - -	vend-	long-
chef	sens	lâch-	oeuf-	gros-	fraîch-
rêv-	gaz	boug-	suiv-	anglais-	rang-
aim-	gên-	saign-	dorm-	brun-	plaign-
brill-	fil	car	vieil-	il	chanter

The second alternative, implicit in the traditional view of liaison and recently formalized by generative phonologists, does not distinguish between stable and latent consonants in underlying forms. All base and word final consonants are subject to deletion by the application of a set of rules analogous to those required for the latent consonant solution. This interpretation was rejected in Chapter 10 because it required marking two sets of items as irregular (idiosyncratic). First, there are items such as *sens, chef, sec, net* and *gaz* whose final consonant is never deleted. Second, the consonant deletion solution necessitates recognizing a special class of consonants—liquids—comprising **l, r,** and **j** that are never deleted. There are, however, items such as *il,* the infinitive ending *-er, vieil,* and, in the plural, *oeil, ail,* etc. which contain deletable liquids and consequently must be listed as idiosyncratic. Within a treatment of French morphophonology limited to inflectionally related forms the number of exceptional items that characterizes the consonant deletion solution looms relatively large. But within an overall treatment that extends to derivationally related forms, the number of forms that require special marking is not inordinately large, and the consonant deletion interpretation is more economical.

Another weakness of the latent consonant analysis is the arbitrary assignment of base final consonants to the stable or latent category. Consider for example the bases of *-er* verbs. If we take into consideration verb forms alone, these bases would be represented with final stable consonants, since their final consonant is always pronounced. This is because all tense-person endings of this group of verbs begin with a vowel: *je pass.e, ils pass.ent, il pass.er.a,* etc. In the case of verbs such as *donner* and *ranger* on whose bases nouns are derived by zero affixation—*le don, le rang*—consideration of verb forms only and imperfect knowledge of the French lexicon would yield the wrong results. In order to derive / dõ /. and / rã̃ / the liaison rule must be applied to bases represented by **dɔN-** and **rã̃ʒ-**; the latent consonants are deleted in the nouns since they occur in word final position before a major syntactic boundary. In the final consonant deletion analysis *-er* verbs are represented by final consonants to which the general final consonant deletion rule applies. In all verb forms the conditions for the application of the liaison rule are never met and the consonant is always pronounced. In the noun forms, as is the case for verbs such as *finir* or *vendre* which take Set B endings in the present tense, the rule applies and the final consonants are deleted. Thus, without previous knowledge of the existence of *don* and *rang* but on the basis of verb forms alone, underlying forms can be posited that yield the correct phonological outputs. *Don* and *rang* differ from most nouns derived from *-er* verb bases by the fact that they are formed by zero affixation rather than by the adjunction of the suffix **-E**: compare *donn.er/don* and *pass.er/pass.e; rang.er/rang* and *song.er/song.e.*

It is important to note that in both the latent consonant and the final consonant deletion analyses the overt forms subsumed by the underlying forms are unquestionably morphologically relatable. Consider, for example, the derivational sets *chanter/chant, donner/don, sortir/sortie, partir/départ.* Even non-educated native speakers of French would agree that members of each pair share primary semantic features and that the second member is included in the first member. According to the latent consonant solution the underlying form of the bases would be ʃã̃T-, dɔN-, sɔrT-, and parT-, respectively. The latent consonant appears as a phonemically manifest consonant in the infinitives since in all of them it is immediately followed by an inflectional ending beginning with a vowel; it is realized as zero in the nouns since these are composed of the bare stem. According to the final consonant deletion interpretation the underlying form of the bases would be ʃã̃t-, dɔn-, sɔrt-, and **part-**, respectively. The final consonant is deleted in the nouns but not in the infinitives since in the latter it is followed immediately by a vowel. In both solutions, the derivation of the noun *don* / dõ / from the underlying form of the base requires in addition the application of the nasalization rule.

17.2   DEEP-LEVEL VOWEL ALTERNATIONS AND NASALIZATION

The nasalization rule, which nasalizes any vowel occurring before a morpheme or word final consonant, was posited to account for such inflectionally related alternant forms as *bon/bonne, sain/saine,* and *paysan/paysanne.* Another rule, nasal vowel adjustment, was posited to account for alternations such as *fin/fine* and *brun/brune* since the simple application of nasalization would result in masculine forms */ fĩ/ and */ brỹ / containing non-existent nasal vowels. Nasal vowel adjustment replaces these non-existent vowels by the phonetically nearest nasal vowels, / ẽ / and / œ̃ /, respectively. There is a sixth alternation between an oral and a nasal vowel attested in verb forms: / ɛn / prennent and / ã / *prend.* As was pointed out, this alternation is idiosyncratic since the application of nasalization to / ɛn / would yield / ẽ /. To summarize, there are six alternations between a sequence oral vowel + / n / (more generally, oral vowel + nasal consonant) and a nasal vowel found in adjective and verb stems:

1.	/ ɔn /:/ õ /	bonne/bon; bon ami/bon camarade
2.	/ an /:/ ã /	paysanne/paysan
3.	/ ɛn /:/ ẽ /	saine/sain; américaine/américain
4.	/ in /:/ ẽ /	fine/fin; voisine/voisin
5.	/ yn /:/ œ̃ /	une/un; brune/brun
6.	/ ɛn /:/ ã /	prennent/prend

Five additional alternations between oral and nasal vowels are found in derivationally related forms:

1.	/ e /:/ ẽ /	plénitude/plain; bénévole/bien
2.	/ a /:/ ẽ /	famine/faim; humanité/humain; sanitaire/sain
3.	/ E /:/ ẽ /	menotte/main; grenu/grain
4.	/ wa /:/ wẽ /	soigner/soin; joignent/joint; poignée/poing
5.	/ œ / or / ø /:/ œ̃ /	jeûner/à jeun

Of these, only the alternation / wa /:/ wẽ / is also found in inflectionally related forms: *ils joignent/joindre* or *je joins.* Two of these alternations can be accounted for by the application of nasalization: if / e / is nasalized, the nearest corresponding nasal vowel is / ẽ /, and / œ̃ / is also the nearest nasal corresponding vowel to both / œ / and / ø /. It would therefore be possible to posit underlying forms common to such alternants as *plénitude* and *plein* on the one hand and *jeûner* and *à jeun* on the other, which, upon the application of nasalization yield the attested alternants:

		Pre-Vowel	Pre-Consonant/Final
Underlying Forms:	**plen-**	plénitude	plein
	ʒoen-	jeûner	à jeun
Nasalization:		- - - -	plẽn ʒõen
Final Consonant Deletion:		- - - -	plẽ ʒõ̃e
Phonological Output:		/ plenityd / / ʒøne /	/ plẽ / / ʒœ̃ /

The postulation of a single form underlying overt forms showing / e / and / ẽ / and another underlying forms containing / œ / or / ø / and / œ̃ / is well motivated since these underlying forms are not highly abstract and permit the derivation of overt forms by the application of a morphophonological rule otherwise required to account for inflectionally related forms.

But the postulation of single underlying forms to account for the alternations / a /:/ ẽ /, / E /:/ ẽ /, and / wa /:/ wẽ / is more problematic. If on the model of the other alternations between sequences oral vowel + *n* and nasal vowels we choose the oral vowel as underlying, application of nasalization fails to yield the correct overt nasal vowel: **fam-** (nasalization, final consonant deletion) →*fã; **mEn-** (nasalization, nasal vowel adjustment, final consonant deletion) →*moẽ; **swañ-** (nasalization, final consonant deletion) →*swã. In order to relate these sequences oral vowel + *n* and nasal vowels, it is necessary to consider the derivationally related sets:

2a.	/ a /:/ ɛ /:/ ẽ /	humanité/humaine/humain; sanitaire/saine/sain
3a.	/ E /:/ a /:/ ẽ /	menotte/manuel/main; grenu/granulé/grain

It is clear that these ternary alternations can be derived from a single underlying vowel only at the cost of great abstraction; the procedure for the postulation of underlying form that can account for such deep-level alternations will be presented in Section 17.3. In a morphophonemic analysis of French in which it is required that underlying forms be relatively concrete, that is, that they permit the derivation of surface forms by the application of only very general phonological processes such as nasalization and mid vowel raising, no attempt would be made to relate *humanité* to *humaine* and *humain,* for example. Instead, two different bases would be posited: **yman-** to account for *humanité, humanisme,* etc. and **ymɛn-** to account for *humaine* and *humain*; the latter is derived from **ymɛn-** by the straightforward application of nasalization.

There are in French many morphemes containing nasal vowels that do not alternate with sequences oral vowel + nasal consonat, e.g., *tomber* / tõbe /, *penser* / pãse /, *rincer* / rẽse /, *lundi* / lœ̃di /. That is to say, the verb *tomber* has no forms that contain the sequence / ɔm /. (Since we are describing Standard French, we exclude from consideration such Southern (Méridional) accented forms as [tɔ̃mbe]. In any case, this is a phonetic variant, not a morphophonemic alternant of / tõbe /.) Should the nasal vowels of such forms as *tomber, penser, rincer,* and *lundi* be derived from underlying sequences oral vowel + nasal consonant and the application of nasalization and final consonant deletion to bring them in line with the nasal vowels appearing in inflectionally (*bon* / bõ /: *bonne* / bɔn /) or derivationally (*plénitude* / plenityd /: *plein* / plẽ /) related forms which do participate in such alternations?

The major problem that such a proposal raises is the assignment of non-alternating nasal vowels to a given sequence oral vowel + nasal consonant. Consider again the various alternations between nasal vowels and sequences oral vowel + nasal consonants:

1.	/ ẽ /:/ ɛn /		**2.**	/ ã /:/ an /
	/ ẽ /:/ in /			/ ã /:/ ɛn /
	/ ẽ /:/ en /		**3.**	/ œ̃ /:/ yn /
	/ ẽ /:/ an / or / am /			/ œ̃ /:/ øn / or / œn /
	/ ẽ /:/ E /		**4.**	/ õ /:/ ɔn /
	/ wẽ /:/ waɲ /			

In only one of these alternations can a nasal vowel be assigned to only one sequence oral vowel + nasal consonant, namely / õ /:/ ɔn /, as in such pairs as *bon/bonne* or *don/donne.* The assignment of the other three nasal vowels (when they occur in non-alternating forms) to sequences oral vowel + nasal consonant can only be arbitrary or supported by orthographical or etymological considerations, both of which are excluded from a strictly synchronic analysis. Consider the assignment of the / ã / of *penser.* In the absence of morphophonemic alternations, one could choose underlying representations in **an** (on the basis of / ã /:/ an /) or ɛn (on the basis of / ã /:/ ɛn /).

The surface nasal vowels of bases without alternants will be assigned to underlying nasal vowels. Surface nasal vowels are thus derived from two underlying sources: (1) underlying nasal vowels in the case of bases without alternants and (2) sequences oral vowel + nasal consonant in bases that show two alternants, one with a nasal vowel and the other with a sequence oral vowel + nasal consonant. In the case of alternating forms one might wish to distinguish between inflectionally related alternants, as in the case of *bon/bonne* or *tient/tiennent,* and derivationally related alternants, as in the case of *plein/plénitude* or *main/menotte.* It may be claimed that since speakers of French probably do not relate the latter type of alternants, there is no justification for positing abstract underlying forms. The surface nasal vowels of forms related only derivationally to others containing sequences oral vowel + nasal consonant will be derived from underlying nasal vowels. As a summary of this section on the derivation of surface nasal vowels, compare the derivation of the nasal vowels of *don, rond,* and *main:*

Morphophonological Level				
Underlying Form:	donn.e	don	rond	main
	dɔn.E	dɔn-	rõd-	mẽ-
Morphophonological Rules:				
Nasalization	- - - -	dõn	- - - -	- - - -
Final Consonant Deletion:	- - - -	dõ	rõ	- - - -
Mute *e* Deletion:	dɔn	- - - -	- - - -	- - - -
Phonological Level	/ dɔn /	/ dõ /	/ rõ /	/ mẽ /

17.3   DEEP-LEVEL ORAL VOWEL ALTERNATIONS

In the description of French adjective and verb morphology presented in Chapters 14, 15, and 16, a common underlying form was provided only for those base alternants which could be derived from the postulated underlying form by the morphophonemic rules of nasalization, nasal vowel adjustment, mid vowel raising, or liaison (final consonant deletion). In addition, in the preceding sections of this chapter, we have taken the point of view that only inflectionally related forms, such as *fine* and *fin,* or derivational forms unquestionably related, such as *donner* and *don,* should be derived from a common underlying base. As a result, the underlying forms we posit have a relatively low degree of abstractness. This term is used here to indicate that surface manifestations and underlying forms are related by a small number of very general rules and that surface alternants of a common base are felt by native speakers to be clearly related semantically and morphologically.

In this section we examine a model of French morphophonology in which more abstract underlying forms are posited and in which an attempt is made to relate derivational alternants whose relationship is not always obvious to naïve native speakers of the language.

It is important to emphasize the difference between the morphophonological rules that will be posited in this section in order to relate various vowel alternations and a rule such as mid vowel raising. It will be recalled that mid vowel raising characterizes the replacement in final free syllables of low-mid vowels by their high-mid correlate, e.g., *première/premier, sotte/sot, veulent/veut.* This rule may be said to have a phonological basis since / ɔ / and / œ / generally do not occur in final free syllables. If mid vowel raising were not applied, after the application of liaison to the underlying forms **sɔT**- *sot-* or **vœL**- *veul-,* these two vowels would occur in final free syllables, i.e., */ sɔ / and */ vœ /. The application of mid vowel raising thus results in forms which are more in accord with the phonological structure of French.

Present indicative forms of many verbs listed as "irregular" in traditional descriptions show vocalic alternations which cannot be accounted for in terms of phonological processes:

1. / u /:/ œ /   mourir/meurt; pouvons/peuvent
2. / E /:/ jɛ /   venons/viennent; tenons/tiennent
3. / E /:/ wa /   recevons/reçoivent; devons/doivent

In the analysis of the present indicative and present tense system of verbs (Chapter 15.9), these alternations were accounted for by setting up two present stems. The regular present stem (equivalent to the bare base) shows the first vowel of each set of alternants: / mur / *mour- (nous mourons),* / vEn / *ven- (nous venons),* / dEv / *dev- (nous devons).* The modified stem on which are formed the 3 pl and the singular forms of the present indicative and the present subjunctive contains the second vowel, or as in the case of / wa /, vowel sequence: / mœr / *meur- (ils meurent),* / tjɛn / *tienn- (il faut que je tienne),* / dwav / *doiv- (ils doivent).* It will be recalled that the singular forms of the present indicative are derived by the application of liaison (and in some cases nasalization) to the modified stem: **tjɛN→tjĕN→tjẽ** / tjẽ / *(il tient).*

It will now be shown how instead of postulating two alternating present stems for verbs such as *mourir, pouvoir, venir, tenir, recevoir, devoir,* etc. one may derive both from a single abstract underlying form by the application of various vowel morphophonological rules. Furthermore, it will be shown that these rules possess a certain degree of generality and result in a well-integrated system of underlying vowels. It should be borne in mind however that these rules do not reflect phonological processes of the French vowel system.

17.3.1   Low Vowel Fronting

The establishment of a system of abstract underlying vowels that would permit the derivation of such alternants as *mour-* and *meur-* or *ven-* and *vienn-* from a single stem requires bringing into relation not only inflectionally related forms such as alternant verb stems but also derivationally related sets of forms from two different lexical layers of French. In view of some of the phonological features they exhibit, their relative frequency of occurrence in texts, the styles in which they appear, etc., French words may be termed **learned** *(savant)* or **non-learned** *(populaire).* Both types of words are inherited from Latin, but the learned vocabulary has been borrowed from Latin at a relatively late date (Middle

Ages to Renaissance period) and does not show the sound changes characteristic of words belonging to the original lexical stock of the language.

Compare the following paired words, the first member of which belongs to the learned vocabulary and the second to the native stock:

flor-aison	/ flɔr- /	fleur	/ flœr /
mort-el	/ mɔrt- /	meurt-re	/ mœr- /
sol-itude	/ sɔl- /	seul	/ sœl /

The bases on which members of each pair are formed differ only by the vowel. Furthermore, / ɔ / and / œ / differ only by the feature of front vs. back. The same relationship obtains more or less between the bases which underlie the following paired items:

sal-é	/ sal- /	sel	/ sɛl /
clar-té	/ klar-te /	clair	/ klɛr /
human-ité	/ yman- /	humaine	/ ymɛn- /

It will be observed that the front vowel of both sets of alternations occurs in stressed (final) position; the back vowel (or the more back vowel in the case of the alternation / a /:/ ɛ /) is found in unstressed (non-final) position. By positing a rule, **low vowel fronting**, that switches the feature [-front] to [+front] for low stressed vowels, it becomes possible to account for the two variant bases. In other words, low vowel fronting has the following effect:

$$
\overset{\text{ɔ}}{\begin{bmatrix} -\text{front} \\ +\text{mid} \\ +\text{low} \\ +\text{round} \end{bmatrix}} \rightarrow \overset{\text{œ}}{\begin{bmatrix} +\text{front} \\ +\text{mid} \\ +\text{low} \\ +\text{round} \end{bmatrix}} ; \quad \overset{\text{a}}{\begin{bmatrix} -\text{front} \\ +\text{low} \\ -\text{round} \end{bmatrix}} \rightarrow \overset{\text{ɛ}}{\begin{bmatrix} +\text{front} \\ +\text{mid} \\ +\text{low} \\ -\text{round} \end{bmatrix}}
$$

In view of the existence of the contrast / a / vs. / ɑ / ([+low, +front] vs. [+low, −front]) and the fact that / ɛ / is specified as a low-mid front vowel, accounting for the alternations / ɔ /:/ œ / and / a /:/ ɛ / by low vowel fronting requires a different set of distinctive features than those posited in Chapter 5. If it is assumed that / a /, / ɔ /, / ɛ /, and / œ / are all "low" vowels, then low vowel fronting derives / œ / from / ɔ / and / ɛ / from / a / in stressed position. In the derivation below, it will be noted that in the forms of the two left columns the vowel of the base is in non-final position (*mort-el*) and the rule does not apply:

			flor.aison	sal.é
Underlying Form:	**flor**	**sal**	**flor.ezon**	**sal.e**
Low Vowel Fronting:	flœr	sɛl	- - - -	- - - -
Phonological Output:	/ flœr /	/ sɛl /	/ florezõ /	/ sale /

The postulation of low vowel fronting makes it now possible to account for such triads as *humanité, humaine* and *humain* in terms of a single underlying form:

	human.ité	humain.e	humain
Underlying Form:	**yman-ité**	**yman.E**	**yman**
Low Vowel Fronting:	- - - -	ymɛn.E	ymɛn
Nasalization:	- - - -	- - - -	ymɛ̃n
Liaison (Final Consonant Deletion):	- - - -	- - - -	ymɛ̃
Mute *e* Deletion:	- - - -	ymɛn	- - - -
Phonological Output:	/ ymanite /	/ ymɛn /	/ ymɛ̃ /

Forms derived from a base containing underlying ɔ enter, in fact, into ternary alternations:

mort-el / mɔrtɛl /   *mour-ons* / murõ /   *meurt-re* / mœrtr /   *meurt* / mœr /

Since, in both *mortel* and *mourons,* the base vowel occurs in non-stressed position, low vowel fronting cannot account for the alternation. Two sets of underlying vowels must be posited: (1) **tense vowels,** which do not undergo changes determined by their position relative to stress, and (2) **lax vowels,** which do undergo these changes. Thus, the base of *mortel* contains the tense vowel ɔ whereas that of both *mourons* and *meurtre* contain lax ɔ. As a general principle, learned derivational forms such as *mortel, solitude, humanité, clarté,* etc. contain tense vowels.

The surface / u / that appears in such forms as *mourons, douloureux,* etc. is accounted for by positing a **raising** rule applicable to lax **o** and ɔ occurring in unstressed syllable. The phonological output of the various *o*-vowels is summarized by the derivations below:

Underlying Form:	coll.e kɔl.E	en.dol.or.i En.dɔl.ɔr.i	doul.our.eux dɔl.ɔrɔz	doul.eur dɔl.ɔr
Low Vowel Fronting:	- - - -	- - - -	dɔl.ɔr.œz	dɔl.œr
Raising:	- - - -	- - - -	dul.ur.œz	dul.œr
Nasalization and Nasal Adjustment:	- - - -	ãn.dɔl.ɔr.i	- - - -	- - - -
Liaison (Final Consonant Deletion):	- - - -	ã.dɔl.ɔr.i	dul.ur.œ	- - - -
Tense Vowel Conversion:	kɔl.E	ã.dɔl.ɔr.i	- - - -	- - - -
Mute *e* Deletion:	kɔl	- - - -	- - - -	- - - -
Mid Vowel Raising:	- - - -	- - - -	dul.ur.ø	- - - -
Phonological Output:	/ kɔl /	/ ãdɔlɔri /	/ dulurø /	/ dulœr /

Recall that the alternation *douloureux* / ø / vs. *douleur* / œ / is determined by a truly phonological process, mid vowel raising. The above derivations emphasize the fact that the consequence of positing abstract underlying forms to relate forms claimed to be morphologically linked is the postulation of a large set of morphophonological rules.

Tense **O** and **ɔ** do not quite parallel the corresponding lax vowels **o** and **ɔ**. The latter are both raised to / u / in unstressed position and fronted to / œ / or / ø / in stressed position. But whereas **ɔ** is always converted to / ɔ /, **O** is raised to / u /. While there are no surface alternations / o /:/ u /, two sets of base alternations not assignable to **o** and **ɔ** are attested:

prouvons	prouve	routier	route
genou	génuflexion	double	duplication

If the alternation / u /:/ y / is assigned to underlying **U**, all surface front rounded vowels are now derived from back rounded vowels. That is, / ø / and / œ / are derived from lax **o** or **ɔ**:

floraison:fleur **flor-**
endolori:douloureux **dɔl.ɔr.ɔz**

and / y / is derived from **U**:

duplication: double **duplikasjɔn**

Thus, the alternation / u /:/ u / found in *prouvons/prouve* cannot be the surface output of **U**. Nor can it be assigned to underlying **u** since there are parallel alternations involving / i / and / y /, on the one hand, and zero, on the other:

popul.aire peupl.e	fabul.eux fabl.e
mobil.ier meubl.e	amabil.ité aimabl.e

These latter alternations / y /:/ ∅ / and / i /:/ ∅ / are assigned to lax **u** and **i**, respectively, and alternations / u /:/ u / can only be derived from tense **O**.

17.3.2   Diphthongization

In addition to the alternations presented in 17.3 involving inflectionally related forms (*venons/viennent; recevoir/reçoivent*) one of whose member contains a **diphthong** (/ jɛ / in *viennent* and / wa / in *reçoivent*), there are derivational sets whose learned member contains a front mid vowel and whose non-learned member contains a diphthong:

(i)	régicide / reʒ- /	roi / rwa /
	espérance / esper- /	espoir / espwar /
	crédibilité / kred- /	croire / krwa- /
(ii)	vétuste / ve- /	vieil / vjɛj /
	pédestre / ped- /	pied / pje /
	bénévole / ben- /	bien / bjẽ /

(Diphthongs in French are defined as combinations of the glides / j / or / w / followed by a vowel.) Although all the learned forms show the same vowel / e /, it is necessary to posit two different underlying vowels, since the non-learned forms contain two different diphthongs. On the basis of other evidence—for instance the fact that in some Northerns French patois / wa / corresponds to / we /—we assign the alternation / e /:/ wa / to **e**, and / e /:/ jɛ / to **ɛ**. We now need to account for ternary alternations such as:

réception / resep- /	reçoivent / rEswav- /	recevoir / rEsEv- /
ténacité / ten- /	tiennent / tjɛn- /	tenir / tEn- /
avènement / vɛn- /	viennent / vjɛn- /	venons / vEn- /

The inflectionally related forms are derived from bases that contain lax **e** and **ɛ** by the application of a **diphthongization** rule whose effect is to insert a / w / before / e / and a / j / before / ɛ /. As was the case for low vowel fronting, diphthongization applies to underlying vowels occurring in the stressed (final) position. In non-stressed position both front mid vowels are reduced to mute *e* (schwa). The learned derivatives contain the tense vowels É and **ɛ** to which neither diphthongization nor schwa reduction apply:

	tén.ac.ité	ten.ons	tienn.ent
Underlying Form:	**tÉn.as.ite**	**ten.õZ**	**ten.Et**
Diphthongization:	- - -	- - -	tjɛn.Et
Mute *e* Reduction:	- - -	tEn.õz	- - -
Phonological Output:	/ tenasite /	/ tEnõ /	/ tjɛn /

The above derivations do not, of course, take into consideration various other morphophonological rules such as nasalization, final consonant deletion, or conversion of tense vowels which are not directly relevant to the present discussion.

Since the abstract morphophonological description of French discussed here eliminates the front rounded vowels **y**, **ø**, and **œ** as well as the nasal vowels, it might be thought that the system of abstract underlying vowels posited is considerably more reduced than the inventory of surface phonemes. In fact, two matched sets of seven underlying vowels—tense and lax—are required:

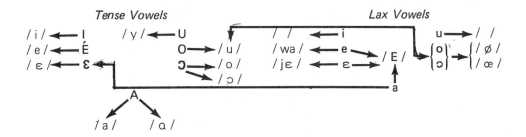

The phonological output of the various underlying vowels is provided; recall that the nasal vowels are derived from sequences composed of underlying vowels + nasal consonant occurring in final position or before certain consonants (for details, see Sanford A. Schane, *French Phonology and Morphology*, Chapter 2; note that lax **i** and **u** underlie zero (/ /) alternating with / i / and / u /, respectively).

17.3.3   Idiosyncratic Formations

A considerable number of forms belonging to the non-learned vocabulary fail to show expected surface vowels in unstressed position. For example, in addition to the predictable alternation *mourir/meurt* resulting from the application of raising and low vowel fronting, respectively, to lax ɔ (underlying form of the base, mɔr-), one finds the pair *fleurir/fleur* instead of expected **flourir/fleur*. Historically, of course, irregular alternations such as this are the result of the generalization of one of the two surface forms of the base, a process known as **analogy**. From a synchronic point of view, forms such as *fleurir* must be marked as idiosyncratic. Other illustrative exceptions to the treatment of lax vowels in unstressed position are:

aimons	/ ɛmõ /	(/ Emõ /)	aime	/ ɛm /
feuillage	/ fœjaʒ /	(/ fujaʒ /)	feuille	/ fœj /
siéger	/ sjeʒe /	(/sEʒe /)	siège	/ sjɛʒ /
poilu	/ pwaly /	(/ pEly /)	poil	/ pwal /

The forms in parentheses represent the expected forms. The form *pelu* / pEly / does in fact occur and has the same meaning as *poilu* "hairy"; the latter has in addition the meanings of "strong man" and was the term given to French soldiers during World War I. In fact, all verbs of the *-er* class whose base contains a lax vowel constitute exceptions to the application of the various morphophonemic rules in stressed syllables:

aimons	aime
pleurons	pleure

17.4   CONSONANTAL ALTERNATIONS

While alternations between surface vowels in derivationally related forms are the most striking aspect of French morphophonology, there also exist alternations between consonants or between a consonant and zero.

Medial dental and velar stops (/ t d k g /) alternate with zero:

vital	vie
nudité	nu
amical	ami
régale	roi

In the case of the last pair, the alternation is really between / g / + non-front vowel (*régale*) and / ʒ / + front vowel (*régicide*) vs. zero.

Sequences of stops + the high front vowels / i / and / y / + / l / alternate with clusters stops + / l /:

populaire	peuple
mobilier	meuble
fabuleux	fable

These alternations stem in fact from the deletion of underlying lax **i** and **u**.

In both derivationally and inflectionally related forms the presence of base final / n / alternates with its absence:

corn-u	cor
journ-ée	jour
hivern-al	hiver
dorm-ir	dor-s

Pre-consonantal / s / alternates with zero; in many instances, the deletion of / s / is replaced by potential vowel length represented in the spelling by the circumflex accent:

festival	fête
costal	côte

In some cases / s / alternates with an initial / e /:

scolaire	école
scripture	écriture

The sequence / al / alternates with / o /. In addition to such derivatives as

alt.itude	haut
fals.ifier	faus.se / fos.E /
sal.é	sau.poudrer,

this alternation characterizes the only major group of nouns and postnominal adjectives whose masculine singular and plural forms differ phonetically:

cheval	chevau-x
principal	principau-x

Finally, the presence of the cluster / ks / alternates with its absence:

destruction / destryks.jõ /	détruire / detryi-r /
jonction / ʒõks.jõ /	joignent / ʒwẽñ /

17.5   HOW ABSTRACT IS FRENCH MORPHOLOGY?

On the basis of what criteria does the analyst set the limits to be placed on the abstractness of underlying forms? Put differently, how does he decide which surface variant forms should be related by the postulation of a common underlying form?

The first criterion in the establishment of underlying forms is the degree of morphological relatedness of the variant surface forms. Consider the surface forms / pã / *paon* "peacock" vs. / pãt / *pente* "slope" and / vã / *vent* "wind" vs. the base / vãt- / occurring in *venter* "to blow (of the wind)." Although the two sets of alternations are analogous from a phonological point of view, one would not postulate a common underlying form **pãt** or **pãT** for *paon* and *pente* because these two forms are too divergent from a semantic point of view. On the other hand, native speakers of French would generally agree that *vent* and the base of *venter* share the same semantic features; they would paraphrase *venter* as *faire du vent,* and this indicates that *venter* is simply the verbal form of *vent.* Thus, to be morphologically relatable forms must share a certain number of semantic features.

Secondly, morphologically related forms must share a sufficient number of phonological features. For instance, although English *kingly* and *regal* are synonyms, no analyst would attempt to derive them from a common underlying form. Obviously, phonologically similar forms must differ by few segments: *roy.al* / rwaj.al / and *roi* / rwa / which differ by only the segment / j / vs. / ∅ / are more phonetically similar than *régal* / reg.al / and *roi* which differ by their vocalism as well as the alternation / g /:/ ∅ /. But phonological relatedness is centrally a function of the **generality** of the rules required to relate variant forms and their **naturalness,** that is, the degree to which they rest on deep-seated phonological processes of the language. Final consonant deletion is the most general morphophonemic rule in French, and forms that differ at the surface level by the presence or absence of a base final consonant have close phonological affinity. Another rule of great generality is mid vowel raising, determined in part by distributional constraints of mid vowels with regard to syllable type.

Thus in French there is strong motivation to relate morphologically related forms that can be derived from a single underlying form by the application of final consonant deletion and nasalization or mid vowel raising. These variant forms fall into three groups: (i) liaison variants of words: *un grand* / grã / *garçon* vs. *un grand* / grãt / *homme*; (ii) inflectionally related forms, either masculine and feminine forms of adjectives or variant form of the base of verbs: *un petit* / pti / *chalet* vs. *une petite* / ptit / *maison; suivre* / syiv.r /, *vous suiviez* / syiv.je / vs. *je suis* / syi /, *il suit* / syi /; (iii) derivationally related forms usually consisting of bases which occur with zero suffixation as nouns or adjectives and with various verbal endings as verb forms: *il donne* / dɔn / vs. *le don* / dõ /, *ranger* / raʒ:e / vs. *le rang* / rã /, *brunir* / brun.ir / vs. *brun* / brœ̃ /, *sottise* / sɔt.iz / vs. *sot* / so /. It is important to note that in the various alternations cited above both forms belong to the non-learned vocabulary. Of course, we would also want to relate forms derivable from an underlying form containing mute *e* (E): *le cheval* / ʃøval /, / ʃœval /, / ʃval /; *le* / lø /, / lœ /, / l /.

There are numerous inflectionally related forms differing only by a medial vowel or a medial vowel and a liaison consonant to which neither nasalization nor mid vowel raising apply. These include (i) verb bases such as *mourons* / mur.õ / vs. *meurent* / mœr /, *tenir* / tEn.ir / vs. *tiennent* / tjɛn /, *devez* / dEve / vs. *doivent* / dwav /; (ii) masculine pre-consonantal and pre-pause vs. masculine pre-vocalic and feminine forms of adjectives such as *beau* / bo / vs. *bel, belle* / bɛl /, *nouveau* vs. *nouvel, nouvelle* / nuvɛl /, *vieux* / vjø / vs. *vieil, vieille* / vjɛj /, *fou* / fu / vs. *fol, folle* / fɔl /; (iii) masculine singular vs. masculine plural forms of adjectives and nouns such as *global* / glɔbal / vs. *globaux* / glɔbo /, *animal* / animal / vs. *animaux* / animo /, *travail* / travaj / vs. *travaux* / travo / *ciel* / sjɛl / vs. *cieux* / sjø /, *œil* / œj / vs. *yeux* / jø /. But the rules that have been posited to derive the variant forms from a postulated underlying form do not have great generality or naturalness. While subsuming variant forms by means of a common underlying form results in a simplification of the lexicon, unless it is accomplished by means of general and natural rules, it entails a complication of the morphophonemic analysis and thus fails to achieve overall descriptive economy and simplicity.

Let us compare the consequences of postulating a single underlying form for the variant forms *sot* / so / and *sottise* / sɔt.iz /, on the one hand, and *mou* / mu / vs. *mol* / mɔl /, on the other. In the case of the first pair of variant forms, their derivation from the postulated underlying form sɔt- requires only the application of final consonant deletion and mid vowel raising, both of which are general and natural rules. With regard to mid vowel raising, it is important to note that it applies to any base containing a mid vowel in the final syllable immediately followed by a final consonant. In the case of the alternation *mou/mol,* the postulated rule—whatever its form—applies only to certain bases which, in the final analysis, must be marked in the lexicon. For example, it does not apply to *bol* whose plural form is *bols* / bɔl /. Whether one marks as idiosyncratic forms such as *mol/mou, ail/aulx, ciel/cieux,* etc. which show alternations, or forms such as *miel/miels, bol/bols, bal/bals, rail/rails* which do not, is inconsequential. The fact remains that whenever one comes across a form ending in vowel + *l,* one cannot tell whether the *l* will be deleted and the vowel shifted or the *l* retained and the vowel unchanged.

The postulation of common underlying forms subsuming derivationally related forms such as *sel* / sɛl / vs. *salé* / sal.e / presents two problems. First, as was the case with the inflectionally related form cited in the preceding paragraph, the morphophonemic rules that would be required lack generality and naturalness. Second, and most importantly, clear criteria are not available in determining whether variant forms are morphologically relatable. It is no doubt the case that French speakers would agree to relate *sel* and *salé* or *mortel* and *meurtre.* But can it be asserted that *clair* and *clarté* or *doléance* and *deuil,* which are derivable by the application of the same rules, show the same degree of morphological affinity? To make such an assertion would require information about psycholinguistic processes that is not available at present, and the wiser alternative is to assume that corresponding learned and non-learned derivationally related forms are derived from different bases. For example, *clair* is underlain by **klɛr-**, *clarté* by **klar-**; *deuil* by **dœj-** and *doléance* by **dɔl-**; nor would any attempt be made to relate *mortel* and *meurtre* to each other or to the verb bases *mour-* or *meur-.* A serious weakness of the postulation of abstract underlying forms subsuming learned and non-learned surface forms is that in all cases the underlying form reflects the learned rather than the non-learned form. That is, the derivation of the non-learned form required a greater number of rules. Finally, in the postulation of abstract underlying forms, it is difficult to know where one should draw the line. At first, it might seem that it is highly artificial and counter-intuitive to derive *mère* and *maternel* from a common underlying form. But numerous examples could be adduced to support the three sets of alternations required to derive *mère* from **matεr-**: (i) / ε /:/ a /—*sel/salé, mer/marin*; (ii) / ∅ /:/ t /—*vie/vital, nu/nudité*; (iii) / ∅ /:final / n /—*jour/journée, cor/cornu*.

As a final consideration, the postulation of abstract underlying forms entails the implicit claim that the system of underlying units (**systematic phonemes**) and the rules required to map them into surface phonemes have some sort of psychological reality for the native speakers of the language. These systematic phonemes and morphophonemic rules are part of the competence of native speakers and are acquired by children during their linguistically formative years, approximately up to age five or six. To posit abstract morphophonemic representations for such non-learned vocabulary items as *mère* or *peuvent* is to claim that French children have the capacity to abstract underlying forms from diverse surface structure data. But the learned vocabulary items *(maritime, potentiel)* required for the postulation of the underlying forms are absent from the productive inventory of young children. One must therefore abandon the strong claim that abstract underlying form and morphophonemic rules of limited generality constitute part of the competence of the average speaker and adopt two weaker sets of claims. First, the ability to relate learned and corresponding non-learned forms is part of the passive competence of speakers. Second, after the linguistically formative years there is a restructuring of the knowledge that speakers have of their language in which underlying forms of a low degree of abstractness are replaced by more abstract underlying forms and new morphophonemic rules. But both of these weaker claims are difficult to substantiate, and we conclude in putting forth a more limited proposal of how French speakers relate learned and non-learned vocabulary.

Learned and non-learned forms constitute two distinct **lexical strata** of French, and the ability to relate corresponding items from the two strata does not constitute part of the linguistic competence of native speakers. This ability is a function of the formal acquisition of certain marginal features of the language which takes place characteristically in the classroom context. As a consequence the ability to effect lexical relationships between words of the language is highly variable among speakers, and it may reflect their level of formal linguistic training rather than their fundamental linguistic competence.

STUDY QUESTIONS

1. Analyze the following words into constituent morphemes. Represent the base with the use of the latent consonant notation.

    a) délicieusement   delis-; delisjøZ-   délic.ieus.e.ment

    b) départ   parT-

    c) abattre

    d) chevalier

    e) rougissant

    f) vendeur

    g) douceur

    h) engager

2. Show why the following bases must be represented at the underlying level by final latent consonants.
   a)   oeuf **oeF-** (in plural) *des oeufs* / ø / **oeF.Z;** (in singular) *un oeuf* / œf / **oef**
   b)   vin **viN-** *vin* / vẽ /, *vinaigre* / vinɛgr /
   c)   rang **rãʒ-**
   d)   plaigne **plɛÑ-**
   e)   vieil **vjɛJ-**
   f)   fausse **foZ-**
   g)   donner **dɔN-**

3. Within an analysis of French in which liaison is interpreted as the deletion or non-deletion of final consonants and in which no distinction is made between stable and latent consonants, how would the base of the following words be represented?
   a)   rond **rõd**   d)   battre
   b)   plomb   e)   suivre
   c)   don   f)   rougir

4. Which of the following words constitute exceptions to final consonant deletion and must be marked as idiosyncratic?
   a)   ail **aj** idiosyncratic since / j / is never deleted in the singular
   b)   plan **plan** regular: / n / appears in derivative *planer*
   c)   sens
   d)   vent
   e)   camp
   f)   chef
   g)   long
   h)   car

5. Provide one additional example of the following ternary alternations.
   a)   / e / : / ɛ / : / ẽ /   plénitude/plaine/plein
   b)   / a / : / ɛ / : / ẽ /   sanitaire/saine/sain
   c)   / a / : / E / : / ẽ /   manuel/menotte/main

6. Provide two additional examples of the following binary alternations.
   a)   / wa / : / wẽ /   poigne/poing
   b)   / a /   : / ẽ /   famine/faim
   c)   / E /   : / ẽ /   grenu/grain
   d)   / ɔ /   : / œ /   floral/fleur
   e)   / a /   : / ɛ /   amabilité/aimable
   f)   / u /   : / œ /   courage/coeur
   g)   / e /   : / jɛ /   lévrier/lièvre

7. Provide a corresponding learned form for the following words.
   a)   soir *sérénade* (alternation / e /:/ wa /:/ E /
   b)   courage
   c)   mer
   d)   loi
   e)   ciel
   f)   double
   g)   piétiner
   h)   soeur
   i)   ils peuvent

8. Indicate the underlying vowel of the base and the rule applied to derive the surface vowel that appears in the forms given.
   a)   courage lax ɔ; Raising
   b)   saine
   c)   menotte
   d)   fièvre
   e)   oeuvre
   f)   royal
   g)   tenir

9. For which of the following words would you posit an underlying base containing a sequence oral vowel + nasal consonant? Assume that all types of forms, inflectional and derivational, would be related in terms of a common underlying form.
   a)   vin **vin-** (since we find alternations *vin* / ṽe / and *vinaigre, vignoble, vinicole, vineux* / vin /)
   b)   manquer **mãk-** (since there are no alternations / ã /:/ an /)
   c)   saint
   d)   rein
   e)   bain
   f)   mont
   g)   an
   h)   son (le son)
   i)   clin
   j)   daim

10. State which of the following variant surface forms are morphologically or lexically relatable. If you think that two forms are morphologically relatable, provide justification in the form of an underlying form and a set of morphophonemic rules on the basis of which the surface forms are derived.
    a)   bain/baigner morphologically; bɛñ Nasalization + Final Consonant Deletion
    b)   père/paternel
    c)   coupable/culpabilité
    d)   an/année
    e)   fête/festival
    f)   blanc/blanchir
    g)   vert/verdure
    h)   bel/beauté
    i)   salaud/salope

BIBLIOGRAPHY

I. GENERAL DESCRIPTIONS OF FRENCH

Dubois, Jean. *Grammaire structurale du français* (Vol. 1: *Nom et pronom*). Paris: Larousse, 1965.

Génouvrier, Emile et Jean Peytard. *Linguistique et enseignement du français.* Paris: Larousse, 1970.

Gougenheim, Georges. *Système grammatical de la langue française.* Paris: d'Artrey, 1939.

Hall, Robert A. Jr. *Structural Sketches No. 1: French* ("Language Monograph Series," No. 24). Baltimore: Linguistic Society of America/Waverly Press, 1948.

Martinet, André. *Le français sans fard.* Paris: Presses Universitaires de France, 1969.

Mayer, Edgar N. *Structure of French.* New York: New Century/Appleton-Century-Crofts, 1969.

Politzer, Robert L. *Teaching French: An Introduction to Applied Linguistics* (2nd ed.). New York: Ginn, 1965.

Schane, Sanford A. *French Phonology and Morphology.* Cambridge, Mass.: M.I.T. Press, 1968.

———. "How abstract is French Phonology?," in Jean Casagrande and Bohdan Saciuk (eds.), *Generative Studies in Romance Languages,* pp. 340-53. Rowley, Mass.: Newbury House, 1972.

Togeby, Knut. *Structure immanente de la langue française* (2nd ed.). Paris: Larousse, 1965.

Valdman, Albert. *Applied Linguistics: French* (with introduction in general linguistics by Simon Belasco). Boston: D.C. Heath, 1961.

II. PHONETICS

Armstrong, Lillian E. *The Phonetics of French.* London: Bell, 1947.

Carton, Fernand. *Introduction à la Phonétique du français.* Paris: Bordas, 1974.

Coustenoble, H. H. *Studies in French Intonation.* Cambridge: Heffner, 1934.

Delattre, Pierre. *Les difficultés phonétiques du français.* Middlebury, Vt.: Middlebury College, 1948.

———. *Principes de phonétique français à l'usage des étudiants anglo-américains.* Middlebury, Vt.: Middlebury College, 1951.

Delattre, Pierre. *Comparing the Phonetic Features of English, French, German and Spanish.* London: Harrap, and Heidelberg: Julius Groos Verlag, 1965.

–––. *Studies in French and Comparative Phonetics.* The Hague: Mouton, 1966.

Fouché, Pierre. *Traité de prononciation française.* Paris: Klincksieck, 1956.

Grammont, Maurice. *Traité pratique de prononciation française.* Paris: Delagrave, 1954.

Léon, Pierre R. *La prononciation du français standard: aide-mémoire d'orthoépie.* Paris: Didier, 1966.

Léon, Pierre R. and Monique Léon. *Introduction à la phonétique corrective.* Paris: Hachette/Larousse, 1964.

Léon, Monique. *Exercices systématiques de prononciation française* (Vols. 1 and 2). Paris: Hachette/Larousse, 1964.

Malmberg, Bertil. *Phonétique française.* Malmö: Hermod, 1969.

Nachtmann, Francis W. *Exercises in French Phonics.* Glenview, Ill.: Scott, Foresman, 1970.

Valdman, Albert, Robert Salazar and Marie-Antoinette Charbonneaux. *A Drillbook of French Pronunciation* (2nd ed.). New York: Harper and Row, 1972.

III. PHONOLOGY

Bibeau, Gilles. *Introduction à la phonologie générative du français.* Paris, Montreal, Bruxelles: Didier, 1975.

Dell François. *Les règles et les sons; introduction à la phonologie générative.* Paris: Hermann, 1973.

Gougenheim, Georges. *Eléments de phonologie française.* Strasbourg: Strasbourg University, 1935.

Martinet, André. "Remarques sur le système phonologique du français," *Bulletin de la Société de Linguistique de Paris* 34 (1933), 191-201.

–––. "Les traits généraux de la phonologie du français, in *Phonology as Functional Phonetics.* Philadelphia: Russell Press, 1950.

IV. MORPHOLOGY

de Felice, Th. *Eléments de grammaire morphologique.* Paris: Didier, 1950.

"La grammaire du français parlé." *Le Français dans le Monde,* 57 (June, 1968). A series of articles describing the morphology of spoken French.

Guiraud, Pierre. *Les mots savants* ("Que sais-je?" No. 1325). Paris: Presses Universitaires de France, 1968.

Mahmoudian, Mortéza. *Les modalités nominales du français.* Paris: Presses Universitaires de France, 1970.

Mitterand, Henri. *Les mots français* ("Que sais-je," No. 270). Paris: Presses Universitaires de France, 1965.

Rigault, André. "Les marques du genre," in *La grammaire du français parlé,* 1968, pp. 37-42.

Trager, George L. "French Morphology: Verb Inflection." *Language,* 31 (1955), 511-29.

–––. "Personal Pronouns and the 'Definite' Article." *Language,* 34 (1958), 225-31.

Ullmann, Stephen. *Précis de sémantique française* (2nd ed.). Bern: A. Francke A. G. Verlag, 1959.

V. SPELLING

Blanche-Benveniste, Claire and André Charvel. *L'orthographe.* Paris: Maspéro, 1969.

Burney, Pierre. *L'orthographe* ("Que sais-je," No. 685). Paris: Presses Universitaires de France, 1955.

Catach, Nina, Jeanne Golfand and Roger Denux. *Orthographe et lexicographie.* Paris: Didier, 1971.

Thimmonier, René. *Le système graphique du français.* Paris: Plon, 1967.

–––. *Code orthographique et grammatical.* Paris: Hatier, 1970.

Valdman, Albert. "Not All Is Wrong with French Spelling." *French Review,* 37 (1963), 213-23.

VI. LANGUAGE VARIATION

Deyhime, Guiti. "Enquête sur la phonologie du français contemporain." *La Linguistique* 1, 2 (1967), 97-108; 47-84.

Dugas, André (ed.). *Le français de la région de Montréal* (No. 4 of *Cahiers de Linguistique de l'Université du Québec*). Montréal: Presses de l'Université du Québec, 1974.

Guiraud, Pierre. *L'argot* ("Que sais-je?," No. 700). Paris: Presses Universitaires de France, 1956.

———. *Le français populaire* ("Que sais-je?," No. 1172). Paris: Presses Universitaires de France, 1965.

———. *Patois et dialectes français* ("Que sais-je?," No. 1285). Paris: Presses Universitaires de France, 1968.

———. (ed.). *Le français en France et hors de France*. Vol. I: *Les créoles et contacts africains*; Vol. II: *Les français régionaux, le français en contact* (Proceedings of the Colloque sur les Ethnies Francophones, Nice 1968). Paris: Belles Lettres, 1969, 1970.

Léon, Pierre R. *Essais de phonostylistique* (Collection Studia Phonetica). Paris-Montréal: Didier, 1971.

———. "Etude sur la prononciation de *e* accentué chez un groupe de jeunes Parisiens," in A. Valdman (ed.), 1972, pp. 317-28.

Malécot, André. "New Procedures for Descriptive Phonetics," in A. Valdman (ed.), 1972, pp. 345-56.

Martinet, André. *La prononciation du français contemporain* (2nd ed.). Paris/Geneva: Droz, 1972.

———. "Pour un dictionnaire de la prononciation française," in David Abercrombie *et al.* (eds.), *In Honor of Daniel Jones,* pp. 349-56. London: Longmans, 1964.

Martinet, André and Henriette Walter. *Dictionnaire de la prononciation française dans son usage réel.* Paris: France-Expansion-Egecena, 1973.

Pottier, Bernard. "La situation linguistique en France," in André Martinet (ed.). *Le langage* ("Encyclopédie de la Pléiade"), pp. 1144-61. Paris: Gallimard, 1968.

Reichstein, Ruth. "Etude des variations sociales et géographiques des faits linguistiques." *Word* 16 (1960), 55-99.

Unité et diversité du français contemporain. *Le Français dans le Monde,* 69 (December, 1969). A series of articles dealing with linguistic variation in France and stylistic levels in spoken and written French.

Valdman, Albert (ed.). *Papers in Linguistics and Phonetics to the Memory of Pierre Delattre.* The Hague: Mouton, 1972.

———. "The Loi de Position as a Pedagogical Norm," in A. Valdman (ed.), 1972, pp. 473-85.

VII. VOWEL SYSTEM

Delattre, Pierre. "La question des deux *a* en français," *French Review,* 31 (1958), 141-48.

———. "La nasalité vocalique en français et en anglais," *French Review,* 39 (1965), 92-109.

Durand, Marguerite. *Voyelles longues et voyelles brèves.* Paris: Klincksieck, 1946.

Høybe, Poul. "Voyelles et semi-voyelles à l'initiale du mot en français," *Travaux du Cercle Linguistique de Copenhague* 5 (1949), 266-73.

Malmberg, Bertil. "Observations sur le système vocalique du français," *Acta Linguistica,* 2 (1940-41), 234-46.

Martinet, André. "C'est jeuli, le Mareuc," *Romance Philology,* 11 (1958), 345-55.

———. "La nature phonologique d'*e* caduc," in A. Valdman (ed.), 1972, pp. 393-400.

Valdman, Albert. "Phonologic Structure and Social Factors in French, the Vowel *un*," *French Review,* 33 (1959), 153-61.

Varney-Pleasants, Jeanne. *Etudes sur l'e muet.* Paris: Klincksieck, 1956.

Zwanenburg, W. "Les phonèmes 'semi-vocaliques' du français moderne," *Neophilologus,* 1 (1966), 28-33.

———. "Quelques remarques sur le statut phonologique d'*e* muet en français," *Word* 24 (1968), 508-18.

VIII. CONSONANT SYSTEM

Bursill-Hall, G. L. "Frequency of Consonant Clusters in French," *Journal of the Canadian Linguistic Association,* 2 (1956), 66-77.

Frei, Henri. "Pour l'*n* mouillé," in *Mélanges de linguistique française et de philologie et littérature médiévales offerts à Paul Imbs* (*Travaux de Linguistique et de Littérature de l'Université de Strasbourg,* 9 (1973), 487-94).

Malécot, André. "Frequency of Occurrence of French Phonemes and Consonant Clusters," *Phonetica,* 29 (1974), 158-70.

–––. "The Glottal Stop in French," *Phonetica,* 31 (1975), 51-63.

Malécot, André and G. Metz. "Progressive Nasal Assimilation in French," *Phonetica,* 26 (1973), 193-209.

Malmberg, Bertil. *Le système consonantique du français moderne* (Etudes de phonologie et de phonétique; études romanes de Lund). Lund: Gleerup, 1943.

IX. SYLLABLE AND JUNCTURE

Arnold, Gordon F. "A Phonological Approach to Vowel, Consonant, Syllable in Modern French," *Lingua,* 5 (1956), 253-81.

Delattre, Pierre. "Le mot est-il une entité phonétique en français?," *Le Français Moderne,* 8 (1940), 47-56.

–––. "Rapports entre la durée vocalique et la structure syllabique en français," *French Review,* 32 (1959), 547-52.

Haden, Ernest F. "Le système accentuel du français," in A. Valdman (ed.), 1972, pp. 209-14.

X. ELISION AND LIAISON

Klausenburger, Jurgen. "Rule Inversion Opacity, Conspiracies, French Liaison and Elision," *Lingua,* 34 (1974), 167-79.

Malécot, André. "The Elision of the French Mute *e* within Complex Consonantal Clusters," *Lingua,* 5 (1955), 45-60.

Malécot, André and M. Richman. "Optional Word-Final Consonants in French," *Phonetica,* 26 (1973), 65-88.

Pulgram, Ernst. "French / ə /: Statics and Dynamics of Linguistic Subcodes," *Lingua,* 10 (1961), 305-25.

Schane, Sanford A. "There is No 'French Truncation Rule'," in R. J. Campbell, M. G. Goldin, and M. C. Wang (eds.). *Linguistic Studies in Romance Languages.* Washington, D. C.: Georgetown University Press, 1973a.

–––. "The Treatment of Phonological Exceptions: The Evidence from French," in Braj B. Kachru, *et al.* (eds.). *Issues in Linguistics: Papers in Honor of Henry and Renée Kahane.* Urbana: University of Illinois Press, 1973b.

XI. JOURNALS

(The following journals are likely to contain articles dealing with French phonology and morphology.)

Le Français aujourd'hui. Paris: Association française des Enseignants de Français.

Le Français dans le Monde. Paris: Hachette and Larousse.

Le Français moderne. Paris: d'Artrey.

Langue française. Paris: Larousse.

The French Review. Chapel Hill, N. C.: American Association of Teachers of French.

Cahiers de Linguistique de l'Université du Québec. Montréal: Université du Québec.

Langages. Paris: Didier-Larousse.

La Linguistique. Paris: Presses Universitaires de France.

INDEX